CALIFORNIA'S MISSION
LA PURÍSIMA CONCEPCIÓN
The Hageman and Ewing Reports

LA PURISIMA CONCEPCION RESIDENCE — SEPT. 1937

An Archeological and Restoration Study of Mission La Purísima Concepción

Reports Written for the National Park Service

BY

FRED C. HAGEMAN AND RUSSELL C. EWING

Prepared and Edited for Publication

BY

RICHARD S. WHITEHEAD

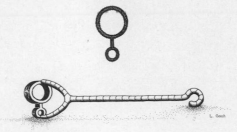

L. Gooch

Santa Barbara Trust for Historic Preservation
P.O. Box 388
Santa Barbara, California 93102
1991

The Santa Barbara Trust for Historic Preservation
Presidio Research Center Publication

Originally published as
Mission La Purisima Concepción
as *Number Five* in
THE SANTA BARBARA BICENTENNIAL HISTORICAL SERIES
1980
Santa Barbara Trust for Historic Preservation

Title page decoration:
La Purisima's Branding Iron
by L. Gooch

INTRODUCTION TO THE
SECOND EDITION

` When visitors to La Purisima Mission State Historic Park step through the line of trees and brush shielding the parking lot from the main mission grounds, they enter a different world. Left behind is the cacophony of contemporary civilization, its constant, pounding dissonance replaced by the bucolic sounds which have echoed in Los Berros Canyon for more than two centuries—the bleat of a sheep startled by the shadow of a circling hawk, the occasional bray of a donkey begging treats, from a passing ranger now rather than a gray-robed Franciscan. Otherwise, only the gentle whisper of the wind through the mission garden, the soothing splash of the fountain, and the welcome chatter of birds flashing a bit of color among the dark and gnarled oak branches disturb the silence. The pleasant shade of the long portico invites present day sojourners, much as it must have enticed early travelers along *El Camino Real,* to rest and refreshment. Even the soft lines of the tile and adobe buildings, the only evidence of human intrusion visible from the floor of the valley, add to the atmosphere of peace and serenity reminiscent of an earlier, less hurried time, when life itself could be savored. For although La Purisima Mission no longer ministers to the religious needs of the population, it continues to provide refuge in a hectic world, offering nourishment for the spirit and counterpoint to the cramped confines of modern life.

That this remarkable island of tranquility exists at all is the result of a serendipitous set of circumstances combined with the extraordinary energies of two individuals separated in time by more than a century, but of a single mind in terms of La Purisima. The first of these uncommon men was Mariano Payeras, O.F.M. Born on the island of Mallorca, coincidentally the birthplace of the founder of the California missions, Junipero Serra, Payeras entered the service of the church at an early age. After completing his advanced education at Serra's *alma mater,* the Convent of St. Francis in Palma, Fr. Payeras was dispatched to the New World in 1793. At the College of San Fernando in Mexico City he was introduced to life in New Spain and the rigors of frontier missionary work before being assigned, in 1796, to the farthest fringe of the Spanish Empire, Alta California. Once on California soil, Fr. Payeras served in the missions San Carlos, Soledad, and San Diego, in the process demonstrating talents for both missionary work and administration which so impressed his superiors that he was placed in charge of his own mission, La Purisima, in 1803.

La Purisima must have been an exciting challenge for the young priest, as it was already one of the most prosperous of the Franciscan establishments, in addition to being one of the most strategic. Founded by Fr. Fermin de Lasuén in 1787 as one of a series of missions located in the vast country inhabited by the energetic and numerous Chumash Indians, La Purisima was originally sited south of the Santa Inés River, within what is now the grid of the city of Lompoc. The rich alluvium of the valley proved amenable to agriculture and the abundant grasses of the region provided fodder for cattle and sheep, thousands of which soon dotted the surrounding hills. An equally abundant labor supply was also available, as La Purisima boasted an enrollment of over 1,500 neophytes at the time of Fr. Payeras' arrival. Under his active direction, La Purisima continued to grow and prosper. As the flocks of sheep increased, weaving became an important industry and, despite the ominous decline in Indian population, the mission continued to be a key element in the plans of both church and state in Alta California.

Nature intervened in Spanish plans, however, in December of 1812, when one of the severest earthquakes ever to strike the West Coast rattled all of southern California. The ground shook violently for a period of ten days, crumbling the walls of La Purisima. That, coupled with the torrential rains which ensued, almost completely destroyed what Fr. Payeras and his predecessors had built.

After surveying the devastation, Fr. Payeras came to a number of conclusions, two of which were of vital importance for the future: one, the mission site would have to be abandoned; and two, La Purisima would be rebuilt on the north side of the Santa Inés River in *Cañon de Los Berros*, a location better suited to the work of the mission and its service to travelers along *El Camino Real*. With characteristic energy, he threw himself and his Indian charges into the daunting task of building La Purisima on the new site. In so doing, Fr. Payeras deviated considerably from standard mission design, for while all the other missions in California, and throughout most of the Spanish Empire, were built in a quadrangular plan, La Purisima was not. Perhaps because of his earthquake experience, and certainly more in harmony with the Los Berros site, Mission La Purisima buildings are individual and strung out along the floor of the tight little valley. Moreover, Fr. Payeras built massively, with huge buttresses supporting exterior walls. The result was not only an efficient and effective mission establishment, but an architectural gem as well.

The future was not kind, however, to Fr. Payeras' labors. The Indian population of the mission continued to decline as forced labor, segregation, the strange diet, and European diseases took a frightful toll, and although there was mutual love and respect between Fr. Payeras and the Chumash, the latter harbored no similar feelings for the Spanish in general or the mission system in particular. Indeed, immediately after Fr. Payeras' death in 1823, the La Purisima Chumash joined a general south coast Indian uprising, a blow from which the once prosperous mission in Los Berros Canyon never recovered. The Franciscans abandoned the site, and later secularization placed mission properties in the hands of private administrators who sold lands and utilized mission buildings for barns, habitations, storage and the like, with no thought for maintenance or preservation. Thus when later Mexican Governor Manuel Micheltorena attempted to salvage something for the church by returning some missions to it, La Purisima was already beyond reclamation. Indeed, when American President Ulysses S. Grant signed the deed of La Purisima over to the church in 1874, there was almost nothing left, and practically all of the lands of the original establishment were in the hands of private individuals. Eventually, the Union Oil Company came into possession of much of the site and, fortunately, had some interest in preserving the few ruins which remained as testimony to Payeras' work.

Fr. Mariano Payeras had set the stage. He had chosen the site for the second Mission La Purisima, developed the plan and architecture, and erected the structures which would become the basis for the present reconstruction. Posterity is in his debt.

That brings us to another set of unusual circumstances leading directly to the emergence of the second extraordinary individual involved in Mission La Purisima, Frederick C. Hageman, architect. Unhappily, much less is known about Fred Hageman than Mariano Payeras, but the events which brought him to prominence were significant enough to mark an entire generation. The onset of the Great Depression in 1929, and its continuation for a decade, devastated the United States as effectively as the 1812 earthquake smashed the original Mission La Purisima. The collapse of the economy called for drastic remedial measures, and among the innovative approaches to recovery implemented by President Franklin D. Roosevelt was the Civilian Conservation Corps, a vehicle for the employment of American youth. Eventually enlisting more than three million young men, the CCC, among many other tasks, was charged with the preservation of historic sites and investigators scoured the nation seeking appropriate projects. One of them, Phillip Primm, happened upon the ruins of La Purisima in his travels and suggested it as a potential site for a camp.

Private, county, state, and federal officials, the latter represented by the National Park Service as the agency designated to supervise historic preservation projects, enthusiastically agreed. With an alacrity rarely seen in governmental operations, the forces were set in motion for the preservation of the La Purisima ruins.

As the project quickly matured, Fred Hageman, then Staff Architect in the National Park Service, was placed in charge. A workaholic by nature, Hageman plunged into the daunting task, marshalling the expertise of archaeologists, historians, knowledgeable locals, and anyone else who had information to offer as he developed his plans. Quickly grasping the enormous potential of the project, Hageman recommended a complete and authentic reconstruction of, if not the entire mission complex, at least its major structures, thus embroiling himself in the age-old controversy over reconstruction versus preservation. The original concept for the mission ruins was simply to stabilize and protect the existing remains—portions of walls, foundations, and the like—but after determining for himself the enormous potential value of a completely reconstructed mission, Hageman charged ahead, gearing the camp for a reconstruction effort. His persistence, and the unassailable logic of this position, won out. The entire concept was changed along the lines Hageman suggested. Then, with historian Russell Ewing looking over his shoulder all the while, Hageman went to extraordinary lengths to ascertain what, exactly, had been there before. That meant not only historical research in old documents, but assessing the architectural and archaeological evidence, visiting other mission sites for comparison and suggestion, and, when all else failed, using common sense, something Fr. Payeras had in abundance and certainly would have appreciated in his modern successor. His methods are well documented in his report and the result of his ideas and labors is one of the finest historical reconstructions anywhere.

However, Hageman's vision would not have become the marvel it is without the dedicated work of the men of the La Purisima Camp of the Civilian Conservation Corps. Those young men, mostly from the Los Angeles area and supervised by local contractors and builders, realized that theirs was not simply a make-work project. They knew they were creating something for the ages. As a result, they learned and applied their skills with enthusiasm, many of them developing successful careers built on their CCC experience. They reenlisted again and again, occasionally even beyond the limit allowed, in order to see the job to completion. Their devotion, too, would have delighted Fr. Payeras.

When the advent of World War II brought an arbitrary end to the La Purisima project and the men of the CCC moved on to military service or war-related jobs, Fred Hageman wrote up his report, crafting it as meticulously as he had fashioned the mission buildings. Like all good government reports, it was filed away and remained relatively unknown, except for devotees of La Purisima Mission, who used it as a bible for the upkeep and improvement of the site. And there it might have remained had not a group of historical reconstructionists from the Santa Barbara Trust for Historic Preservation become frustrated in their own attempt to find relevant information for the rebuilding of *El Presidio de Santa Barbara*, the military headquarters of the district in which La Purisima stood. The Hageman report proved to be a godsend, and some members of the Trust realized that the report had implications far beyond the reconstruction of a single mission. Led by a past president, the late Richard S. Whitehead, the Trust raised the funds to publish *An Archaeological and Restoration Study of Mission La Purisima Concepcion* (Santa Barbara, 1980).

All copies of that first edition have since been distributed, but, given the burgeoning interest in historic preservation and reconstruction, the Santa Barbara Trust for Historic Preservation is offering this new printing as a tribute to all those, past and present, who contributed to the reconstruction of Mission La Purisima and to all of those who would preserve our rich historical heritage. It is a document upon which to build dreams

Richard E. Oglesby
Santa Barbara, 1990

ACKNOWLEDGEMENTS

The original edition of this book was part of *The Santa Barbara Bicentennial Historical Series,* a collaborative publishing effort among six Santa Barbara organizations. That effort was made possible by grant support from The Thomas More Storke Fund of The Santa Barbara Foundation. Participating organizations at that time agreed that all monies accruing from the sale of publications in the series would be applied to future scholarly works. This edition of *La Purísima Concepción* is funded in part by the Storke Publication Fund of the Santa Barbara Trust for Historic Preservation, established as part of that original agreement and administered by the Presidio Research Center.

As Doyce B. Nunis, Jr. stated in the original edition, the "guiding spirit" behind *The Santa Barbara Bicentennial Historical Series* was "a lady of grace and dedication," Mrs. Ernest F. Menzies, daughter of the late Thomas More Storke. We acknowledge with deep gratitude the continuing generous support and encouragement of Jean Storke Menzies, who has been instrumental in making this reprint possible.

We also wish to acknowledge the assistance of Prelado de los Tesoros, that superb group of dedicated volunteers who put the "living" in living history at La Purisima Mission State Historic Park.

Lest we forget, it took someone with the dedication and talents Santa Barbara Trust for Historic Preservation Life Honorary Trustee Richard S. Whitehead possessed to shepherd this volume through its original publication. Always obsessed with getting the facts right, Whitehead was the perfect person for the task.

Jarrell C. Jackman, Ph.D.
Executive Director
Santa Barbara Trust for
Historic Preservation

TABLE OF CONTENTS

PART ONE

AN ARCHITECTURAL STUDY OF MISSION LA PURISIMA CONCEPCION

By Frederick C. Hageman

PART TWO

MISSION LA PURISIMA CONCEPCION, CALIFORNIA
By Russell C. Ewing

LIST OF PLATES

EDITOR'S INTRODUCTION

Between 1769 and 1830, twenty-one Franciscan missions and four presidios or forts were built in Upper California to promote and protect Spain's program of colonizing and Christianizing the west coast. Some of these establishments had to be rebuilt several times due to earthquake damage, faulty workmanship, fire, weather and the need for expansion of facilities to accomodate growth. Most of the missions still stand although some have been almost completely rebuilt, and many are being used daily as parish churches, but the presidios have all but disappeared. Only at Santa Barbara are efforts being made to reconstruct the entire presidio complex.

Reliable information detailing the materials used in the buildings, their furnishings and the construction methods used during this period is meager. The padres and soldiers saw no reason for recording their routine day by day activities and practices, and so the written accounts are almost non-existent. Historical documents such as annual and progress reports provide generalized information, but little detail. The surviving buildings and ruins tell part of the story if one can distinguish between the original work and later reconstruction. Archeological investigations and findings during repair and restoration work, if properly recorded, provide valuable detail. When the Hageman and Ewing reports on La Purísima Mission were "rediscovered" therefore, they proved a bonanza to those interested in rebuilding the Santa Barbara Presidio. Recognizing the value of these reports to historians, archeologists, architects, engineers and those interested in building and furnishing adobe structures of that period in an authentic manner, the Santa Barbara Trust for Historic Preservation, sponsors of the program for reconstructing the Santa Barbara Royal Presidio, decided to publish them as part of the Santa Barbara Bicentennial Historical Series.

During the forty years since these reports were written, new discoveries at Mission La Purísima and elsewhere have been made which could provide additional information on the subject. It seemed best, however, to publish the two reports essentially as they were originally written, leaving the up-dating to a supplementary publication. The only changes made from the original manuscript, therefore, were those necessary to eliminate errors in typography and spelling, including the insertion of accent marks where needed, the correction of obvious errors in quotes and sources, and the addition of an index. Every effort was made to verify quotations and notations, but some sources could not be checked. A few photographs accompanying the Ewing report were omitted because they were duplicated in the Hageman report.

Except as noted above, we have faithfully tried to reproduce as accurately as possible the original text and illustrations. The numerous photographs and their figure numbers appear in the same order as in the manuscript. Many are not specifically referred to in the text although inserted in such a location that they will illustrate the accompanying subject matter. For this reason, some references to illustrations by figure number occur long after the photo or drawing appears in the text.

Plate XI in the original manuscript contained nine canvas swatches in color to illustrate its title "Interiors and Color Treatments". Cost of color printing and the difficulty of duplicating exactly the original shades made reproduction of the colors impractical. Only the Plates are listed in the Table of Contents. Where appropriate to the Index entry, the subject of figures is listed by page in the Index.

I am deeply appreciative of the confidence placed in me by Mrs. Ernest F. Menzies and the other trustees of the Santa Barbara Trust for Historic Preservation when they accepted my offer to prepare these reports for publication on a volunteer basis. This granted me the privilege of working with Dr. Doyce B. Nunis Jr., Professor of History at the University of Southern California, a noted author and historian, and Editor-in-Chief of the series of which this book is a part. His encouragement and patient guidance were invaluable and I am most grateful to him for his help.

For their assistance in obtaining permission to publish these reports, thanks are due to Theodore Wilson, Herbert L. Heinze, Jack Mason and James P. Tryner of the State Department of Parks and Recreation, and to Robert M. Utley and Gordon Chappell of the National Park Service. Mr. Chappell was especially cooperative in loaning one of the original copies of the manuscripts which included the numerous photographic prints.

In the early stages of the project, photographic copies of the original reports had to be made, and this was accomplished through the volunteer help of Brian Kennedy who made positive prints from the negatives sent us through the cooperation of the Sacramento office of the State Department of Parks and Recreation. Mrs. Henry Griffiths, Executive Director of the Santa Barbara Historical Society, arranged for us to use the Society's excellent darkroom facilities. My thanks are extended to both of them.

Because of the limited number of available copies of the original manuscripts, it was necessary to find and use duplicate prints from the archives of Mission La Purísima. Where none were available, photographic copies had to be made from the prints in the original manuscript. The tedious chore of matching prints with negatives and of finding duplicate prints and negatives fell to Dick Edwards and Harold Hallett, State Park Rangers at Mission La Purísima. They spent many hours at this task which yielded the benefit of a well-organized photographic archive. Their dedication to this job is gratefully acknowledged. William Dewey, photographer for the Santa Barbara Historical Society, is to be thanked for the excellence of the duplicate prints of the illustrations he made when none were available for the printer.

Last, but far from least, I want to acknowledge my indebtedness to Mrs. Muriel Fuller who spent countless hours at the typewriter, all without remuneration, to produce drafts and letters related to the project. Without such dedicated help, a task such as this could not be completed.

Her advice and wise counsel stemming from her years of experience as an executive secretary made the undertaking possible.

I was privileged to know some of those who instigated the Mission La Purísima restoration project and others who participated in the investigative and construction phases when, in the 1950s and 60s, I served as secretary of the La Purísima Mission Advisory Committee to the State Park Commission. My work in editing these reports has evoked a new feeling of esteem for their dedication and competence. But it also has aroused a new respect and admiration for the men of the Civilian Conservation Corps who worked on the La Purísima project. Their ability to help salvage from a worthless ruin the invaluable information contained in these reports and to create from that ruin the historical monument to the Mission period that can be enjoyed by this and future generations for all time has not, I believe, been adequately recognized. I would like to add my "Salute" to those men.

Richard S. Whitehead

PART ONE

AN ARCHITECTURAL STUDY
OF THE
MISSION LA PURISIMA CONCEPCION
CALIFORNIA

By Frederick C. Hageman

LETTER OF TRANSMITTAL

National Park Service
Region Four
San Francisco, California
April 25, 1939

Memorandum for Regional Director Frank A. Kittredge:

A report, "An Architectural Study of the Mission La Purísima Concepción, California," prepared by Mr. Frederick C. Hageman, Architectural Foreman under my supervision is herewith submitted for your approval.

This report was prepared in accordance with arrangements whereby the Director of the National Park Service approved our request that Mr. Hageman be detailed to this assignment. This was encouraged by State Park Authority Dan R. Hull, Inspector Phillip T. Primm and Superintendent H. V. Smith, who urged that such a report should be prepared by Mr. Hageman before he resigned from the Service, which he has since done. He has summed up herein the results of his work and conclusions.

The history of Mission La Purísima Concepción has already been treated in considerable detail in one of Father Engelhardt's publications (1932), and in a monograph (1937) by Dr. Russell C. Ewing, formerly Associate Historian of the National Park Service. The present report was planned, therefore, to provide a comprehensive study of the physical aspects. Through a review of the project, attention is brought to steps by which this mission came into public ownership as a state historical monument. A summary of archeological work at the site by the Civilian Conservation Corps indicates the valuable knowledge gained from material remains uncovered by excavations. A discussion of documentary, photographic, archeological and architectural sources reveals information on which plans for individual buildings and the mission as a whole have thus far been reconstructed. Data from laboratory analyses of old materials suggest how problems encountered in discovering and emulating original adobe construction, wall surfaces, tile and woodwork were solved.

Letter of Transmittal

The intensive study of the physical aspects of Mission La Purísima has suggested comparisons and conclusions regarding California mission architecture in general and has corrected misapprehensions as to the plan and construction of particular buildings and the mission as a whole. The report explains former erroneous conclusions, especially in regard to the enlarged chapel, usually believed to have been the church.

Because of favorable comment that the restoration has received from eminent authorities in the fields of architecture, archeology and history, and from the Franciscan order, it is hoped that the report will also promote what Dr. M. R. Harrington has called "The right kind of restoration." Old methods of making tile and adobe and constructing buildings by the use of such materials are suggested by the study. Attention is also given to furnishings and hardware copied from originals recovered at La Purísima or in use at other California missions.

Cost of reproduction has limited the number of copies of this report to seven. In addition to two copies each to the Washington and Fourth Regional Office of the National Park Service, and the State Division of Parks, approval is requested for the deposit of one copy at the Bancroft Library. The historical materials of this library and the assistance of its staff are constant aids in historical work on this and other projects. If the Service approves, directo prints of any part of the report, or photographs contained therein, and copies of detailed drawings of furnishings can be provided at cost. A still wider service would be rendered if the study could be published. This has been discussed with Associate Director A. E. Demaray and Mr. Conrad S. Wirth, Supervisor of Recreation and Land Planning.

Olaf T. Hagen
Associate Research Technician

ACKNOWLEDGMENTS

The past four years has been a fascinating adventure, made doubly pleasant by the unfailing interest and courtesy on the part of those many persons who have cheerfully and generously contributed time and information toward the undertaking at La Purísima Concepción.

Dr. Herbert E. Bolton, and Dr. Owen C. Coy, have both lent the benefit of their wide experience to advise how best to guard and develop the principal values of the monument. Expert archeologists and museum men such as Arthur Woodward of the Los Angeles County Museum, and Dr. M. R. Harrington of the Southwest Museum have travelled long miles to advise on correct procedure.

For the courtesies extended, this writer, as a member of the National Park Service, wishes to express appreciation to His Excellency, the Most Reverend J. J. Cantwell, Archbishop of Los Angeles. A debt of gratitude is due to the *Padres* at the various missions which have been visited in the search for original material, particularly the Franciscan Fathers of Mission Santa Barbara and San Miguel. Throughout the work, Father Roddy and Father Maynard Geiger have opened to us the resources of the Santa Barbara Mission Archives and have been a constant source of aid and sympathetic advice. Father Wand, pastor of the old Mission San Miguel, has also been most helpful, and has acted more than once as my genial host, and as mentor on reconnaissance expeditions. To the Capuchin Fathers of Santa Inés, Purísima's neighbor, our heartfelt thanks are also extended for their never failing hospitality during many visits there for the purpose of measuring and photographing details, and to film the original record books which are in their care.

Most particularly do I express gratitude to Mrs. Edith Webb, who has contributed so largely from her detailed and intimate knowledge of mission lore and from her extensive documentary and pictorial collection, accumulated through long years of research. Her continued interest and periodic visits have counted heavily in prosecuting the work.

The region of Santa Barbara County treasures its Spanish background and traditions. Much history is stored in the minds and memories of the older residents, who have been a very real source of detailed local knowledge. Among these is Mr. Emmet O'Neil, who lived as a boy close by the mission. He has supplied much information from his amazingly accurate memory — information not in books or documents, which could be and was, many times corroborated in the field. Many other local residents have manifested their interest and contributed most valuable data. Space does not permit mentioning individual names, but to them all our thanks are rendered.

Many societies and organizations, whether primarily interested in historical matters or not, have cooperated. Among them should be mentioned the California State Historical Society, for the use of pictures from its collection, the Society of California Pioneers, for permission to photograph certain documents; the Pioneer Society of Lompoc Valley; the Amer-

Acknowledgments

ican Index of Design for contribution of technical assistance and information resulting from its study of mission decoration; the Union Oil Company for photographs and other aids; the Southern Pacific Railroad Company for furnishing the Tibbets series of photographs; and the Bancroft Library, for the use of its facilities. To Professor George Hendry, University of California, and his colleague, Mr. J. N. Bowman, we are indebted for information on early adobes and on the Spanish-Mexican land grants. The W.P.A. unit under the direction of Dr. Aubrey Neasham has performed a most valuable work in translating the recently filmed copies of the La Purísima annual and biennial reports, and in addition has transcribed and translated in full, for the first time, the La Purísima account books and other records.

The sources of the historical pictorial collection have not been detailed in this report. However, precise information as to whereabouts of original negatives will be found in the photographic file at the La Purisima Camp, and later will be on file at the Regional Office in San Francisco. The greatest number of photographs were secured from Messrs. C. C. Pierce and Company, Los Angeles; Putnam Studios, Los Angeles; Tibbitts, San Francisco; the Southwest Museum, Los Angeles; together with some miscellaneous views by private individuals which had not found their way into the historical collections.

It needs scarcely be added that the work of Father Zephyrin Engelhardt, the Franciscan historian, has been a constant guide and reference. More recently the sound historical account by the former Regional Historian, Dr. R. C. Ewing, has supplemented the earlier work.

The members of the La Purísima Advisory Committee have given careful and sincere attention to the problems presented, and their continued interest and desire to bring about the most desirable development of the monument has been exhibited in many ways. Mr. Wallace C. Penfield, its chairman, has ably correlated many opinions into concise form to enable the State Park Commission to formulate proper policies.

Finally, and perhaps one of the most essential factors in the success of such an undertaking has been the close cooperation of the local Park Service personnel, of which each and every one has conscientiously and loyally worked toward a common goal for nearly four years.

This page would be incomplete were the name of Inspector Phillip T. Primm omitted. His vision of the possibilities for a splendid work caused him to make initial recommendations to start the work, and the brightness of that vision has not dimmed in the time since.

For advice and active assistance in organizing and preparing this report I tender my very great thanks to Regional Historian Olaf T. Hagen. The benefit of his broad knowledge of historic sites, and his wide experience has effected a marked improvement, which he would, I know, modestly deprecate.

Frederick C. Hageman,
Senior Foreman, (Architect)
July 26, 1938

A SALUTE TO THE CIVILIAN CONSERVATION CORPS

When the stir of activity has ceased, and the dust of reconstruction has settled at La Purísima Concepción, California should long remember the Civilian Conservation Corps, which regained a splendid monument from a desolate ruin.

To a task of heroic proportions they brought the confidence and enthusiasm of youth — unconscious that they mastered problems that perplexed many an expert.

They met an intricate job, and they did it well. Let him who views the restored mission, and whose thoughts turn back to the gray-robed *Padres* and their dusky toilers, pay tribute also to these youthful builders of today who so ably played their part.

INTRODUCTION

Immediately north of the promontory formed by Point Conception and Point Arguello, which marks the western end of the Santa Barbara Channel, a coastal valley famed for its broad acres of flowers meets the sea. This fertile Lompoc Valley of prosperous farm lands extends eastward for more than ten miles before being hemmed in by the Santa Rita Hills.

Spanish missionaries and military officials quickly recognized that this valley possessed qualities essential to a successful mission — a large native population, a promising agricultural area of large extent, ample pasturage, and an abundance of water, both for domestic use and for irrigation.[1] Building materials were also conveniently available: timber, stone, and lime rock were nearby, and firewood could be secured from the valley bottom and from the rolling mesas to the north.

Eight years of missionary activity in *Alta California* had convinced religious and governmental officials that the Santa Ynez, then called the Santa Rosa country, was of strategic military and administrative importance to the whole California mission system. The main north and south line of communications must pass very close along the Santa Barbara Channel through the country of the *Canaliño* Indians, and should be controlled.

Therefore, the plan of Governor Neve, dated June 3, 1777, calling for the founding of a mission and presidio at Santa Barbara, and a mission at each end of the channel, to be known as San Buenaventura and La Purísima Concepción respectively, found favor with the Mexican authorities.[2]

After the establishment of Mission San Buenaventura in 1782, and Santa Barbara in 1786, the third step in the plan was carried out by the founding of Mission La Purísima Concepción by *Padre Presidente* Fermín de Lasuén on December 8, 1787. The site selected lay close to the hillslope south of the river Santa Ynez, and about ten miles distant from the sea, within the city limits of what is now the town of Lompoc, California.

For the first twenty-five years, success attended the venture and La Purísima Concepción grew to occupy an important place in the mission chain. The number of natives living under the protection of the mission increased to 1,520; their agricultural developments and cattle raising activities extended many miles in all directions. In 1812 activities at this site were suddenly halted by the unusually violent earthquakes which occurred along the entire California coast. At La Purísima the buildings were so badly damaged and the natives so badly frightened by the catastrophe, that the *Padres* seriously considered the advisability of abandoning this site.

Across the valley, on the north side of the river, a small *cañada* runs to the north. It was called by the Spaniards Los Berros, a name attributed to the water cresses found there. The highroad of California, the *Camino Real,* winding its way from mission Santa Inés through the rolling Santa Rita hills on the northern side of the river, entered the Lompoc Valley near the mouth of Los Berros. Here the old road turned sharply to the north, passing up the little *cañada*, on its way to San Luis Obispo, La Purísima's neighbor mission fifty-five miles to the north. To reach old La Purísima or the "Mission *Vieja*", as it was later called, it was necessary to cross the river, which during flood stage was impassable. With the approval of the new location in March 1813, Los Berros became the site of the second Mission La Purísima Concepción. Future travelers would thus be saved a detour of about four miles, the distance which the old site was removed from the highway. With courageous and vigorous effort, an extensive group of buildings was erected there in a remarkably short time.

In the decline of California missions that followed with the close of the mission period, the subsequent decay and their secularization, Purísima fared ill, indeed. One by one her buildings were reduced to ruin, until, in 1933, even her principal edifice, the Residence, was an unroofed ruin, and the Church had fallen into such a state that only portions of adobe walls indicated its outline. Two or three rubbish filled masonry reservoirs and pools — remnants of the former water system — indicated here and there the elaborate system once existing.

Efforts had been made in 1905 to undertake to repair and restore the Residence. The proprietors of the area embracing the mission succeeded in interesting the Landmarks Club of California in its preservation. On the condition that a certain sum be spent, the Residence and five small ruins were deeded to the Club. Plans for this work were never carried out, and each passing year further reduced the ruin.[3]

When the County of Santa Barbara acquired the ruin in 1933, the monument passed into public hands. Not certain of what could be done toward its preservation or restoration, the county supervisors felt that the opportunity for public ownership was one to be grasped.

The Civilian Conservation Corps proved to be the answer. Here was a group of young, untrained laborers, needing only proper direction to accomplish what all else had failed to do. Here was a monument, built in its day by untrained labor — the Indians — directed by intelligent leadership it was obvious that here was an analogous situation.

Could they undertake the tremendous archeological investigations? After the necessary field information had been secured, analyzed and related to the research information by competent technicians, could these young men successfully carry out the complicated task of restoration? Many believed they could, and acting on favorable recommendations the Department of the Interior granted the petition of the County to establish a CCC camp in the area.

To acquire land considered most essential for development as an historical monument the County of Santa Barbara and the State of California jointly purchased about forty acres of the mission site. To this nearly 470 acres of rolling mesa land was added as a gift. In 1935 title to the whole area was vested in the State and designated the La Purísima State Historical Monument, to be administered by the Department of Natural Resources, Division of State Parks.

Actual development has resulted through the cooperation of three separate agencies. The County of Santa Barbara, the original owner of the main ruin and several smaller isolated ruins, relinquished its title and furnished one half of the sum required for the purchase of additional land. The State of California has assumed responsibility for the administration and for the proper development of the area. The Federal Government, cooperating with the State through the National Park Service of the Department of the Interior, has supplied technical advice, funds and labor; and has supervised development jointly agreed upon.

The immediate objective when work at the site was begun was investigation of existing remains with a view to permanently recording historical and archeological data. This, it was hoped, would be the initial step in the restoration of the main building.

Informed residents of Santa Barbara County indicated their interest in the undertaking and desired that any proposed restoration be carefully handled. The State Park Commission, desiring serious study of the broad problems presented by the newly acquired monument in March, 1935, named a group of persons qualified in different pertinent fields to act in an advisory capacity.[4]

Meanwhile, the excavation and reconnaissance of the site begun in November, 1934 had been restricted to minor structures pending the acquisition of additional land by the State. The land transfer, completed in January, 1935, permitted the archeological investigation of the mission Residence, the principal ruin.

In the meantime, research had been carried forward. Historical societies, museums, and writers contributed information in the form of drawings and photographs. Published materials and original documents were examined for descriptive and historical information. Old residents, who remembered the building as children, were interviewed, many came forward with reminiscences and descriptions. Gradually a fund of varied and valuable information was compiled.

In the spring of 1935, the Advisory Committee met with technicians of the local National Park Service staff to review the information available and to consider policies for guiding contemplated development. The committee recommended that work on the restoration of the Residence be undertaken as soon as necessary plans could be prepared.

By June, 1935, plans for the first unit had been approved by the State authorities and by the Washington Office of the National Park Service. Nearly a year had passed since the occupation of the site, but the time had been well spent in reconnaissance, investigation and research.

In the spring of 1937, the restoration of the Residence building had been completed, except for minor details. Completion of this unit requires the acquisition or duplication of mission furnishings, an undertaking which continues in progress.

Meanwhile, the wide interest in this project has enlarged the scope of the ultimate plan for the development of the monument. Instead of confining the undertaking to the one major building as originally planned, prominent authorities in fields of history, architecture and archeology have confirmed earlier recommendations for the restoration of a complete mission establishment at La Purísima.[5]

Investigation required for the work thus far accomplished has added to our knowledge of the materials and methods of California's Spanish builders who established a simple architecture so pleasing and eminently suitable to the country that it continues to be a guiding inspiration.

To relate the story of the restoration; to present the information gathered during three and a half years of study; to frankly state the problems encountered and the reasons for the solutions adopted is the purpose of the following report.

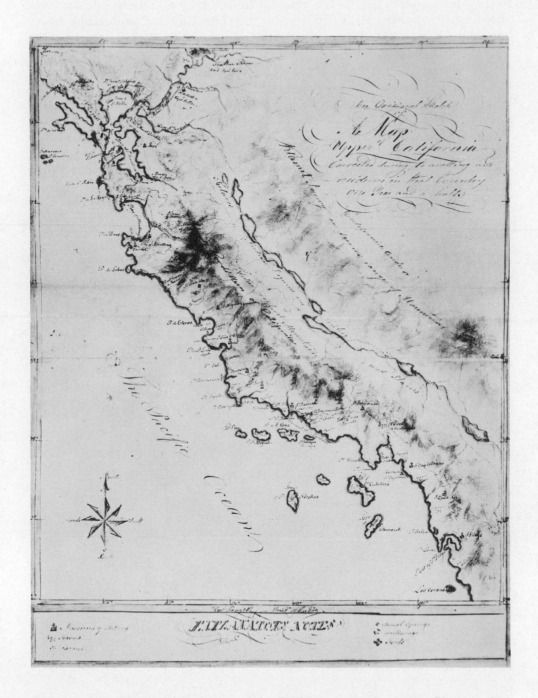

Figure 1. The "King's Orphan" map of the California coast about 1842. Photographed from the original in the possession of the Society of California Pioneers, and copied through their courtesy. Published in the *Quarterly* of the Society, June 30, 1926.

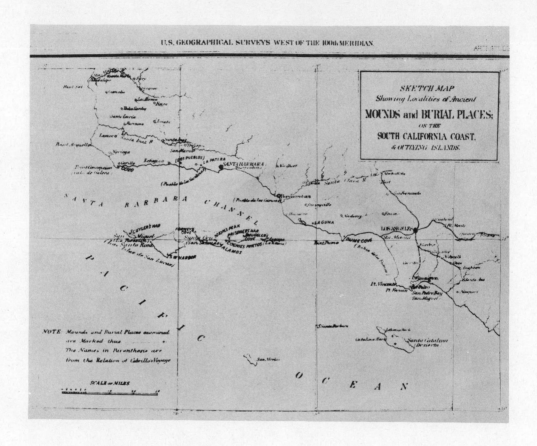

Figure 2. U. S. Geographical Survey of the channel region published in 1879. The roads of this period are clearly shown. Note that the original *Camino Real* no longer extended beyond Casmalia, and the stage route passed through Los Alamos and Santa Ynez. *U. S. Geographical Surveys West of the One Hundredth Meridian.* Washington, 1879. Vol. VII, Part I.

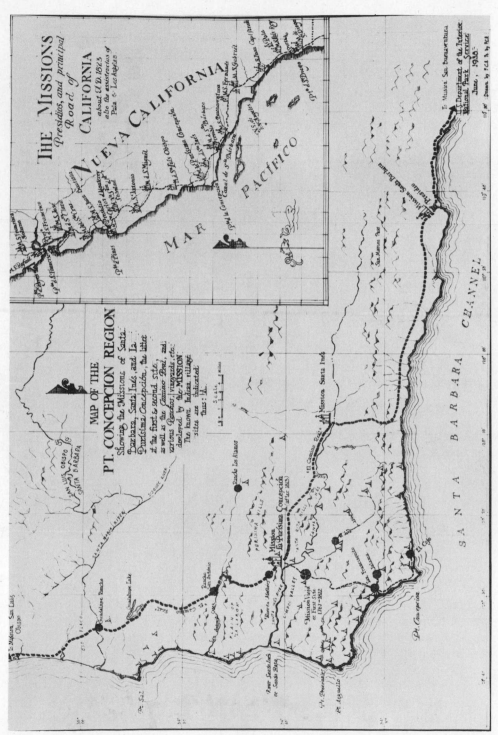

Plate No. I

"Malo House" Ruin: In a field about three-eighths of a mile north of the Residence building explorations uncovered the foundation of a small structure. The foundation measured about twenty-three by thirty-three feet, and was divided into four small rooms or spaces. The top of the stonework was approximately eighteen inches below the present grade.[4] The U.S. patent map (Figure 6) indicates a small house at this point, marked "Malo's house," but details of its history are not known. Work on the water system was suspended in January, 1935, when the excavation of the Residence was commenced.

The Mission Residence: On January 4, 1935, according to the entry in Field Book number 2, a party of seventeen men began the investigation of the Residence ruins. Authority for proceeding with this work had been eagerly awaited and it had been decided that as soon as the land status had been settled, the investigation should be started without further delay. Consequently, it was with the greatest enthusiasm that the entire personnel received the news that the property was now State-owned, and that the excavation of the main building had been approved.

Following methods that had been used in the exploration of the water system, archeological excavation was commenced. The architectural foreman was assigned to supervise the work and record the information. For assistance in surveys and measurements the survey party under the direction of the engineering foreman was available. Mr. E. D. Rowe, the landscape foreman, was delegated to make necessary photographic records because of his equipment and experience. Enrollees assigned to archeological jobs were instructed in the work and in the history of the ruin. They were especially cautioned regarding the paramount importance of not destroying the very fragile remains that it was expected would be encountered.

Mr. Arthur Woodward, Archeologist for the Los Angeles County Museum had previously visited the site in company with Dr. Owen C. Coy, Chairman of the Department of History at the University of Southern California, and had suggested to members of the staff proper methods of procedure, and impressed them with the need for great caution in every phase of the undertaking. It was with a wholesome respect, therefore, that the party approached the grass-grown mound and the precarious walls which were still standing.

The objective of the investigation was to obtain all available information as to plan, elevations, materials, and details of all parts of the original construction. It was hoped that artifacts recovered would add to our knowledge of mission life, and would indicate the original use of the rooms.

The decomposition of the walls had proceeded to a point where in some instances they were invisible above the resulting earth mound. At the north end of the building the earth mound was approximately five feet above the original floor line, and extended outward for a distance of nearly fifty feet, diminishing in depth away from the building. In some parts, particularly the southwest portion, the mound reached heights of nine to ten feet above the floor level. It was estimated that between four and five thousand yards of material would have to be moved in order to expose all the remains of the original structure.

The seventeen men assigned to the excavation were divided into two groups. After establishing the main corners of the building, men trenched the overburden at carefully chosen points in order to expose the cross section down to the floor lines. These trenches extended transversely through the entire building, including the east and west corridors, and beyond the building lines for a reasonable distance. Thus the floor levels were established at fixed points. It was found that the floor in the east corridor and the walk on the west side of the building had been covered with tiles. The first floors uncovered inside the rooms were badly decomposed redwood.

After the extreme corner measurements had been accurately established by survey, dimensions were taken so that a rough field plan could be drawn up at the scale of one-eighth inch to the foot. On this plan, the existing walls, openings and other features were entered in ink. Additional plan information was added in pencil as it was determined by the excavation. The plan drawing was supplemented by details and notes entered in the field books by the architectural foreman, and these are to be found in Field Book Number 2. The enrollee leader kept a daily work diary, or log, giving such information as the size of the crew, location of work, what was established by the day's work, etc.

After preliminary explorations had established main features of the structure, the interior of each room was encircled by a narrow trench started a few inches away from the wall. The earth separating the trench from the wall was carefully removed by the men who had proved themselves most dependable and cautious. This work was necessarily slow and painstaking, and the tools that were used might vary from a pocket knife and a whisk broom to a brick mason's trowel. In many cases the findings were so fragile that the information they yielded had to be recorded immediately, for only a few hours of exposure totally destroyed the evidence. This work of carefully following up each wall surface actually revealed the ground plan of the building. It was surprising how much information existed below the surface of the earth mound. In all but a few locations, the plan could be established with precision. Floor levels and floor materials could be readily distinguished in most instances. Certain rooms contained no trace of the original flooring, but even in some of these it was possible to fix the level by the point to which the whitewash of plaster extended.

In two parts of the building it proved difficult to determine the former wall openings with any degree of accuracy because of the almost complete disintegration of the walls above the foundation. These portions were the northwest corner and along the west wall, starting about fifty-six feet from the south end, and extending about eighty-eight feet. Almost no trace of the adobe wall was found along this entire distance. Pictorial evidence indicated that this wall had disappeared before 1892.

[3]

The existing walls yielded considerable definite information, which was recorded. Door and window openings, door and window locations, and very often the horizontal dimensions could be determined even though the upper portions of the opening had disappeared. Dimensions of the wall openings recorded on charts and additional data about them were entered in the field books. Thirteen doorways and ten window openings were thus quite fully described.

The height of the ceilings could be established in the south end of the building and from the north end down to approximately the center. A few rotted ceiling beams were still in place, and even where these beams had disappeared the wooden sills and the beam sockets permitted accurate measurements of the spacing. Existing beams were salvaged and stored. It was interesting to observe that the ends which had been set in the adobe walls were well preserved and provided information about the appearance and shape of the originals. These will later be discussed in detail.

The walls clearly indicate the former surface treatment. It was found that all of the front row of rooms, from the north end to the passageway separating the chapel from the living quarters, had been plastered with lime plaster, whereas all of the rear row of rooms and the rooms south of the passageway had been plastered with mud and whitewashed. The surfaces of the exterior walls on the sides receiving the full force of the southeast rains were protected by a substantial lime plaster coat, while those on the west had received the more economical mud and whitewash treatment. Traces of color decoration were carefully filed in envelopes and recorded. Samples of the plaster were removed and stored for the information that they gave as to material, method, texture and color.

The elevations of wall and column tops, doors and windows, floors, beams and sockets had to be established at important points, because it was found that the entire structure was built to follow the natural grade of the site. The exterior stone wall enclosing the east corridor was found to slope downward from the north end of the building to the south, a total of 3.87 feet, in the total distance of 315 feet. Consequently, elevations of ceiling or floor levels at any particular point could not be indicated as typical for the whole building.

Of the tile masonry columns of the colonnade fronting the building, nine of the original nineteen were standing. In addition to these there was also the extra stone column, which is generally credited to the Mexican period, and which was not a part of the colonnade proper. All of the columns showed the effects of time and weather, and some had been damaged by vandalism. Only one remained intact, with the cap, base and fluted shaft complete. The other columns had been either completely removed, or as in the case of one, pushed over, and some of the tiles picked out of the shattered mass and carried away.

Other details of stonework, buttresses, steps, drains were entered on the plans and elevation drawings. From the data thus accumulated, a more carefully drawn plan was prepared and measurements were rechecked by the surveying party. Errors were corrected, desired additional data was obtained when possible and many of the elevations were established again. By the end of March, 1935, the recording of data yielded by remains was complete except for further detailed information found necessary for the preparation of the restoration drawings. The huge accumulation of earth had been removed from the ruin and hauled away into stock piles. The excavated walls, no matter how hazardous their condition, were left unprotected, pending final decision on policies to be pursued.

The recovery of artifacts in the excavation proved disappointing. During the long period that the building had been abandoned, most things that appealed to souvenir hunters had been removed and carried away. The excavation did yield many evidences of architectural importance. These findings, along with others found elsewhere on the site, have been catalogued and classified.[5] Details of hardware, such as hinges, locks, strike plates, decorative nails and bosses were helpful in providing detailed information for the restoration. Since no complete doors or shutters existed, fragments of shutters, frames, panels, etc., were regarded as treasures. Some examples of old tools and other equipment were unearthed. Saws, axes, mattocks, garden tools, an interesting wood auger and leather tools are all listed in the catalogue. Of special interest was an obsolete tool formerly used for boring holes in adobe. The artifacts recovered were too scattered to constitute any conclusive evidence of the original use of the different rooms. In determining the usage of different parts of the buildings, recorded archeological findings can at best corroborate conclusions arrived at from other sources.

The investigation occupied approximately three months and the work of an average of twenty-five men during that time. Over four thousand yards of earth were moved and dumped into stock piles, awaiting further disposition. The possibility of screening the lower strata in the hope of recovering additional artifacts was reluctantly dismissed because the results of the material thus carefully sifted did not yield any information of value. During the excavation the strata close to the floor had been carefully worked and any artifacts discovered removed.

Tallow Vats (Structure Number 6):

In February a crew of seven men was assigned to investigate a ruin visible on the hillslope about seventy-five feet west of the Church. Excavation revealed a masonry structure of stone, tile and copper, unquestionably the early soap and tallow vats. Similar structures exist at other California missions, but in less complete form. Its preservation can be attributed to the protection of the sandy hillside, which had covered all but a few stones. No evidence was at first found to indicate that this structure had been connected with a nearby spring, as was conjectured. However, in 1938, remains of an aqueduct, made of inverted roof tile, helped explain the choice of this location. This ruin deserves further detailed study in connection with historical references in order to gain a more complete picture of how the vats were operated.

The area lying between the tallow vats and the Church was found to contain a foundation of poor quality and small size containing two rooms. That one of the rooms had been added to the other was indicated by the addition lapping over the earlier structure. (Figure 50). The soil inside this foundation appeared to be in greasy layers, which alternated with less greasy layers. Although this structure appeared to connect with the Church, investigation was not completed at that time, since title to the Church ruin had not yet been acquired. Later study proved that the building was not a part of the Church, and the greasiness of the soil suggests that it probably served in connection with the nearby tallow vats, possibly as storehouse or candleroom. Other evidence indicates that this building had either been destroyed or removed prior to 1821.[6]

Workshops and Quarters Building (Structure Number 2):

On February 14, preliminary reconnaissance was started on the second major building which begins at a point twenty-six feet six inches south of the Residence. This is an L-shaped building, the main wing of which continues the axis of the Residence for a distance of 323 feet, where a minor wing extends to the west, almost to the northeast corner of the Church. At the time the work began this ruin was completely covered with earth, although the top of the east wall foundation was but very few inches below ground level. Along both sides of the main wing, foundations of the former colonnade were found at regular intervals. On the west, foundations of walls indicate a double patio, or walled enclosure, extending from the west wing to the north end of the building. The entire ruin covered an area approximately 323 by eighty feet. When the results of this work were checked against the original reports of the missionaries it was found that it agreed with the building reported in 1816 as the guardhouse, workrooms and living quarters for the soldiers, the *mayordomos* and families, although the report mentions no patio.[7] Findings indicate that the early plat of the Mission ruins known as the Alemany plat (Figure 3) was incorrect in its representation of this building, suggesting that it was in an advanced state of ruin by 1853. In February, 1936, remains were more fully excavated and detailed measurements were recorded. The study of this building was completed in the Fall of 1937.

Church:

A reconnaissance of "what is thought to be wall surrounding Church," was begun on February 28, 1935.[8] The limits of the building, and trenching within the nave, exposed the tile flooring and some of the plaster of the walls. Since the building had not yet been transferred to the State, work on this site was delayed until May of the following year. The detailed excavation was recorded and reported in archeological reports for June and July, 1936.

Buildings 7 and 8:

The hillslope to the west of the Church, Workshops, and Residence was explored by means of a continuous zig-zag trench, starting from the tallow vats. Several important items of information were secured by this procedure. First was the discovery of the two minor buildings Nos. seven and eight at the base of the hillslope west of the Residence. The north end of building No. eight coincided with the north line of the Residence and consisted of two rooms, with a large opening on the south end. This building measured twenty-one feet by fifty-one feet. The other building (No. seven) consisted of one room, with heavy walls three and a half feet thick and overall dimensions of thirty-five by forty-two and a half feet. The side nearest the hill was buried by sand to a depth of nearly ten feet. On this site a large millstone, a stack of unburned tile water pipe and the remains of what apparently were two grinding mills were uncovered.[9] A number of pieces of raw gypsum were also found in this ruin, and between the piers of one of the "mills" was a thin layer of the same material which had been ground to powder. The floor was of adobe bricks laid flat. In the area between the two buildings considerable rubbish in the form of animal bones, broken pottery, etc., suggested that the space had possibly been used as a "backyard." Small cooking places resembling barbecue pits were also found. A little to the north, and about thirty feet west of the west porch of the Residence a group of four fire places, or places arranged to support a large caldron on three upright stones, were uncovered.[10] It has been conjectured that these may have been places where the food for the Indians was prepared. The staple food was a sort of porridge of grains, called *atole*, or when meat was added, *pozole*. If it can be definitely established that this was the purpose of these small ruins, it forms an interesting sidelight on the life at this mission.

The relationship of the buildings once occupying the western side of the valley was greatly clarified by the explorations described. The major group of three buildings and the cemetery was clearly defined. Discovery of the tallow vats and the two smaller buildings west of the Residence and the miscellaneous smaller finds definitely indicated that the plan of this mission was not the usual rectangular patio type, and that the conjectures of earlier writers and investigators concerning the "connecting wings" running outward from the main building were groundless. Instead, it appeared to be a community grouping; that is, buildings which had a definite relation to each other, but were actually unconnected.

The area occupied by the CCC Camp as well as the whole opposite side of the valley remained to be explored. It was anticipated that in that area some of the original Indian dwellings would be located. Accordingly, a crew was moved over to the east side of the valley to do reconnaissance work in unoccupied areas. Excavations were begun near the circular fountain beside the county road. In tracing out the pipe lines running through the camp area, two problematical structures were encountered. On March 27, about eighteen inches below the surface, a rough bed of mortar and rubble about six inches thick was struck starting about fifty-three feet south of the fountain. The outlines appeared to be very indefinite, although it covered an area of over twenty-five feet square. An open aqueduct line from the northeast, which terminated a few feet away, could be said to have come into, or through, this area. Also, the mortar and rubble mass extended toward the fountain, and apparently was a sub-base for a tile drain line. A broken stub projected from the wall of the fountain.[11] This problem still remains unsolved, but it seems reasonable to assume that it had to do with the arrangement of the water system.

A second problematical structure of minor importance was a small masonry circular mass, whose top was approximately eighteen inches below the surface, roughly twenty-eight inches in diameter, and twenty-one inches in height.[12] It enclosed a rectangular hole, with no bottom, 12 x 15 inches, which immediately suggested that it once was filled by an upright timber. It was made exactly as though someone had planted a post, and filled around it with pieces of tile, rock and mortar to make it secure. It was further conjectured that it might have been the location of a cross, which had the upright been 12 x 15 inches, must have been of good size. This structure lies about fifty feet west of the fountain (No. 12) and has been backfilled. Excavations in this area proved the location of a tile pipe line running from this fountain to the central fountain (No. 9) which still remained in good condition. This was noted and immediately backfilled.

The next operation was centered in the area south of the camp, down to the south boundary of the park, and from the county road on the east over to the drainage ditch, which ran north and south a short distance from the main ruins. It was proposed to explore this entire area by means of trenches which would be started at fifty foot intervals, and if nothing was found, intermediate trenches would be placed, reducing the interval to twenty-five feet. Then the process would be repeated with trenches at right angles, forming a gridiron of the entire field. In but a short time, however, the initial trenches ran into foundations of two buildings, lying parallel to, and seventy five feet west of the county road, and about opposite the Church.[13] The larger of the two measured about 19 x 113 feet, divided into two spaces, and the foundation had an average width of two feet three inches. About fifty feet south of this a second foundation of smaller size, but similar in arrangement and appearance was discovered.[14] This building was approximately 19 x 60 feet. A closer examination of the foundations showed that there were regularly spaced holes occurring in the stonework, about ten feet on center. These holes were about nine inches in diameter and had no bottom. The reasonable inference to be drawn was that the buildings originally were of post construction, with probable thatch walls, and that they were later converted into adobe walled buildings by placing the stone foundations and building around the posts with the adobes. More complete investigation of the interiors showed evidences of small fires at various points in the rooms, and the shells and other small crude articles recovered were suggestive of Indian habitation. It has been assumed that

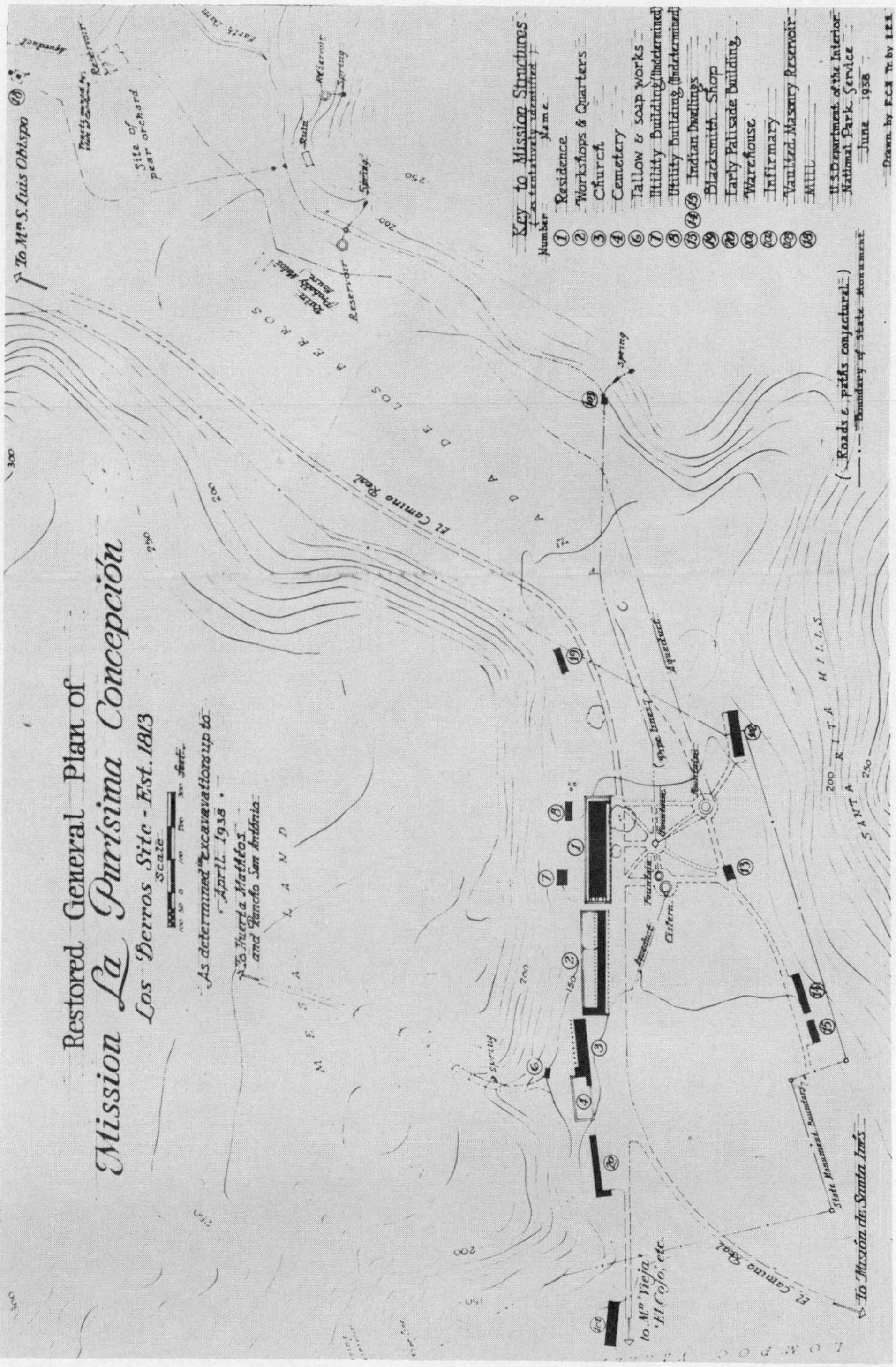

Restored General Plan of
Mission *La Purísima Concepción*
Los Berros Site - Est. 1813

Scale

As determined by excavation up to
April 1938.

By Huerta Mathtes
and Pancho San Antonio

Key to Mission Structures

As tentatively identified

Number	Name
1	Residence
2	Workshops & Quarters
3	Church
4	Cemetery
6	Tallow & soap works
7	Utility Building (undetermined)
8	Utility Building (undetermined)
13 14 15	Indian Dwellings
19	Blacksmith Shop
22	Early Palisade building
23	Warehouse
24	Infirmary
25	Vaulted Masonry Reservoir
28	Mill

U.S. Department of the Interior
National Park Service
June 1938

(Roads & paths conjectural)
-··-··- Boundary of State Monument

Drawn by F.C.H. Tr. by L.F.H.

Plate No. II

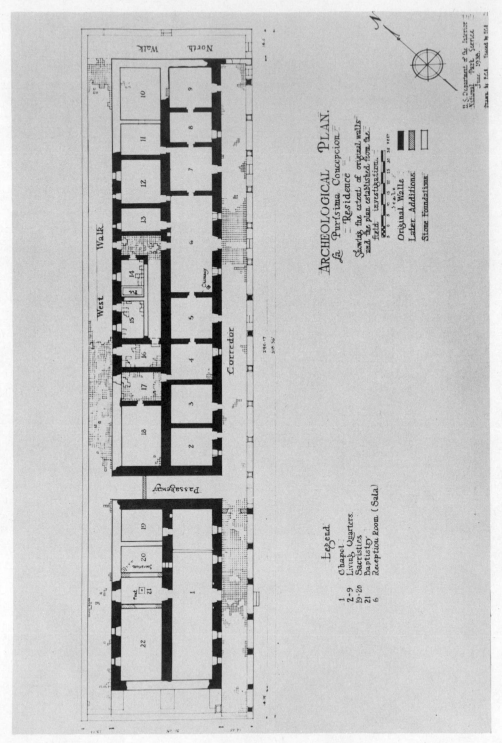

ARCHEOLOGICAL PLAN.
La Purísima Concepcion
Residence
Showing the extent of original walls
and the plan established from the
field investigation.

Scale

Original Walls
Later Additions
Stone Foundations

Legend

1 Chapel
2-9 Living Quarters
19-20 Sacristies
21 Baptistry
6 Reception Room (Sala)

U.S. Department of the Interior
National Park Service
June 1936.

Plate No. III

[10]

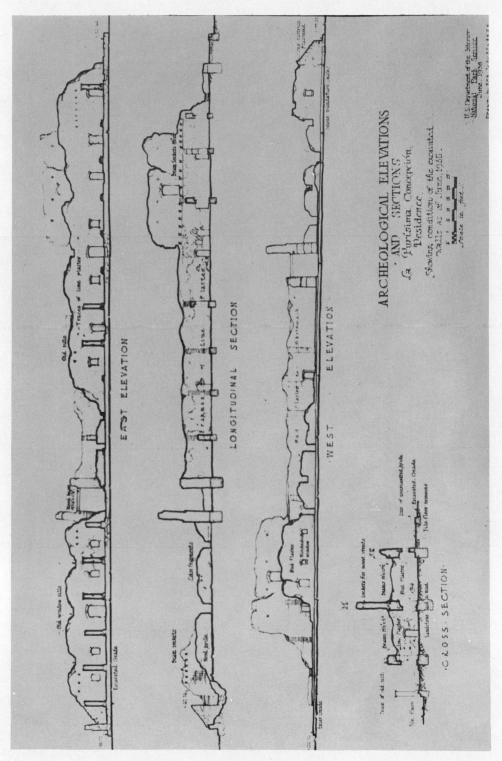

Plate No. IV

Figure 4. A section of typical tile pipe line with protective rock casing.

Figure 5. A section of open irrigation aqueduct with stone walls and tile bottom.

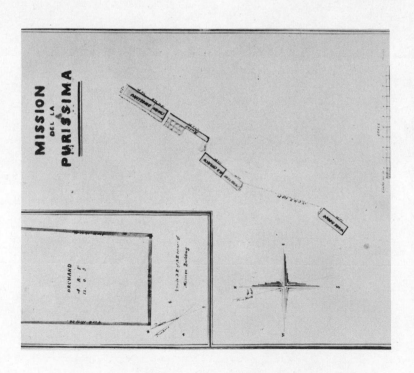

Figure 3. "Alemany Plat," so called, earliest known map of the La Purísima site. This map accompanied the petition of Bishop Joseph Sadoc Alemany to the U.S. Land Commissioners, in 1853, for the settlement of land claims of the Roman Catholic Church.

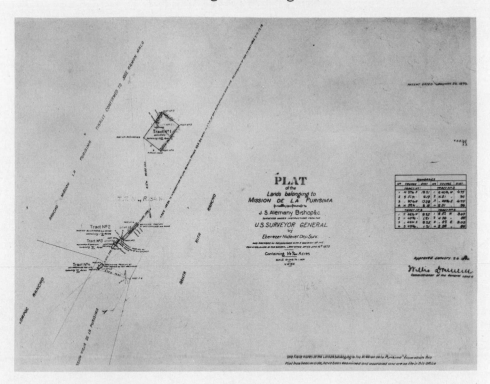

Figure 6. U. S. Surveyor General's plat of the 14.04 acres, confirmed to J. S. Ale-many, Bishop of Monterey. At its height the mission had undisputed control of thousands of acres. This map, dated January 24, 1874, shows the relation of the Orchard (Tract No. 1) to the Residence.

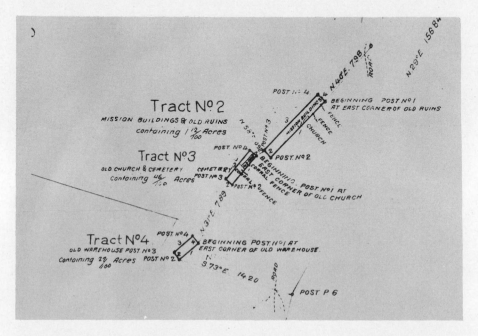

Figure 7. A detail of the above survey showing the location of the principal mission buildings. Tract No. 3 was retained by the Church until 1935.

Figure 8. The ruins of the Residence as it appeared prior to excavation, September 1934.

Figure 9. Residence ruin, from the southwest, prior to excavation.

Figure 11. Two of the nine surviving columns of the corredor.

Figure 10. Residence ruin looking northeast from about the middle of the building, showing accretion of overburden from eroded walls. September, 1934.

Figure 12. Beginning trenching operations in the north end of the Residence building. Depth of overburden about three feet.

Figure 13. Trenching along walls of chapel. Note the moistened condition of base of walls and fragments of whitewash still remaining.

Figure 14. Condition before excavating, room Number 14. Note eroded condition of ceiling beams.

Figure 15. Room Number 14, excavated, exposing a masonry cooking, or fire-pit across the south end.

Figure 16. Southwest end of Residence, April 1935, after being excavated.

Figure 17. Residence ruins from the east, May 1935.

Figure 18. Southwest end, showing Chapel, Baptistry and Room No. 22, after excavation. Note foundation of baptismal font enclosed by fence. April, 1935.

Figure 19. The center wall from about the center of the building, looking north. Almost this entire wall was preserved. Foundations and absence of plaster on parts of the wall seen above gave clues to the location of partition walls, which had earlier disappeared, probably because they were not as thick as the main walls.

Figure 20. TOOLS: axe, No. 1055; hoe, No. 1052; mattock fragments, No. 1004, No. 1058.

Figure 21. Whalebone mallet, No. 68; Pestle, No. 14.

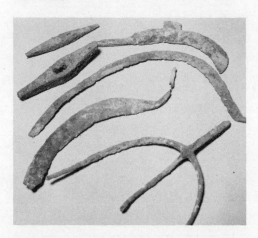

Figure 22. TOOLS: fork, No. 1053; sickle, No. 1091, No. 1092; hook, No. 1088; brick hammers, No. 1086, No. 1087.

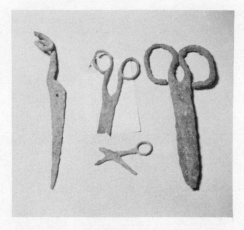

Figure 23. SCISSORS: 1 sheep shear blade No. 1139.

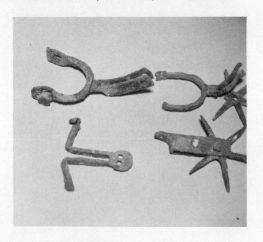

Figure 24. SPURS: No. 1005, No. 1009, No. 1280; Bit, No. 1021.

ORIGINAL TOOLS AND IMPLEMENTS

Representative articles recovered during archeological investigation.

Catalogue numbers from *Catalogue of Historical and Ethnological Objects.*

Figure 25. TOOLS: 2 machetes, No. 1095, No. 1096; auger, No. 1144; hook, No. 1137, trowel, No. 1142.

Figure 26. EATING IMPLEMENTS: spoons, No. 1180 - No. 1182 inc.; knives, No. 1128, to No. 1130 inc.

Figure 27. COPPER OBJECTS: buttons, No. 5002 - No. 5007 inc.; medallion, No. 5001; cup, No. 2025; copper fragments, No. 2091.

Figure 28. GUN PARTS: No. 1272, No. 1273; canister shot, No. 1277; bullet mould, No. 1275; musket balls, mould, and box, No. 1276; rifle barrel, No. 1274.

Figure 29. China fragments, No. 3011; Puebla ware fragments, No. 3043.

MISCELLANEOUS ARTIFACTS

Types of articles recovered included tools, knives, spoons of iron and copper, buttons, medallions, cups, and fragments of copper pots, musket parts, musket balls, moulds, and dishes of China and earlier glazed Puebla ware.

(Numbers given from *Catalogue of Historical and Ethnological Objects*.)

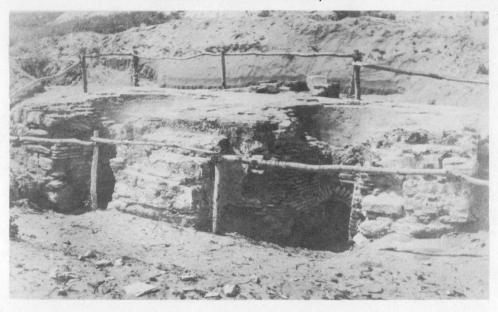

Figure 30. Excavated tallow and soap vats.

Figure 31. Opening to fire chamber. The arches are constructed of tile set in clay. The vat is placed above the chamber and separated by a copper disk.

Figure 32. Excavated foundations of Building No. 2, the "Shops and Quarters," looking south. Church restoration in progress, upper right. The temporary fence surrounds ruins of ovens in the Patio area.

Figure 33. Building No. 2, looking northeast from Church. Note L-shaped form of the building and numerous partition walls.

Figure 35. Base of *corredor* column, east side, building No. 2.

Figure 34. A storm drain through the west wing of building No. 2. Exploration trenches in the area to the southwest, upper portion of picture.

Figure 36. Remains of piers for grinding machine in building No. 7, west of the Residence.

Figure 37. Findings in excavation of building No. 7. Extreme right, portion of masonry pier seen in Figure 36, adobe floor, a mill stone, and stack of unburned tile pipe.

Figure 38. Arrow straightener, No. 180; Pestles, No. 44, 46, 47, 96; Pipe, (not in catalogue); Beads, No. 164, 165, 168.

Figure 39. Crucifix.

Figure 40. *Mano,* No. 6; Pestles, (21), 34.

Figure 41. Mortar, No. 70.

MISCELLANEOUS ARTIFACTS

Indian artifacts were numerous. At the left, the strings of beads were donated by Mr. Clarence Ruth of Lompoc, tagged as surface findings on the hillside east of the mission, and represent the trade beads and native Indian shell beads of the period. The arrow straightener was also donated by Mr. Ruth.

Upper right is one of the most interesting objects, an early crucifix of bronze, found west of building No. 7, eight feet below grade. The length of this cross is three and three eighths inches.

Numerous pestles, mortars and *mano* stones are included in the catalogue, a few of which are pictured here

Figure 42. General exploration work in area south of the CCC camp which can be seen at the right. Trenching was carried on in general east-to-west trenches at 50 foot intervals.

Figure 43. Trenching in area east of Residence after removal of camp buildings. The pieces of pipe were remnants of culverts formerly used in the camp streets.

Figure 44. Building foundation No. 13. Looking south. Top of foundation approximately 18 inches below present grade.

Figure 47. Excavated nave of Church looking southwest toward the altar wall. The tile floor was found to be in good condition for nearly one half the length of the nave.

Figure 46. Foundation of building No. 19, (Blacksmith shop). The raised portion lower right showed evidence of great heat, and was capped with tile. Possibly the original forge.

Figure 45. Trenching in area northeast of Residence. Trenches were run at 25 foot intervals. The larger excavation in the foreground caused by investigation of rock deposit.

Figure 48. Removing of overburden west side of Church and in sacristy No. 2.

Figure 49. The foundation of the Bell tower of the Church. This great stone foundation was a solid mass of rock 9 x 21 feet and over 7 feet in depth. The tiles on edge were originally the veneering of the adobe mass, and their position as shown in this view indicated that the veneering had fallen away from the structure.

Figure 50. Excavations on west side of Church. The foundation in the foreground is that mentioned on page 6 unidentified, but believed to have been used in connection with the nearby tallow vats.

Figure 51. Remains of post holes of building No. 20, south of the cemetery, looking northeast toward Church.

Figure 52. A detail of one of the post holes. These holes occur nine feet on center in three parallel rows. The holes are approximately 9 inches in diameter.

Figure 53. The straggling line of foundations, contiguous to the line of post holes of building No. 20. This foundation evidently supported the adobe veneering applied outside of the palisade structure.

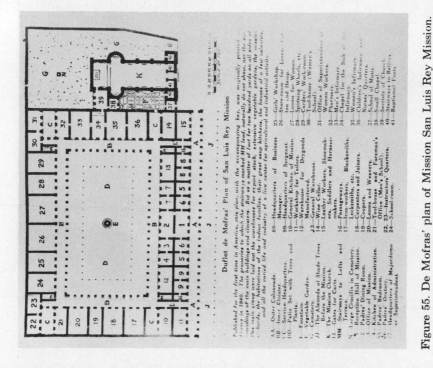

Duflot de Mofras' Plan of San Luis Rey Mission

*Published for the first time in America, this plan, with the accompanying key, was originally printed
in France in 1840. The granaries to which the stairways marked MM lead, naturally do not show, nor the
surroundings of the main buildings and cloisters. But as a matter of fact for two hundred yards on all sides of
this main group were laid out the warehouses for export stock, extensive vegetable gardens, the numerous adobe habitations of the Indian families, their great soup kitchens, the houses of a few colonists
and all the sacred life and industry of a live center for agricultural and industrial activity.*

AA · · Outer Colonnade.
BB · · Inner Cloister.
CC · · Service Headquarters.
DD · · Patio Set with Trees and
Plants.
1 · · Fountain.
2 · · Vegetable Garden.
3 · · Cemetery.
JJ · · The Alameda of Shade Trees
Before the Mission.
k · · The Mission Church.
1 · · Gate for Carts.
2 · · Stairways to Lofts and
Terrace.
N · · Large Crucifix in Cemetery.
1 · · Reception Hall of Mission.
2 · · Office of Administration.
3 · · Kitchen of Administration.
4 · · Padres' Bedroom.
5 · · Padres' Oratory.
6 · · Headquarters of Majordomo
or Superintendent.

88 · · Headquarters of Business
Manager.
99 · · Headquarters of Sergeant.
10 · · General Kitchen of Mission.
11 · · Workshop for Tailors.
12 · · Warehouse for Drygoods
Manufactured.
13 · · General Warehouse.
14 · · Wine Cellar.
15 · · Leather Workers, Shoemak-
ers, Saddlers and Harness-
makers.
16 · · Passageway.
17 · · Iron-workers, Blacksmiths,
Locksmiths, etc.
18 · · Carpenters and Joiners.
19 · · Coopers.
20 · · Looms and Weavers.
21 · · Tool-room and Foreman's
Office (Men's School).
22, 23 · · Instructors' Quarters.
24 · · Schoolroom.

25 · · Girls' Workshop.
26 · · Store-room for Linen, etc.
27 · · Looms for Women.
28 · · Spinning Wheels, etc.
29 · · Carders' Work-room.
30 · · Tool-house (Women's
School).
31 · · Office of Superintendent of
Women Workers.
32 · · Pharmacy.
33 · · Men's Infirmary.
34 · · Chapel for the Sick of the
Infirmary.
35 · · Women's Infirmary.
36 · · Children's Infirmary and
Nurses' Quarters.
37 · · School of Music.
38 · · Small Chapel.
39 · · Sacristy of Church.
40 · · Stairways to Belfry.
41 · · Baptismal Fonts.

Figure 54. Restored plan of Mission San Juan Capistrano.
From Newcomb, *The Mission Churches and Historic Houses
of California.*

Figure 55. De Mofras' plan of Mission San Luis Rey Mission.

COMPARATIVE CALIFORNIA MISSION PLANS

These missions typify the patio type plan which was used so
extensively in California.

Figure 56. Henry Chapman Ford's etching of the original site in the town of Lompoc. This picture is dated 1883. The general quadrangular plan of this mission is evident. The ditch, lower right, was the *zanja* or aqueduct supplying the mission. Portions of it still exist.

Figure 57. A rare photograph of the mission ruins at the original site in the town of Lompoc, taken about 1880. The early settlers of the town utilized the ruins for stock corrals and roofed one portion to serve as a hay barn.

Figure 58. The original site from the hillside looking north toward the newly started town of Lompoc. The gully in the foreground is said to be a result of the earthquake of 1812.

Figure 59. The Lompoc site as it appeared about 20 years ago. The fissure in the hillside is plainly visible.

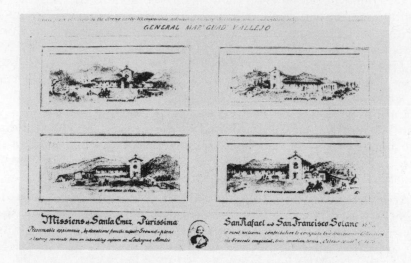

Figure 60. Sketches by Eduard Vischer (about 1878) of the Missions Santa Cruz, La Purisima, San Rafael, and San Francisco Solano. These sketches were made from verbal descriptions furnished to Vischer by General Vallejo.

Figure 61. An enlargement of the La Purisima sketch in the above view. This indicates Vischer's picturization of the "presumable appearance" of the original mission. It is interesting, but probably inaccurate.

these were neophyte dwellings. The archeological report of December, 1936 reviewed these findings in detail.

The removal of the CCC camp from the area in the summer of 1935 permitted exploration of the four acres in the foreground of the Residence. On November 25, cross trenching was started.[15] The same system was employed as for the other large area to the south, except that the east and west trenches were placed at twenty-five foot intervals, whereas the north and south trenches were fifty feet apart as shown on the archeological map. The exploration in this section continued until January, 1936. The major result of the work was the location of a small building foundation (No. 13) about 375 feet east of the south end of the Residence. This building was approximately 25 x 39½ feet. These foundations of rock and mud, of shallow depth and poor quality, indicated but a single room. The top of this foundation was approximately eighteen inches below the surface.

About twenty-five feet west of this building, a deposit of animal bones and rocks was exposed.[16] The rocks took no definite shape, but the field entry reads, "uncovered this area for about 12'. Believe that it might be some sort of a cooking pit. Three nails and a piece of an old bottle were found in this area."[17]

In November, 1936 the same crew made a more thorough investigation of the central fountain[18] and the system of water pipe coming into it.

During the following months exploration of the balance of the camp area and the area north of the former camp was completed. These explorations had no significant result. The archeological report for February, 1936, describes this work.

Building 19:

The triangular space north of the Residence now remained the only area in the immediate vicinity of the major mission structure not yet explored. Work was not taken up here until January, 1937, when work on a park fence led to the investigation of a deposit of tile and debris which proved to be the site of a building foundation now partially covered by the county road. The depth to this foundation, below the existing grade, on the side toward the hill, which rises abruptly immediately behind the foundation, was five feet eight inches.[19] On the opposite side it was about eighteen inches less. This ruin measured 20 x 76 feet, and was divided into two unequal parts by a foundation wall. Evidence of heat, particularly near a raised and tile covered area in one corner, together with the numerous metal artifacts, supported the local report that the old blacksmith shop had occupied this site. The artifacts removed consisted principally of broken tools, mostly agricultural and metal fragments, both iron and copper. The existing county road prevented complete investigation of this structure, but the extent of the foundation was located by borings made with a two inch soil auger. The balance of the triangular area to the south of this ruin, although explored by trenches spaced at approximately twenty foot intervals, yielded little except occasional tile fragments and other scattered building materials.

Church and Cemetery:

Work in and around the Church and Cemetery was resumed in May, 1936. The area in front of the structures was explored by trenches, spaced at twenty-five foot intervals in both directions.[20]

The Church floor was buried to an average depth of four feet necessitating the removal of approximately 2000 yards of material before it could be fully investigated. The cemetery level lay approximately three feet below the existing grade, thus requiring the removal of an estimated additional 1000 yards. Excavation was carried out along the lines described for the Residence building. The walls at the south end of the nave and sacristy and along the southern one-third of the west wall existed in places to heights of thirteen feet. These contained one complete doorway (except for the door and frame) and one complete niche on the right hand side of the altar location. Remains of the niches above the altar were sufficiently well preserved to allow partial measurement. The jambs of a window in the sacristy existed up to the skewback of the arch. The detailed record of the progress of this investigation is to be found in the archeological reports of May 6-June 15, 1936, and July 1936.

Building 20:

Trenching operations in the area between the south end of the cemetery and the south monument boundary, begun early in 1937, resulted in a "remarkable discovery,"[21] shown on Plate II as structure number 20. At a point about fifty feet south of the cemetery, three parallel lines of post foundations were found, approximately nine feet on center each way. On the outside of the east line of foundations a very straggling rock footing continues until it meets the south wall foundation of the cemetery. The excavations revealed an L-shaped structure the main wing of which is 177 feet long. From its south end a minor wing extends about forty-five feet eastward. In the space between the north end of this ruin and the south end of the cemetery are two small stone foundations as yet unidentified. One of these, located fifteen feet south of the cemetery, is T-shaped, and is solidly built of stone. The long bar of the T is nearly twelve feet long and over three feet wide, and about three feet deep. A short stem projects west three feet four inches. A few feet to the south, and about ten feet north of the end of the building wing is a smaller, irregularly shaped foundation, four feet ten inches in one dimension and four feet eight inches in the other, but not so solidly built as the former.

The larger of the above described foundations is reasonably believed to have been the remains of one of the older and more temporary types of construction, and the mission records suggest the probability that it was the earlier Church which collapsed in 1817. The straggling footing along the outside of the post holes is interpreted to be the footing for the adobe veneer which the mission accounts relate was placed around the Church to strengthen it.[22] Whether the smaller foundations described above had any relation to the building, or to each other is unknown, but the heaviness of the larger one might lead to the supposition that it supported a bell, or group of bells. Such a conclusion would, however, require further corroborative evidence and more definite proof that adjacent remains are those of the temporary Church.

Whether or not a positive identification of this ruin is ever made, it remains one of the most interesting archeological finds of the entire site, for it furnishes information of a method of construction employed in the earlier buildings in California, which, by the very impermanency of their nature, have disappeared to the point where this remain is possibly unique. This ruin has been backfilled, and the foundation locations temporarily marked with wooden stakes.

Area south and west of building 20:

In the hillside to the south and west of building No. 20, at a depth of thirteen inches, a stratum of lime mortar, tile fragments and rock was found scattered over an area about fifty feet square. The mortar layer averaged an inch or less in thickness. This area will require stripping of all overburden before any conclusions as to its significance can be reached.

The whole hillside in this section appears to have been used as a source for clay, which is plentiful at this point. The sharpness of the bank suggests that its natural slope has been altered at some former date. If it was used as a source of material for tile products, it is possible that the above mentioned undetermined findings on the lower slope are evidence of former activity in this connection.

For its water supply the Mission not only utilized the springs in Los Berros Canyon, but also relied on more distant sources. The writings of the Fathers show that the water of the river (Santa Ynez) was utilized for irrigation, but no indication of the nature of this development can be found. However, two other major water systems had been completed while at the old site and one of these systems was diverted to the new site, according to Payeras.[23] One was a system of dams and aqueducts originating in the Salsipuedes Canyon, and was brought to the old mission a distance of over six miles. In tracing this system, parts of the dams impounding the water of the Salsipuedes Creek were found, and here and there traces of the aqueduct indicate its course. These fragmentary portions of this very interesting system have been measured and surveyed, and recorded. In addition, a second series of structures built to bring water from the Miguelito Canyon to the old site have also been investigated and recorded.

Concluding Observations:

Intensive archeological investigations of the sites of the major mission buildings and supplementary reconnaissances have revealed the general plan of the second Mission La Purísima. The plan and layout differs materially from the other missions of California. The evolution from the quadrangular, or patio, type plan which was universally employed by the California missions to the community type plan, exemplified by this group, forms a very interesting point in California's architectural history.

The investigation can be said to have contributed new and important information to the previous knowledge and conception of the mission, showing, as it has, that all of the mission plans cannot be classified as a single form. La Purísima shows admirable thought and careful planning, as well as a feeling for architectural composition. Each of the buildings was designed to meet its needs with simplicity and straightforwardness, yet a care for excellence of workmanship and good design was also distinctly evident. The scale of the buildings, notably the Church, was not so grand as others in the chain, but here again the sound and careful judgment of Father Payeras was influenced by reasons which made his decision thoroughly logical.

The above narrative summarizes the activities down to March 31, 1938, at which time the investigation is still obviously incomplete. Other known locations will require investigation if all the information available at the site is to be secured. Certain circumstances especially ownership, have prevented any systematic excavation of these locations. When conditions permit, further investigation of the following areas is suggested:

1. East of the county road, a structure on property owned by the State, John De Costa, and Santa Barbara County, and possibly Walter Ziesche. Pictures taken in the 1880's show this building very plainly. Figure 62 shows some of the tile roof and door openings. Dimensions ascertained by test borings suggest that this structure is the one described in the mission records as the infirmary.[24]

2. The hillslope, on property of Walter Ziesche and L. Rivaldi facing the mission contains many surface indications of building fragments and Indian artifacts. The hill belonging to Rivaldi has been described by early residents as a cemetery; in fact, one man who plowed the slope in early days states that as a boy he plowed up skulls and other bones. The cemetery adjoining the Church was not built until 1821, and as yet the earlier cemetery location is not known. The little side canyon owned by Ziesche should also be explored for Indian dwellings. 1000 Indians could scarcely have been accommodated in the dwellings thus far found.

3. The area south of the garden might yield further information if north and south test trenches were run at fifty, and then at twenty-five foot intervals. Figure 70, although of questionable accuracy, shows a ruin in this area. It is therefore recommended that before the final development is made in this area, it be so handled.

4. Further work on the water system through the De Costa property should contribute more detailed information desired on this phase of the development. Special investigations should be made to determine the relationship of the water system to structure number 18, as yet not positively identified.

5. The tract known as tract "F" on the deed to the State is a plat twenty-five feet square which contains the "ruined pillar" (Structure number 18.) Some investigation here proved a second pillar foundation and a round stone foundation between the two pillars existed. The top of the stone pillar which is standing was made to receive a heavy cross beam, which doubtless extended to the other. The whole arrangement is suggestive of a mill. A more exact knowledge of the water pipe lines in this vicinity might determine whether or not this is the "Mill" mentioned in the inventory of August 18, 1935.[25]

6. A masonry structure recently has been observed on the eastern hillside opposite the large reservoir, known as Tract E in the State's deed. This ruin, due to its recent discovery, has had no investigation whatever. It is on the property of De Costa.

7. The site of the old warehouse, shown on the patent surveys by Nidever in 1874, also on the "Alemany plat", is on the property of Basil Fox. Close to this building, a little to the southeast was the reputed location of a large circular stone floor, said to be a "matanza" or killing floor. Also near it, according to old residents, was a large corral, of palisade type, but it is unlikely that any trace of this structure would be found.

8. The spring and reservoir also on the Fox property has a pipe line extending in the general direction of the warehouse. Its relation to those other structures should be determined.

9. Further investigation of the ruin known as the "smithy" (No. 19) should be made when conditions permit.

10. Test trenches should be run in the De Costa property, particularly in the site of his present orchard. This is purely exploratory.

11. The property of the Lompoc Produce Company, north of the De Costa north line should be explored. There are indications of ruins directly under one of the outbuildings. This is in addition to the known water lines running through the farmyard.

12. Exploration should be undertaken in the property of John De Costa, now occupied by the "schoolhouse", at the southeast corner of the Monument. In excavating the basement of the schoolhouse, years ago, it is reported that burials were encountered. When possible, test trenching in both directions at fairly close intervals should be done in this area.

There were also *estancias*, or structures away from the mission used for farming, orchard, vineyard and cattle operations. These include the Jalama site; the vineyard and wine vats about two and a half miles west from it, known as the San Francisquito; and the rancho San Antonio, where farm buildings and a granary were erected in the mission period. Also falling in this category is the site known as the *"Huerta Mateo"*, in Lompoc Canyon, a few miles west of the mission. Near the region known as the *Oso Flaco* was a rest house, and on the Guadalupe Rancho was another large development. These names are mentioned as historic sites, which, if the investigations are to be carried to completion should be studied. Most of these sites contain but the merest traces of the former development, but it is possible that a more thorough investigation of them would reveal valuable data about less generally known activities of the mission's development and life.

The original site of the mission in the town of Lompoc still remains as one of the important historic sites in California, and one which has been largely untouched since its destruction in 1812. Up to the present date, nothing has been found which indicates its plan or appearance, except in the most general way. In 1883 it was described by a writer in the following terms:

> The grand square or quadrangle was about 400 feet each way. . . . The walls (of the Church) being thirty feet high.
> . . . Large rooms, sometimes 100 feet in length and 25 in width, indicated extensive dining rooms and work shops. . . . The quadrangle was also flanked by numerous buildings of adobe, probably intended as Residences for the Indians or other members of the mission with families.[26]

Ford's etching of this site, made in 1883, indicates that the foregoing description is correct, for the general quadrangular plan can be quite plainly distinguished. Two rare photographs taken of this ruin also confirm this arrangement (Figures 57 and 58). Obviously the buildings covered a very large area.

There is every reason to believe that the site should be very rich in artifacts of the mission period, for as Payeras wrote, after the earthquake:

> . . . The inclemency of the weather, and the very heavy rainfalls that followed, prevent digging out of anything or covering what lies exposed. For the present we have nevertheless dug out the most valuable things and we have secured what is most urgently needed.[27]

Other evidence shows that during the following year materials were salvaged for use at the new site, and it probably served as a quarry for some years thereafter. Nevertheless, a wealth of material undoubtedly still remains buried by several feet of overburden. Some of the area is unoccupied, but the gradual expansion of the town has encroached more and more into the heart of the site, until during the past year a seven room residence has been built within twenty feet of the sole remaining adobe wall visible above the present earth mound.

Excavation of this site would offer a great opportunity to add to our present knowledge, not only of this mission, but the architecture and life of the whole chain. Broadly speaking, it is evident that while history has recorded the events of the mission period, the specialist and student of the architecture and art of early California finds exact, detailed knowledge woefully incomplete when any exhaustive study is attempted.

The opportunity is therefore taken to endorse recommendations already made that the investigation of the original mission site in the town of Lompoc be arranged for.[28]

CHAPTER 2

HISTORICAL COLLECTION OF PHOTOGRAPHS, DRAWINGS AND SKETCHES

Photographs, drawings, and renderings of the site and the principal buildings of the Mission La Purísima Concepción, arranged chronologically to show the progressive stages of ruin of the Residence.

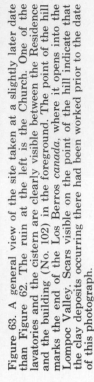

Figure 63. A general view of the site taken at a slightly later date than Figure 62. The ruin at the left is the Church. One of the lavatories and the cistern are clearly visible between the Residence and the building (No. 102) in the foreground. The point of the hill marks the end of the *Los Berros canada,* where it opens into the Lompoc Valley. Scars visible on the point of the hill indicate that the clay deposits occurring there had been worked prior to the date of this photograph.

Figure 64. Early photograph of the Residence, about 1890.

Figure 62. The earliest known photograph of the Residence, taken about 1880. The building in the foreground numbered 102 on Plate II, has been tentatively identified as the "Infirmary". The fence is believed to be of post-mission period. The roof at the north end of the building (right edge) was destroyed by a fire a few years earlier.

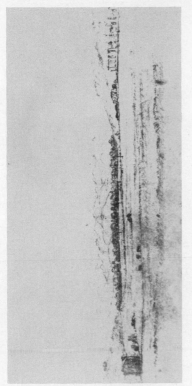

Figure 66.

Figure 68.

Figure 65.

Figure 67.

THE FORD ETCHINGS AND SKETCHES

Henry Chapman Ford, whose etchings and sketches of historic sites in California are well known, visited La Purisima in 1881. A photograph of his published etching is shown in Figure 65. Three pencil sketches made by this artist were secured through the courtesy of the California Historical Society. Figure 66 represents the site from the northeast, with the Lompoc hills in the distance. Figure 67 is a sketch of the *corredor*. Figure 68 is the Los Berros *canada* north of the main group, indicating a few trees of the pear orchard. The small house is probably that shown in Figure 6 as "R. Malos House."

STOCK RANCH OF JESSE HILL & MISSION LA PURISSIMA, NEAR LOMPOC, SANTA BARBARA CO. CAL.

Figure 69. La Purisima from the south about 1883. The property at this time was privately owned and used as a sheep ranch. A fragment of what was evidently the Church appears at the extreme left. The small buildings in the distance are said to have been built by Mr. Hill.

(From Mason, J. D., *A History of Santa Barbara and Ventura Counties*.)

Figure 70. A sketch similar to Figure 69, showing the mission about the same period. Certain differences in these two drawings are noticeable, particularly the representation of the ruin in the lower right corner. Existence of this building has not been confirmed by archeological investigations to date.

(From: Engelhardt, *La Purisima Concepcion*.)

Figure 71. A view similar to Figure 64 taken about 1890. The disrepair of the roof is noticeable.

Figure 72. An undated photograph of the Residence with one of the masonry lavatories in the foreground.

Figure 73. By 1892, the roof of the main portion was in an advanced stage of ruin and a break appears in that of the *corredor*. Note the adobe piers and grille forming an entrance to the Chapel in the third bay of the *colonnadem* and the unusual arch of the window in the section of the wall lighted by the break in the roof.

Figure 74. Detail of the southwest end, 1892, clearly showing the underside of the gable, the beam and detail of the corbel of the *corredor*. The two end columns of stone are considered to be additions made after the secularization of the missions. The difference in workmanship between the *corredor* columns and these later ones is interesting.

Figure 75. In 1903, eleven years after the photograph shown in Figure 74, the southwest end was unprotected by any roof and exposed to the attacks of winter storms. This photograph was particularly helpful for restoration purposes. (See Plate XIV.)

Figure 76. By 1904, the condition of the west side of the building was that of a ruin. The remaining tiles had been removed and stacked in piles about the building, some of which can be seen in the left foreground.

Figure 77. Condition of the Residence about 1905.

Figure 78. West side 1892. This side apparently had received less attention than the east side, and disintegration was more advanced.

Figure 79. View from the west. Precise date unknown; about 1895.

Figure 80. The roof tiles had been removed and stacked about the building. Disintegration was rapid from this time on. (about 1904.)

Figure 83. Southwest end about 1904.

Figure 82. 1906.

Figure 81. 1904.

Figure 84. June 27, 1909.

Figure 85. October 22, 1908.

Figure 86. June 23, 1906.

Figure 87. June 27, 1909.

Four comparative views, 1906, 1908 and 1909. From the *Outwest* magazine, August, 1909, showing the "swift ruin wrought by the elements" in three years. (From the report of the Landmarks Club.)

Figure 88. West side, about 1908. This photograph was valuable for locating and illustrating the window and door treatment of the rooms west of the Chapel.

Figure 89. By 1912 the west wall had collapsed revealing the center wall. This photograph shows the opening to the pulpit, the door from the sanctuary to the sacristy, and the opening to the choir loft (lower right hand corner).

Figure 90. Undated photograph. About 1910-1912.

Figure 91. West side 1916. Note the uncultivated areas in the field beyond marking the location of the fountains and cistern.

Figure 92. Detail, west side, about 1916.

Figure 93. Undated photograph. Probably about 1920. Several columns have fallen and are lying on the ground (right center).

Figure 94. Northwest end, February 17, 1916.

Figure 95. North end of colonnade. Note the adobe filled end opening.

Figure 96. An excellent view of the north end indicating the jambs of two of the windows (left center). The scheme of the story and a half construction is clearly shown in this photograph. (Date unknown.)

Figure 97. North end about 1912.

Figure 98. The columns terminating the *corredor*. (Date unknown.)

Figure 100. The colonnade about 1912. (Courtesy Southern Pac. Railroad Co.)

Figure 101, (left). The *corredor* from the north end. The carefulness of the workmanship in the execution of beams, rafters and corbels is very noticeable in this picture taken about 1892. The two transverse beams across the *corredor* in the upper part of the picture are of a later date.

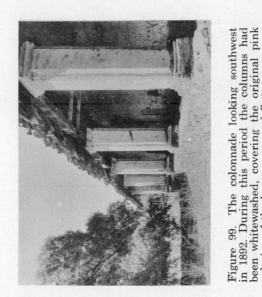

Figure 99. The colonnade looking southwest in 1892. During this period the columns had been whitewashed, covering the original pink coloring of the bases, caps and flutes.

CHAPTER 3

THE MISSION RESIDENCE

Early Descriptions:

The construction of the proudest building of his new establishment during the year 1815, was laconically reported by Padre Mariâno Payeras in the following words:

> We have built a wing 100 varas long, containing a double row of rooms, with walls an adobe and a half thick, and a roof of tiles, which serves as dwellings for the Fathers, with all their help (servants), rooms for guests, a chapel, and the rest for work shops.[1]

It represented a tremendous amount of work in planning, manufacturing and transportation of materials in addition to the considerable task involved in the construction. One can imagine the pride and satisfaction that filled his soul as he penned these lines, doubtless occupying his new study at that very moment. Perhaps he would have considered it unwarranted boasting unbecoming in a Franciscan to have elaborated his report, yet how often later investigators wished that his description had been more detailed and explicit, as they tried to solve the riddle of those ruined rooms!

The correct name by which this building should be designated has been the subject of much discussion. It will be noted that the Fathers themselves gave it no precise name, but rather listed the types of rooms the new building contained.

In the mission community such a structure served a number of purposes. Primarily, it was a residence for the friars in charge. Had it served only this purpose, an exact term could easily be assigned. While many writers refer to such a building as a "monastery", the name "friary" is preferred by the Rev. Dr. Maynard Geiger, Franciscan historian of Santa Barbara Mission.

In his discussion of the background and organization of the Franciscan Order, he says:

> Just as the diocese is the administrative unit of the church, so the province, or *provincia* is the administrative unit of the Franciscan Order. The normal social unit of the province is a convent or friary under a guardian. . . . In official Latin documents, such a house is also designated a convent. In Spanish records, dwelling places of the friars are refered to as monasteries, *monasterios,* or convents, *conventos.*[2]

He draws the distinction between monks, occupying monasteries, secluded and retired from the world, and friars, for, "The characteristic of the monk is monastic life and stability of abode. This is the ideal of the Benedictines."[3] In contrast, the Franciscan friars, "were neither to be monks nor hermits, but active apostles, who yet from time to time would renew their vigor in retirement."[4] Therefore, Dr. Geiger prefers the word friary, for, "since 'monastery' is correlative with 'monk' and since only certain dwellings of friars are convents, *conventos,* the word friary is the best all around word for the abode for friars."[5]

It may be objected, however, that when friars were serving at a mission, they were, so to speak, "on duty"; that is, were administering the secular affairs of the mission and not retired in the seclusion of a monastery. They lived in a building of the mission group which served as their dwelling. This building functioned as the administrative center of the community, in much the same capacity as a provincial or insular governor's Residence, which is clothed with the dignity and authority of government.

In the Mission Residence, dignitaries of military government and of the Church were entertained and temporarily domiciled. Chance visitors and travellers were also welcomed; in fact, rooms were set aside for that purpose. The missions were the hospices of the time. The mission accounts were kept therein, and business affairs transacted. Servants quarters and workrooms were provided. Finally, a chapel, for the private use of the friars was added. To the writer, the word friary suggests a more restricted use, and for the purpose of this discussion the term "Mission Residence" or simply "the Residence" will be used.

Just how many rooms the building originally contained is problematical, because in the course of time the plan was altered, and no record of its original plan has been found.[6] After these alterations were made, it contained a total of twenty-one rooms on the ground floor, and above the rooms, the loft, or *tapanco,* added nearly an equal amount of area. This upper space could be used for living, storage, or other purposes. The plan of the building, like others, was simplicity itself. As Payeras said, it was a double row of rooms; that is, two parallel series divided by a center wall, which extended up through the loft to support the ridge of the roof. At a point about one third the length of the building a passageway led from one side of the structure to the other, separating the living quarters from the chapel. The portion of the building north of the passage could best be described as the dwelling, containing the reception room, rooms for the Fathers, guests, servants, work and storage-rooms. The portion to the south contained the chapel (which later was converted to serve as the church) two sacristies, a baptistry, and, it is said, a room for school purposes. The original plan and use of the rooms west of the chapel is not known. The partitions found in the archeological investigation were clearly of a later date.

On the east side was a generous *corredor,*[7] or colonnaded porch, from which the Padres could view the central area, with its fountains and pools and keep a watchful eye on their Indian charges housed in the buildings on the opposite side of the "patio". It was the *corredor* which lent this building its chief architectural distinction, for Payeras, with characteristic simplicity and direction, chose to employ a column and a beam style in contrast to the arcaded *corredores* which characterize many California missions. The column and corbel that was evolved for this purpose was unique in California, and the design and proportions are so satisfying that they have served, and probably will continue to serve, as models for modern architects. Certainly it is an index to the character of these early builders, for it has dignity, yet charm; sturdiness, yet grace; simplicity, yet delicacy of detail, and the quiet rhythm of the whole facade creates a sense of repose. In its spacious width, one finds relief from the hot summer sun, shelter from the winter rains, and when the disagreeable spring winds blow, it offers welcome protection. On the west side and north end there was also a walk, or terrace, but it was not covered.

With the terrible earthquake which they had experienced three years before strongly in mind, great stone buttresses and a heavy bulkhead braced the south end of the building. "Experience", wrote Payeras, sadly, after seeing the destruction of his mission in 1812, "may teach us the best method for constructing other buildings".[8] This heavy stonework, whose meaning and purpose often is questioned by the visitor, was also contrived to shed the water quickly from the adobe wall, moisture being a serious problem in this type of construction.

The total length of the structure is three hundred eighteen feet, four and one half inches. Of this total length, which includes the buttresses and the north porch, the building itself is two hundred ninety feet and two inches, or slightly more than the 100 varas (about 275 feet), reported by Payeras. In width the building measures fifty one feet three and one half inches, not including the porches. The front *corredor* is fourteen feet five and one half inches overall, the west walk thirteen feet and nine inches, making a total overall dimension of seventy nine feet six inches.

The main walls are four feet four inches thick. The interior partitions average two feet one and one half inches. A total of nearly 140,000 of the large adobe bricks, weighing no less than 4,235 tons, were required in the construction. A few of the larger door arches were constructed of tile, while all the other door and window openings employed segmental adobe arches. The columns supporting the roof of the *corredor* were all of tile, and special shapes were made for the fluted shaft, the ogee cap and base moldings.

The building was observed and described with varying degrees of accuracy by numerous writers. Helen Hunt Jackson, of Ramona fame, visited the building while gathering material for her book, published in 1883.[9] She wrote:

> . . . Nothing is left there but one long, low adobe building, with a few arches of the corridor; the doors stand open, the roof is falling in; it has been so often used as a stable and sheepfold, that even the grasses are killed around it. The painted pulpit hangs half falling on the wall, its stairs are gone, and its sounding board is slanting awry. Inside the broken altar rail is a pile of stones, earth, and rubbish thrown up by seekers after buried treasures; in the farther corner another pile and hole, the home of a badger; mud-swallows' nests are thick on the cornice, and cobwebbed rags of the old canvas ceiling hang fluttering overhead. . . .

Another writer, in the same year, described this building thus:

> This . . . is a very imposing building, with its brick arches, wide verandas and extensive facade. The walls, as a result of the earthquake experience, are very massive, and bid fair to last as ruins many years after the timbers, which are now rotting and giving away, shall have ceased to exist. Many portions of the tile covered roof have fallen in, but the general design and uses of the building can be easily determined. The sacristy, with its carved doors, making pretensions to elegance; the pulpit with its painted canopy; the organ loft, approached by a ladder with wide steps, where the half-civilized, half-imbecile natives essayed, with violin, horn, drum and voice the solemn Gregorian chants, are in tolerable preservation. Standing in the rickety pulpit, which looks as though it might fall and tumble one on the rotten floor below, and recalling to mind the scenes of half a century since, when the floors were covered with the half-naked natives, saying their *Pater Nosters* and *Ave Marias,* we may well ask, "What of it"? [10]

In 1903, the San Francisco *Chronicle* published a series of mission pictures with accompanying articles. Under date of September 10, 1903, in an article entitled "Another Mission Picture Ready", the following description of the Residence appeared:

> . . . In architecture this home of the padres is quite different from the others; it is less pretentious, in fact the building is one long, low rambling house, built like the cloistered habitations which are always to be found nestled beside the mission churches. This building was quite as impressive, however, in its very simplicity, as the more notable places where high towers rose above gables and ornate facades. The long stretch of plain tiled roof was distinctly picturesque and the place most inviting with its long porch within the arcades.

The picture was published September 13, 1903, and the historical sketch accompanying indicates that the writer was under the impression that this building was the Church:

> . . . On it (the Church), the friars, and neophytes worked and in 1817 they dedicated the new Church, the ruins of which stand today. It is of stone, exceedingly simple as there was no attempt at the handsome architecture of the earlier Churches. The padres, out of their experience, built the place that was best suited to the needs of the time and calculated to withstand destruction from the things that wrought such havoc. It did, and time and the neglect of man has brought the ruin of today, almost as complete as when the terrific earthquake dashed the place into pieces.

George Wharton James, however, described the colonnade with a greater degree of accuracy, but he also, was apparently unacquainted with its true purpose as a dwelling:

> . . . The Mission of La Purísima Concepción was built in a canyada not far from the river. It stands northeast to southwest, the southwest end buttressed with solid and wellbuilt masonry. The main walls are of adobe, plastered over. Parts of the building are in two stories, but everything

now (1905) is in sad ruins. Though it is as solitary and deserted as San Antonio, it does not make the pathetic appeal that venerable and dignified structure does. And it is hard to say why. The photograph shows that it is not so striking a building, still there seems to be no reason why one should not feel so sadly at its desolation as one does at San Antonio. It is pathetic enough. The tiles have been taken off the roof, except where they have fallen in and been broken to pieces; some of the walls have tumbled down; others are rapidly crumbling away; some of the pillars of the corridor have fallen; weeds have grown everywhere, and instead of giving the feeling of kindly covering the desolation they serve only to accentuate it.

The corridors of La Purísima extended only in front of the building. The pillars are square with chamfered corners, and were built of the material that happened to be readiest to hand at the moment, for some are of stone, others burnt brick, and still others are of adobe. At the time of my last visit in May, 1904, eighteen pillars were still standing, and two had fallen. These pillars are about three feet square. The corridors are ten feet wide and extend the whole length of the building, which is about three hundred feet. The width, without the corridor, is about fifty feet.

The church is at the southwest end on the southeast side. It is about eighty feet long. The windows are low and arched, but there is little left to show what were the attractions of this church, so different from any of the others. At one corner, doubtless where interested neophytes have stood, looking with luminous eyes upon the movements of the officiating padre, now stands a growing tree.

The peculiarity of La Purísima is in the architectural arrangement of the building. The church is a part — one large room merely —, in a structure that contains many rooms. There is nothing that remains of the wings that used to connect, and the ploughing up of the field near by has doubtless destroyed the foundations of walls, did any ever exist.[11]

Mr. James' puzzlement over the arrangement of the Church, and his speculations concerning the "wings that used to connect," are entirely understandable and logical. Familiar as he was with other mission plans, he naturally expected that La Purísima would follow a plan which was considered the general California mission type. His error in describing the colonnade as consisting of materials most conveniently available is less understandable.

Rexford Newcomb, in his study of the California missions and historic houses, made the same assumptions regarding the wings and the Church. He described the columns as did James:

La Purísima lays little claim to architectural distinction. The ruins indicate that the main mission-house, of which the Church was simply one of the larger rooms, was a block some 300 feet long by 50 feet wide with a colonnade, ten feet wide running along its front side. It is to be presumed that wings originally connected with this block at either end and projected in such a way as to give us the semblance of the usual *patio* arrangement, but these wings no longer remain and all traces of their foundations has long since been obliterated by the cultivation of the fields at the rear of the structure. The mission house was mainly of adobe, roofed with tiles, but it was buttressed here and there with masonry. The great piers of the colonnade across the front were built mainly of stone and brick, but a few of them were of adobe.

The Church, a simple apartment some 80 feet long, occupied a room on the colonnade side at the southwest end and its architectural treatment varied little from that of the other rooms of the structure. The windows, rather low in the walls, are arched, but there is little left in the unroofed apartment to testify to any glory the ancient Church might have had.[12]

A misconception had thus become general concerning the Church, which was usually described as "simply one of the larger rooms". It is true that in the mission's later stages, this "apartment", which was the original private chapel of the friars was used for Church purposes. In order to understand clearly the peculiar situation which eventuated with respect to the Church proper and this chapel in the Residence building at La Purísima, it is necessary to have the function of the chapel explained, and to trace the history of the Church proper.

The Rev. Maynard Geiger, O.F.M., Archivist of the Santa Barbara Mission gives the following clear statement of the functions of the house chapels found in Franciscan friaries:

In practically all our larger friaries, besides the public Church or chapel, there is also a private chapel, located in the living quarters of the friary. This chapel is usually small and is called into being for reasons of convenience. It saves the friars walking a long distance to make private visits to the Blessed Sacrament which is kept in such chapels just as in a public Church. It also obviated the necessity of a long distance in inclement weather. Moreover, it can be kept warmer when he is recovering from a cold, etc., can say Mass therein without the necessity of going to the main Church for the same reasons as given above. We have such a chapel in the friary at Santa Barbara and is used in the same mentioned capacity practically everyday. . . . The word convenience will cover the entire situation.[13]

Therefore the private chapel was not intended to be nearly as large nor impressive as the public Church, nor were the appendages which the Church requires, such as lofts, sacristies, a baptistry, etc., to be found in these chapels. Usually these private chapels were much smaller than those found at La Purísima. Archeological evidences did not indicate that it had been enlarged, but its dimensions, eighteen feet and seven inches by seventy-seven feet and seven inches are unusual.

The Church proper, which lies southwest of the Residence about four hundred and twenty-five feet, was of a size comparable to other California Churches, the nave being twenty-five [by] one hundred and forty-four feet in the clear.

For the first five years of the mission's existence at this site, services were held in a temporary building of poles, later veneered with adobes. During the year 1817 foundations were being laid for a suitable permanent Church.[14] Work on the new Church was accelerated during the year 1818 by the collapse of the palisade Church, and it appears, according to Engelhardt, that a new adobe Church was erected on the same site. Recent findings at the site lead to the belief that the new Church was erected on the foundations built during the previous year, but, whatever the truth of this matter, it is entirely possible that the friars modified more ambitious plans for their permanent Church in order to press completion of this one during the summer of 1818. Engelhardt says that it was not to be the permanent Church.[15] Hence Purísima was never noted for an elaborate Church at this site, although we now know that it was spacious enough although lower and less impressive than the one at the old site, (and other of the later mission Churches.)[16]

There can be little doubt that this building was damaged considerably during the quelling of the Indian revolt during 1824. After the seizure of the mission by the Indians:

> . . . The Purísima neophytes now prepared to defend themselves against the soldiers, who they well knew would be sent from Santa Barbara or Monterey. They erected palisade fortifications, cut loop-holes in the adobe walls of the Church and of other buildings, and mounted two swivel guns which had been used to make appropriate noise on feast days.[17]

Troops were sent from Monterey, numbering 109 men (including infantry, cavalry, and artillery consisting of a four pound cannon.) Lieut. Estrada reported the resulting engagement as follows:

> . . . step by step, we approached the mission until we were within shooting distance of our cannon. Protected by thirty three infantrymen, this began firing at about 8 a.m., always advancing until we reached within shooting distance of our muskets. From their loop-holes the Indians poured out a lively gun-fire at us with their one pound cannon, and also sent out a shower of arrows. Boldly despising that resistance, the artillery replied with brilliantly directed shots, and the musketry with a not less active firing.[18]

How much damage the building suffered from this engagement was not reported, but Bancroft stated that in 1835 the "building of a new Church was contemplated this year (1835), the old one being in a sad state; but nothing was apparently accomplished".[19]

The exact date at which the holding of religious services in the Church proper were discontinued is unknown. Engelhardt cites the Baptismal Register as a clue to the time when this occurred:

> . . . the phrase 'en la iglesia de esta Mision de la Purísima Concepción' was used by Fr. Arroyo de la Cuesta in connection with No. 3338 on Mar. 30, 1836. . . . Thereafter the entries always read, "en la iglesia de esta Mision", then "en la capilla pública de esta Mision" or "en la iglesia de esta Mision", doubtless Santa Inés was meant, where the Fathers resided.[20]

H. C. Ford, whose etchings and sketches form one of the most interesting collection of California missions, visited La Purísima in 1883. In his comments which accompany the published group, he supplies the information which he obtained concerning the Church. After describing the earthquake, and the destruction of the first mission he says:

> . . . Here again they were unfortunate, for, after having rebuilt, the Church walls were rendered unsafe by the breaking forth of a stream of water from the adjacent hills during a severe storm. Several workrooms of the mission were enlarged and thrown together and the altar removed thither. A few years since a portion of the mission was destroyed by fire, and it is now used as a stable and storehouse for the neighboring ranch.[21]

The changes that took place in order to convert the private chapel of the friars to a place of public worship could be clearly read in the ruins of this portion of the Residence building.

Some of the changes that were made are:

1. The ceiling was raised about four feet above its original level to the greatest possible height, that is, the eave level. At the original ceiling level the wall stepped back some nine inches, and here a wooden sill at the same ceiling level as found elsewhere in the building was left exposed. (See Figure 102).

2. A choir loft was also added. Of two rows of beam sockets in the east wall of the chapel, one obviously had held the original ceiling beams. The other row, slightly lower, was that for the beams supporting the choir loft, showing that the loft was not original.

3. The door into the chapel had been widened and increased in height. Traces of the earlier arch were visible in the wall.

4. The windows on the southwest end had been altered. Originally, the windows in the end of the chapel were smaller, higher and arched in form. With the raising of the ceiling, and the installation of the choir loft, the beams ran across in front of the opening. The arches were torn out, the windows enlarged, and the arches were replaced by wooden lintels. This is clearly shown in numerous photographs (Figures 75 and 83).

5. The partitions forming the sacristies and the baptistry were added after the original building was built. This was shown by the fact that these partitions did not bond into the earlier main walls; in fact the whitewash and the plaster ran straight through behind the end of the partitions. Also, two of these partitions had no footings whatever, and the third had but a very light rock footing of different character. The openings in these partitions had wood lintels, rather than the arch which characterized all of the original doors and windows (see Figure 108).

6. The exterior lower openings in the two sacristies were blocked up with adobe, the ceilings were raised, and the former openings into the loft were enlarged so that all the light came from above. This would be desirable in order to place the necessary vestment and Church furnishing

cases against the wall, as well as preventing a view into the rooms from the west walk.

7. The large exterior doorway into what became the baptistry was walled up with adobe, the ceiling raised, and the upper window was treated in the same manner as in the sacristies (see Figure 108).

Other evidences confirm the statement of Ford that the Church altar was removed to this building. There is little doubt, however, that this chapel was the original chapel, but the statement that "several workrooms were enlarged and thrown together" can best be interpreted as being the space converted into the sacristies, baptistry, etc.

In short, the conversion of the chapel was dictated solely by reasons of expediency. The mission had been secularized; its affairs were in the hands of political administrators whose concern was not for the Church; its population had dwindled to about 200 souls; and the prospect of improved conditions appeared remote. Therefore, this step was perfectly logical.

The larger room at the southwest corner was the only room which retained the original ceiling height. Consequently, the stair to the choir loft led up from this room to the upper loft, and an opening through the center wall led to the choir. The use of this lower room is problematical, but early residents in the district seem to be in general agreement that the room was a school room. Mr. Emmet O'Neil, an early resident, states that the words, *"Escuela a Mercal"* (Day School) were painted on the wall.

The altar wall probably was fitted up with the niches from the old Church. The central niche which can be seen in the early photograph, (Figure 105) was a rather clumsy effort to simulate the larger, more classical niche which had been built into the wall over the main altar of the Church, which being simply a part of the wall, could not be removed. The two smaller side niches, which were of wood could easily have been removed and brought to the corresponding location in the chapel. The niches which can be distinguished in the above mentioned photograph are obviously out of harmony, being rather more elaborate than one would have expected for a furnishing that would be made for the chapel. It seems reasonable that these were originally the ones over the altar of the Church.[22] The same supposition might be made with regard to the pulpit. The pictures of this pulpit show that it was well executed, and was of a design requiring considerable craftsmanship. The ornamentation was of carved wood with painted decoration. To move the old pulpit rather than build a new one would have been the natural and logical thing to do.

Nothing was found in the north sacristy, but the second sacristy, (room 20) contained the remains of the old sacrarium.[23] From this sacristy, steps also led upward through the dividing wall into the pulpit. The steps, carved out of the adobe, were found in the wall. The treads were covered with tile.

Some alterations to the exterior of this portion of the building also date from about this time. Most noticeable are the two end columns or piers, crudely built of stone and tile fragments. These stand slightly beyond the extreme end of the colonnade and were obviously not a part of the original plan. Their purpose was evidently to support a transverse beam on which were hung the bells formerly occupying the belltower of the Church. The workmanship in these added piers is noticeably different from that in the colonnade, and offers an illuminating comparison with the careful design and execution of the original columns. By 1935 only one of these piers remained intact.

A further alteration was the separation made in the *corredor* between the religious portion of the building, and the remainder which continued to be used as a dwelling. An adobe partition was extended from the wall of the building to one of the *corredor* columns. Figures 111 and 112 show this partition, the height of which extended only to the top of the column cap. Another extraneous construction was the creation of a sort of an entrance-way to the chapel. This was formed by placing a short piece of adobe wall on each side of the columns of the third bay of the colonnade, which was approximately opposite the entrance door of the chapel (Figure 73). This narrowed the opening sufficiently to impart the appearance of a vestibule opening, and the effect was increased by reducing the height of the opening with a wooden grille, extending from the beam overhead to a transom bar. It is possible that the stone steps which approach this bay were also added at this time, although this had not been definitely determined. These extraneous features have been omitted in the restoration. Those charged with the architectural responsibility have felt that beyond a desire for technical consistency in "period" nothing would be gained by their restoration and that the loss of the architectural effect of the uninterrupted sweep of the *corredor* more than offset the desire for technical consistency. Should it prove that this is a mistaken viewpoint, these features can be added as well, ten years or more years hence, as easily as during the present restoration.

The usages of the rooms in the religious portion of the building, at least from the time of the alterations, can be determined with reasonable accuracy. The historical accounts and the illustrative material have dealt with the ecclesiastical features in greater detail than those of the dwelling which occupies over two thirds of the area of the building. The archeological investigation, also, was perhaps more fruitful in this section. Devoted to religious purposes, it naturally received more attention and respect and so tended to retain its original character and architectural features longer than other portions which were cheerfully altered or destroyed during the period after secularization, when they were made to serve varied purposes.

The plan of the section north of the passageway, which can generically be termed the dwelling, since that was its principal function, is more difficult to analyze.

Before attempting a discussion of these numerous rooms, the passageway separating the chapel so definitely from the dwelling deserves explanation. This passage measures eleven feet in the clear, and the openings in the exterior walls leading into it are spanned by two heavy segmental arches which spring from rudimentary caps, or rather, simple fascia moldings, placed slightly above the true spring line. The arches are therefore segmental, but approach very nearly a "full" semicircular arch. The central or interior wall was also arched to permit clear passage through the building, but this arch occurred well above the floor of the loft, and the crown was within a few feet of the ridge (Figure 77). Only a few photographs show this arch. The passage was ceiled with beams and planking. According to an early resident, it was penetrated by a trap door near the west side. Below and above was a large wheel with a rawhide rope which acted as a sort of dumbwaiter for elevating produce to the loft for storage.[24] No evidence to support this statement has been found. To get onto the *corredor* easily, the exterior stone foundation wall is cut, forming a ramp.

In more recent days a partition had been built across the passage slightly over halfway of its length, and a domed adobe oven had been built in one corner. It is said this was used as a bakery after it was occupied by private ranchers.[25] This extraneous construction was also omitted in the restored building.

The Dwelling:

The remainder of the plan consisted of seventeen rooms; eight being on the east, or *corredor* side and nine on the back, or west side. The largest of these rooms occurs as the fifth room north of the passage on the east side, (room no. 6) and was unquestionably the *sala*, or reception room. Its entrance was a large opening with double doors, and it contained two window openings symmetrically placed, one on each side of the entrance. Doorways lead to the adjoining rooms on each end, to two rooms on the west side, and to a corridor, or hallway. This hall provided access to the west walk, and apparently to three other small rooms. In the *sala*, remains of a chimney flue and evidences of a former fireplace were found in one corner. This fireplace was associated with the only chimney shown by early photographs. Evidence available indicated that the fireplace was built at a later date than the original walls.[26] Nearly opposite the *sala* entrance was a niche, apparently intended for a religious figure.

Faint traces of red ochre were found at a few points near the floor indicating that this room had received some color treatment, although an all-over decoration was not discernible in a large plastered area remaining.

At each end of this room is a suite of two connecting rooms. These two suites are similar in treatment, and suggest that they were used for similar purposes. The first adjoining room, in each case, has only a door opening on the *corredor* to provide ventilation, light and access, (rooms 5 and 7). Room 7, however, does have an extra door in the northwest corner in addition to the one which connects to rooms 6 and 8.

Authentic plans of mission Residences made during the period and listing original usages of the rooms are exceedingly rare. It is difficult to make an accurate comparison. However, Duflot de Mofras, whose observations of *Alta California* were published in 1844, recorded the plan of Mission

San Luis Rey. This plan is reproduced in Figure 55 for the purpose of comparison. The plan of the Residence wing presents certain points of similarity to the building at La Purísima. It will be seen that it, too, was formed by a double series of rooms, the central room being the reception room (number 1). At each end an apartment of two rooms each is to be found. These were listed as the oratory, or study, (number 6), and a bedroom, (number 5), for each friar. It would seem probable that at La Purísima this scheme was also followed. Therefore, these rooms might reasonably be assumed to be the "Padre's apartments". The rooms numbered 5 and 7 are believed to have been the studies, and the rooms numbered 4 and 8 the bedrooms.

As a rule, one room was generally reserved for visiting officials or Church dignitaries. One of the better rooms was selected for this purpose.[27] A suitable room for such a purpose was possibly the north end room, which opened on the *corredor*. It also connected to the Padre's apartments, providing interior access from the *sala*. The holy water stoup, found in the reveal of the entrance door suggests such usage.

Two additional rooms complete the series on the east side; rooms numbered 2 and 3 immediately north of the passageway. These do not connect with each other, nor with any other room. In the writer's opinion, these were probably two rooms reserved as "Rooms for guests" as Payeras reported.

The rooms on the west side are more difficult to identify. The original report mentions rooms for servants, and workshops. No doubt these were in the rear. The small room opening off the hallway, (number 14), contained remains of a cooking pit, and evidence of fire, as well as many animal bones. Some sort of kitchen apparently existed here. While it appears to have been a general rule for most of the cooking to be done outside, the presence of kitchens in the buildings was not unknown in California missions.[28] It seems entirely reasonable that this room served as a small kitchen for the friars. The two small remaining rooms opening off this same hallway may well have been servants rooms, but no definite information about these has been found.

The two rooms to the south (number 17 and 18), are indeterminate, but may have been work-rooms or store rooms. In the case of number 17, access has been provided to the Padre's apartment.

Two other rooms on the west side open from the *sala*. One is small, the other of more generous proportions. From their connection to the main room it would be safe to assume they were primarily for administrative purposes, or for the direct use of the friars. The small room could have served as an office, or possibly as a library.[29] The larger room may have served one of these purposes, or it may have served as a dining room for the friars and their guests.

The use of the various rooms is indeed very conjectural. The opinions hazarded here do not pretend to be more than that. It is to be hoped that time and more study of similar dwellings may throw more light on the problem. The rooms have all been used for so many different purposes by the various occupants that only the vaguest conjectures can be secured from persons who lived in the building as far back as 1855.[30] Archeological findings have not offered conclusive evidence either.

The use of rooms number 10 and 11 remain unexplained. During the excavation numerous iron fragments were uncovered in the southwest corner of number 10, but these were identified as American workmanship. The items included China door knobs, cast iron locks, cast iron pot fragments, etc.

One interesting point of the plan remains to be discussed. This is the flanking wall which enclosed the north end of the *corredor*. The photographs of this wall show that the original opening was blocked up with adobe brick. The face terminating the *corredor* was treated with a very shallow panel, circular in shape at the top. This panel was apparently added after the opening was closed, for the lower right hand corner projects into the adobe-filled opening.

In the restoration, the panel was replaced, but the opening was not walled up. The stone spring house, about a quarter mile northeast, is directly on axis with this opening, and provides a very pleasing terminus to the view from the *corredor* at this point.

The Architecture and Structural System:

While the arch, the vault and the dome were to be found in a number of California mission structures, these features cannot be said to be characteristic of the architecture of California, as they are of the Churches of Mexico, Texas, and Arizona. Professor Newcomb has traced the background and development of the style of the California missions in his volume "The Old Mission Churches and Historic Houses of California." After analyzing the complex influences which have touched the architecture of Spain and showing how these influences affected the Spanish colonial Churches and established the prototypes for much of the subsequent work on the new continent, he says:

> Now while great sums of money and infinite pains were expended upon Mexican Churches, little or no attention was given to the Church architecture north of Mexico so far as the royal officials were concerned. Any study which the Churches received was bestowed by the Padres-in-charge. The Texan and Arizonan Churches, however, being in lands more accessible to Mexico, caught by reflection some of the splendor of the Mexican edifices, and in such structures as San José de Aguayo, near San Antonio, Texas, and San Xavier del Bac, near Tucson, Arizona, provincial as they were, we find the same attempt at magnificance, the same decorative fachadas, terraced towers and bare walls. These Churches have also, due to the use of domes, the same oriental atmosphere that characterize their Mexican prototypes, although the use of glazed tiles did not extend into these more northern provinces.
>
> These two edifices are, on the whole, much more elaborate, both in outline and decoration, than either the Californian or New Mexican mission Churches. Therein, perhaps, lies the chief charm of these

Franciscan edifices of California; simplicity, and straightforwardness. The intrinsic quality of good proportion, a trait generally characteristic of the work of Mexico at its best, is there, while much of the foam and froth of degraded decoration is absent. Since it was difficult to get artists and artisans to come into the country, the Padres and the Indians, with humble materials and unskilled hands, were compelled to build simply. Thus we are spared much of the degradation of the Mexican Churrigueresque. Meeting frankly their problem as they saw it, the padres evolved an architecture which, for the country in which it was developed, has not been excelled.

The Californian style is not a decorative style in any sense, but a style that makes its appeal through picturesque composition, good proportion, and structural frankness.[31]

The material which determined the architecture of California more than any other single factor, was the adobe brick. Structures of stone masonry or burned tile were the exception, rather than the rule. To the adobe brick can be attributed the use of heavy walls, the arched openings, the wide, projecting eaves of the roof, the plain wall surfaces, and indirectly, the popular use of the porches. With the development of methods for producing roof tiles from the native clays, as well as for structural and paving brick, the elements of the California builders were completed. Thus, sloping tile roofs; plain, heavy walls, undecorated except for painted or colored surface treatments, timber beams, ceilings and roof structures; and wide porches for circulation and protection from weather, either arcaded or colonnaded, became the dominant characteristics of both ecclesiastical and secular architecture of the New California.

Because the Residence building at La Purísima typifies the construction methods of the mission period in its mature stage, and illustrates the absolute straightforwardness of design which Professor Newcomb praises, it serves as an excellent example for study.

It is axiomatic that the limitations of the materials employed in a building affect and limit its design. The materials the *padres* had to work with were almost entirely those native to the country, and those were few in number; timber, earth, stone, (which was very often poor in quality), and lime, which could be manufactured from seashells or, if present in the locality, limestone. To these fundamental materials, native mineral and animal coloring agents were applied to produce simple decorative treatments. Iron, copper, and bronze were utilized sparingly, since they all had to be imported at great cost.

It is due to their skillful handling of their materials, and judgement in their employment that these early builders command our respect. With a material of such low strength as adobe brick, it was impossible to build light walls, or to build with a system of isolated supports. Therefore, heavy unbroken walls are required.

In the case of wooden members, these were of a size adequate to carry the loads placed on them. An idea is prevalent that such members in mission architecture were made unnecessarily and extraordinarily large.

The reverse is more nearly true. Timber supplies were often many miles distant and could be secured and worked into the desired structural shapes only after considerable effort. Consequently members are apt to be too economical in section to be considered satisfactory for modern safe design.

The limitations of timber beams very definitely affected the character of the buildings. Trussing, as such, was either unknown or merely not practiced due to lack of artisans familiar with those principles. Almost without exception, simple beams were used. This determined the practical limits of width of rooms and buildings. As a result, the Churches of California assume a long narrow shape; a simple nave, without side aisles.[32]

In the case of simple buildings, a recurring dimension of width is six varas, or about seventeen feet. This is a net dimension of the room, and was, no doubt, found to be convenient for use, and one which timbers of reasonable size could span. The simplest examples are one roomed dwellings, store houses, or the like. By joining a number of rooms together, a building of any length could be produced.

The roof rafters, in a structure of this kind, usually span the distance from wall to ridge without intermediate support. If, however, rafters of sufficient size were not available, a purlin was introduced at midspan. At the ridge, a heavy girder supported the upper end of the rafter. In the case of short rooms, i.e., around twelve to fourteen feet in length, the girder simply spanned the distance from the gable of one adobe cross wall to the next without additional support. If the distance was too great to do this, lower transverse beams were introduced, with a post at the mid-point, which supported the girder above.

If the rafter is firmly anchored to the ridge girder, this construction results in no thrust outward on the adobe sidewalls; that is, all the loads taken by the wall are vertical. Care was taken to see that this was done. Different means were in use; one was to notch the girder in such a way as to leave a projecting "tooth", which fitted into a notch made in the rafter. The rafter from the opposite side lay alongside, rather than butting into the end, and it, as well, was fitted into the girder similarly. The whole could be lashed with rawhide, forming a firm anchorage. In instances as at Mission San Carlos at Carmel, a double "tooth" and notch was employed on very large girders.

Where two series of rooms are placed side by side, as in the case of the Residence at La Purísima, the building was more than doubled in width. The rafters, of course, were incapable of spanning the entire distance from wall to ridge, and were supported at the midspan by the usual purlin. The loads from the purlin were transmitted by posts onto the midpoint of the ceiling beams, resulting in considerable deflection, or sag, at least in the chapel. This can be clearly seen in Figures 102 and 103.

An additional member was used in this structure which does not appear to be common elsewhere. Its purpose is not entirely clear. Struts were provided at intervals into the central wall. The upper end of the strut projected into the adobe wall at a point about four feet from the top. Its location in the outer wall is not known, whether close to the floor line, or near the eave. It appears to have been added as an additional brace to secure greater stability of the high adobe center wall. Figure 104 shows the remains of one of these struts, and shows clearly that it was not a continuous member, but composed of two poles halved together, and probably lashed with rawhide.

Plate number V gives a reconstructed cut-away view of the original scheme, illustrating the scheme of support and the location and use of these various members.

The Corredor:

In all but the more primitive houses, or in buildings of a more utilitarian character, the *corredor* was a customary feature in early California, and persists to a great extent up to the present time. For the Spanish word *corredor,* English has no exact equivalent. It is at once a porch, a corridor, a loggia, or an entrance. It may be anything from a splendid masonry arcade, to a simple porch-like structure of wooden posts and roof. Essentially, it is a covered walkway, extending along the side of the building, and onto which various rooms of the building open. In patio type plans, the *corredor* usually occurred on all sides of the courts; the finest and most pretentious of the mission examples were those of San Luis Rey and San Juan Capistrano, whose arcades of brick masonry enclosed very large courts. In simple rectangular structures, the *corredor* was used on one or both sides.

The Californians lived an out-of-door life. The patios and *corredores* were the scene of many of the domestic activities. When the hot sun was uncomfortable, the shaded *corredor* was cool and inviting; in rainy weather, it offered protection in going from one part of the building to another.

The *corredor* was planned with a very practical structural value as well. Adobe construction demands protection from moisture. Therefore, a covered porch placed on the south or east side was of great value for protection from the driving rains, which came from those directions. That the friars had this idea very much in mind is indicated by the report from Santa Barbara mission:

> In this year was built the front corridor facing the presidio. It measures one hundred and twenty-four feet in length and about eight and one half feet in width. The pillars were of brick and mortar, and the roof of tiles. *This corridor was erected to protect the wall of the mission structure that faced the southeast against the rains.* Another corridor similarly constructed, and measuring fifty by eight feet was built in the patio, or inner court, along the weaving rooms.[33]

The last sentence of the above quotation is also significant. It was placed "along the weaving rooms," for a great deal of the work could be accomplished on the *corredor.*

Thus the *corredor* served many purposes: for increased structural safety; for beauty; as a covered passageway; for working purposes; for enjoyment; and, where reserved for the private use of the friars, as a cloister.[34]

In the case of La Purísima, the *corredor* faced the southeast, protecting the weather side of the Residence. The careful design of the columns, the decorative corbels, the simplicity of construction, and withal the dignified yet hospitable character achieved, marks it as one of the outstanding examples of this feature of California work. Restored details of its construction are shown on Plate X. It may be noted that the rafters of the original, approximately five by five and one half inches were undersize for the load imposed. Originally, these rafters were lashed to the main rafters resting on a buried wooden plate, or sill. Over the rafters wooden strips, laid about four inches apart supported the tile (see Figures 112 and 115).[35]

Figure 102. The earliest known photograph of the chapel, about 1875-1880. A valuable picture, although details of the altar, which had been removed, are missing. Above the altar space are remains of the niches. Valuable information regarding the chancel rail, pulpit, floors, steps and decoration is contained herein. Leaning against the railing is one of the window sashes. Note the deflection of the ceiling beams.

Figure 103, (right). The chapel, looking toward the choir loft at the southwest end. An illustration by Henry Sandham. Although less accurate than a photograph, this drawing gives excellent details of the loft, railing, the pulpit and sounding board, the decoration of which can be dimly seen. From: Hunt, *Glimpses of California and the Missions.*

Figure 104, The chapel as it appeared in 1892. The line of the lower original ceiling is clearly defined by the ledge in the wall. A few of the tiles can be seen lying precariously on the rafters.

Figure 105. The altar wall of the chapel in its semi-final stage of ruin. The niche arrangement is clearly defined. Undated, probably about 1916.

[77]

Figure 107. The center wall, dividing the sacristies from the chapel, viewed from the northwest. The lower original ceiling line is visible, as well as the later sockets for the ceiling beams at the upper level. The upper openings, which formerly were archways giving access from one side of the loft to the other were then filled in.

Figure 106. The chapel by 1904 looked very little like the chapel in Figure 102. Note the rawhide lashing hanging from the rafters.

Figure 109. Remains of original sacrarium uncovered in Room number 20, Plate III. The receptacle had disappeared. The inverted roof tile were arranged as a drain.

Figure 108. The Baptistry, 1892. Original door blocked up, and the upper opening enlarged, after raising the ceiling.

Figure 111. The partition built across the *corredor* at the north end of the chapel, obviously not a part of the original plan. (1892)

Figure 110. The baptistry of Mission San Gabriel showing the baptismal font, and sacrarium in the corner. The sacrarium at La Purisima, while located in the sacristy occupied a similar corner position.

Figure 113. The archway from the *corredor* to the passageway separating the chapel from the living quarters of the building. An excellent detail also of the wooden grille of the opening to the loft above. Note the wooden lintel lashed together with rawhide.

Figure 112. The same partition and arch of the passageway. Note the collapse of the rafters. (1892)

Figure 114. The partition and oven in the passage-way are believed to have been added after the building was sold to Ramon Malo in 1850.

Figure 115. A view looking northeast along the *corredor* about 1906. The shallow panel on the enclosing wall at the north end is plainly shown. The line of the door opening can be distinguished with difficulty.

CHAPTER 4

ORIGINAL MATERIALS AND METHODS OF CONSTRUCTION

Foundations:

All foundations examined to date employed native stone. The Lompoc region is poor in stone of a good building quality, either from quarries or from the river.

In areas where large quantities of river boulders are available, the mission builders had no hesitancy in using them for foundation purposes, indeed, they found surprisingly many uses for even small pebbles. Santa Inés, located but twenty miles further up the same river, made extensive use of round river rock, which is abundant in that location.

In the Purísima area, however, quarried rock was used. According to Dr. J. Volney Lewis, Regional Geologist, National Park Service, the Monterey shale formation constitutes the bedrock in large areas of the region about Lompoc.[1] Of six specimens of different types of stone from the foundation work submitted to Dr. Lewis for examination, two were limestone and four were sandstone. Two of the sandstone specimens were calcareous and two non-calcareous. A complete technical description of these specimens will be found in Appendix A.

One of the two limestones is found to have been used principally in aqueducts and in foundations. It is a dense, firm stone, fairly strong, but chalky and whitish in appearance. It does not appear to have been used in exposed locations, except in the aqueducts. The second limestone is a stratified material, suitable for sills, thresholds, steps, and flagging. Occasionally smaller pieces of this type of stone were used for the tops of foundation walls.

The exact location of the quarries from which these rocks were obtained is not precisely known, but it is probable that the sandstones were secured from quarries located about three miles northeast of the Mission, in the Purísima Canyon.[2] Limestone occurs in quantity in the Miguelito Canyon, about two and a half miles south of the town of Lompoc. Lime was produced commercially in the early days of the town's existence. It is probable that this was the location where lime rock was secured. The flagstone occurs in outcrops in several locations nearby. Similar material was secured for restoration purposes from the outcrop on the J. J. Hollister property about one and one half miles northeast of the town of Lompoc.

For mass foundations under adobe walls sandstone was used. The calcareous and non-calcareous materials were intermingled. The rock was not dressed, but was laid in rough chunks anywhere from six inches to two feet or larger, with the smaller stones used to fill in the interstices. The mortar used in such a wall was mud. Because of the rough shapes of the stones a high volume of mortar was required.

Foundations of the Residence were of the same width as the wall and were of considerable depth. In the case of the center wall, which extended to the ridge of the roof and carried the greatest loads, the stone foundation is over seven feet in depth. Other foundations average from four and one-half to five feet in depth.

The top of the stone work was, in general, adjusted to approximately six inches above floor lines, and the top was found to slope. It will be noted on Plate IV that the top of the foundation wall of the colonnade at the southwest end is three feet and ten and one-half inches lower than the corresponding northeast corner. Since the columns were found to be of uniform height, it follows that the entire building was built on a gradient of slightly more than one percent. This was not unusual in California mission structures.

The slope of the Workshops and Quarters building, adjoining the Residence, was found to be five feet, in a distance of three hundred and twenty-three feet, or about one and one-half percent. The Church was found to drop but nine inches in its length of one hundred and seventy-four feet, or forty-three hundredths of one percent. Thus is appears that the controlling factor was the natural gradient of the site.

Floors were adjusted to meet the slope, either with a step between rooms, or at times with a slight ramp. The floors themselves were made level, except for exterior walks and those in the *corredor.*

In order to form an even surface to receive the first course of adobe brick, chips of roof tile, about two inches in diameter, or chips of flat stone of larger size were grouted in with mud.

Despite the large proportion of mud mortar and rough character of the work, these foundations proved remarkably strong, and have remained in an excellent state of preservation. The great thickness of the walls, compared with modern work, reduces the proportional square foot loading to safe limits.

Where stonework was to be exposed, more attention was given to the dressing, laying and finishing. The outer walls supporting the colonnade, walls, and buttresses were built of more carefully dressed sandstone, coursed, and laid in a lime mortar of excellent quality. Even in more careful work, however, no great trouble was taken in dressing the back faces of the stones, which resulted in the use of a relatively large amount of mortar. Realizing that the kind of stone used required protection it was finished with a plaster coat about one quarter inch in thickness.

An examination of the construction of one of the exterior walls showed that the foundation trench received a six inch bed of sand, then a setting bed of lime mortar and small rock nearly six inches in depth and extending on each side of the walls about nine inches.[3] On the base, stones averaging eighteen inches by twenty inches by fourteen inches in size were laid.

The edges of the stones are not sharp, due to the softness of the material. The work was pointed up flush, producing a rather unsightly jointing but since exposed parts were plastered, it was of small matter. The plaster coating has now very nearly disappeared on all exposed locations, and the masonry work is weathering rapidly.

Adobe Work:

Bricks: The word "adobe", according to Mr. J. D. Long,[4] is derived from the Spanish verb *"adobear"* meaning "to knead." This is the name given to green, or unburned brick, "moulded from a stiff mud, dried in the sun, and laid up in a wall by methods similar to the laying of standard burned brick. Straw is usually added to the mud mixture from which the bricks are moulded."[5]

The bricks may be made any practical size. A common size in early work was ten and one-half inches by twenty-one inches by four inches — roughly one-third by two-thirds of a *vara*, the Spanish yard. At La Purísima, the size employed in the residence and in the Church was eleven by twenty-three by four inches.[6]

The weight of each brick is about sixty pounds. The soil composing the bricks is a sandy, fine textured loam. Fifty-eight and fifty-four percent, respectively, of two specimens analyzed passed a two hundred mesh screen. The crushing strength was found to be about one hundred and ninety pounds per square inch.

The source of soil material was at the Mission site, being merely the sub-surface material below top-soil level. It is difficult to arrive at methods for measuring the amount of straw binder material, but the amount recovered in the tests ran between two and two and three-tenths percent by weight. The material used was principally wheat straw and horse manure. The wheat straw is in very short lengths, suggesting that it was probably the chaff from threshing floors.[7] Interesting specimens containing perfectly preserved wheat heads and other matter have been collected and saved for reference at the Mission.

After being molded and thoroughly cured, the bricks were laid in the wall according to the thickness of wall desired. In this building, the main walls were made four feet and three inches thick, being the distance occupied by two stretchers and one header. Partition walls were made the thickness of one header, or approximately two feet using alternate header and stretcher courses. The method of laying these walls is illustrated by the diagram of Plate V. It will be seen that the wall is bonded at each alternate course.

The outside wall thickness is reduced to three feet and six inches above the ceiling level, and the center wall from the same level to the ridge was made three feet. This dimension was obtained by using the header and stretcher, reversing each course to secure maximum bonding.

The practice of making the length of the brick slightly over twice the width is therefore a sensible one, since it works ideally for laying up the various thicknesses described with a maximum of bonding. Modern adobe bricks are generally made twelve by eighteen inches, which does not offer the same advantage.

The mortar used was substantially the same soil as contained in the bricks except that it contained no straw. The average joint is about three-quarters of an inch — a course averaging throughout many measurements four and seven-tenths inches.

Construction Methods: The construction of door and window openings was simply and effectively worked out with adobe brick. Typical original openings are given in Plate XII. No two arches were exactly alike in all particulars, and a great variety of treatment is found in the design of the interior of window openings; some had seats, others ledges, and others a combination of both. The openings in room No. 6, is of the latter design, and makes a very attractive, yet practical arrangement. The outer jamb and arch was usually made eighteen inches thick. The inner arch was splayed out to admit a greater amount of light, not only to increase the width of the opening, but because the white-washed reveals reflect a great deal of light. The setback of four inches at the face of the outer jamb provides the space for the wooden frame of the shutter.

The arch construction is carried out very simply. The arch bricks were roughly shaped as voussoirs, but the joints were not exactly radial. This necessitated fitting a keystone to the arch which was usually formed from two or three bricks. The characteristic method of doing this can be clearly seen in Figure 121. The construction of the inner arch is slightly more complex. The inner arch is sprung from eight to twelve inches higher than the outer arch to permit the head jamb of the wooden frame to be fitted in. Generally the soffit slopes upward toward the inner wall face two to three inches.[8]

After the centering was removed, the arch was trimmed with a tool to a smooth line, and in so doing the first brick was shaped to form a gentle curve to meet the vertical line, producing a somewhat elliptical shape which is more pleasing and graceful than the mechanical segmental arches found in much of our modern work.

All the window arches which existed were of adobe, but two doorway arches of larger span were constructed with burned tile. One is the entrance into the *sala*, where the exterior arch was of tile and the interior of adobe. The other is the entrance into the chapel, which was enlarged from its original size. Here the outer arch is composed of two separate rings — one of tile and one of a narrow ring of adobe brick. A wooden lintel composed of three pieces about six inches thick is substituted for the interior arch. This arrangement apparently dates from the period of the other alterations to the chapel described above.

Floors:

Five types of floor materials have been recorded in the Residence. These are as follows:

1. Redwood planking
2. Tile
3. Adobe brick
4. Tamped sandstone
5. Earth

(1) *Redwood plank floors:* This type of flooring was found in the chapel and seven other first floor rooms.[9] The table on Plate VIII gives the location of this material.

Although in a greatly disintegrated condition, the general method of laying plank flooring was evident. No good specimens of the planking could be obtained, due to its rotted condition, but the indications were that its thickness was about two inches. Details of the width of the plank, method of joining, and finish were lacking. The only positive statement that can be made is that certain rooms had been floored with redwood planking.

Fragments of redwood sleeper beams approximately eight by ten inches were found buried in the earth, and projecting from these fragments were large forged iron nails. In one case (room No. 4) under the remains of the redwood floor, fragments of an earlier tile floor were found. This suggests that this material was not used during the first years and that its use was either a development of the later mission period, or post-mission period. An example of this type of flooring, though badly worn, still exists, in the Residence wing of Mission San Juan Bautista. Those planks vary in width from ten to nineteen inches.

(2) *Tile Floors:* Tile was used principally for the corridors and walks. Very few rooms contained evidences of former tile floors.[10] The floor of room No. 17, and the corridor was of tile although in poor condition. Traces of tile flooring were also found in rooms 10 and 18, and under the redwood floor of room No. 4. The tiles are ten and one-half by ten and one-half by two inches, laid with close joints, and somewhat irregular in pattern; that is, the joints do not form straight lines, but are broken. This is due for the most part to the fact that the tiles are handmade, and vary slightly in size. Tests for weight, size, strength, and water absorption, of the tiles are given in Appendix A. The cross section of nearly all of these tiles shows a black core, indicating incomplete burning. This characteristic black center, and "soft burning" of the exterior would be considered defective, or at least unsatisfactory for present day use, yet the strength developed is fair (1900-2800 pounds per square inch) and the water absorption is quite low (14-17%). Shapes and dimensions of the various tiles which were found during investigation are to be found on Plate number VI.

When better floors were desired, the tiles were laid on a bed of lime mortar and small rubble, about two and one-half to three and one-half inches in thickness. Surviving examples were in a good state of preservation, and can be seen still in the west walk, in room 17 and in the floor in the short hall west of room 6.

There is reason to believe that some tiles were laid without a mortar bed, using merely a sand cushion. In the southeast corner of room 18 a few floor tiles were found laid thus.

A point noted in the method of laying floors was that exposing the edges of tiles had been avoided, wherever possible, by allowing adjoining stonework to project above the surface of the floor. On thresholds, the use of stone flagging was preferred. The padres well knew that tile was too soft to be satisfactory in such service locations.

(3) *Adobe brick floors:* The use of adobe brick floors appeared to be confined in this building, to the smaller rooms of the west side, (rooms 14, 15 and 16). Better examples of this type of flooring were found in other structures and locations. The best preserved example was the floor of building No. 7, which is clearly shown in Figure 37. Adobe was used extensively as paving for the west *corredor* of building No. 2, and in the open patio area No. 1 of this building, around the cooking ovens. Another interesting note is its use as paving for a roadway connecting the north end of the Church to the area west of the Residence. For interior locations it would appear to be a feasible material, but for exposed locations such as those it is surprising that this material withstood the mechanical wear and the weather to which it was subjected.

The adobes used were the standard wall brick, eleven and one-half by twenty-four inches, laid flat on a sand bed, but without great attention to the jointing.[11]

(4) *Tamped sandstone:* A soft yellow sandstone known by geologists as "Vaquero Sandstone" is to be found in this region. This material has much the same appearance as the harder varieties, but it is soft enough to be easily broken into sand by mauls or by tamping. When a layer of this material is tamped into place, it serves as an excellent walk or floor, since it contains enough binder to give the floor a firm "set." The north walk was found to be composed of this material, in a layer approximately two inches thick. Even wet weather conditions do not appear to cause it to wash or to make it slippery or disagreeable to walk on. This same type of flooring was found in the two front rooms north of the passage (rooms 2 and 3).[12]

(5) *Earth floors:* No trace of any floor except earth was found in rooms 7, 8, 11, 12, 13 and 14.[13] In room 9, a few tiles and flat stones were loosely laid across the northeast corner, but findings were not considered adequate for conclusions as to the original floors. Traces of tiles remaining in room 10 were not sufficient in quantity to be conclusive. Whether the floors of any of these rooms had never been anything other than earth is problematical.

Timber and woodwork:

The lumber used in the Residence included both local materials and redwood. The scene of the local lumbering operations is not definitely known, but is believed to have been in the forest on the San Rafael range in Santa Barbara County.[14]

Species of timber in this region include western yellow pine (*Pinus ponderosa*), big cone spruce (*Pseudotsuga macrocarpa*), incense cedar (*Librocedrus decurrens*), Coulter pine (*P. coulteri*), Cottonwood (*Populus fremontii*).

Local material was used for beams, rafters and other framing timbers. Fragments recovered from various locations have been identified as big cone spruce, cottonwood, and Ponderosa pine.[15] A fragment of ceiling planks has been identified as big cone spruce. Apparently any suitable tree was felled and utilized for beams, however, for one specimen was identified as cottonwood. No rafters remained.

Ponderosa pine was used for door and shutter frames, grilles, and other minor details where the excellent working qualities of this wood made it especially desirable.

Redwood was found to have been used in floor planking, door panels, sleeper beams under floors, and in a small fragment of panel and molding believed to have been an original panel from the pulpit.

While identification is not positive, it is Dr. Cockrell's opinion that the redwood specimen submitted is coastal redwood, (sequoia sempervirens) rather than the valley big tree (sequoia gigantea). The coastal redwood was known and used extensively in the northern missions around San Francisco Bay, and certain presidial buildings.[16]

Since the southern limit of coastal redwood was the Santa Lucia mountains in northern San Luis Obispo County, the supposition is that redwood was probably furnished from the Santa Cruz region, shipped by the sailing vessel that plied coastwise to some convenient point on the coast, from whence it was hauled to the site.[17]

All of the timber details show an excellence of workmanship not generally associated with California mission work. In earlier examples, where smaller trees were roughed into shape with axe and adze, the primitive character of the workmanship is marked. By contrast, the smoother finish and greater expertness of the work on the Residence at La Purísima is noticeable. Corners are square, even sharp, and beams maintain an unusual uniformity in size. Figures 99 and 101 illustrate the quality of work, and sharpness of detail of the beams and shaped corbels of the *corredor*. In fact, from these photographs, it is impossible to say whether the corbels were sawn to shape, or cut with a chisel.

From the ends of the beams which still remained, it appears that the original surface had not only been adzed, but planed as well. The method apparently utilized a whipsaw, then either an adze or a plane, or possibly in instances both. Planking was whipsawn and possibly adzed or smoothed on the exposed face.[18]

General practice in timber framing work shows carefulness in arrangement and in connections. Beams did not bear directly on adobe, but on sills or plates which generally were buried in the adobe wall. Ceiling beams rested on a continuous wooden sill, about four and one-half by ten inches, laid in the wall and flush with its surface. This was plastered over or whitewashed. Elsewhere in California work the surface of the sill was roughened and covered with the finishing coat of plaster. This practice was not observed here.

Throughout most of the building, the spacing of the ceiling beams was about two feet and eight inches on center. An exception was in the ceiling of the altered chapel where the beams were about three feet and six inches apart. Measured specimens of the beams used indicated a variation in size from eight by ten and one-half inches to eight and one-half by eleven and one-half inches. The closeness of spacing can probably be attributed to the fact that ceiling beams also had to support the floor of the loft, which served for storage purposes. The ceiling of the Church, which did not serve such a dual purpose, was supported by beams spaced approximately five and one-half feet apart. Corbels, which were often used elsewhere to reduce the effective span, were not found in the Residence, since timber of adequate size for the span was available.

Fragments of plank recovered, one and one-eighth inches thick, white washed on the exposed face were assumed to be ceiling boards.

Although no rafters were found in the ruin, from photographic evidence they can be judged to be about four and one-half to five by five and one-half inches.[19] These rafters were notched into the ridge pieces as explained in the discussion of the structural scheme.

Roofing: Two methods of sheathing or stripping were used in the Residence building. Over the building proper solid sheathing consisting of round branches tied to the rafters with rawhide was used. Since no remains of this material were found it is not possible to state precisely what the original method was. In some photographs it appears to have been hollow, such as bamboo. Some persons who saw the ruins years ago, state that they remember it as chaparral (the branches of the native cover). From photographs the material used appears to have been about an inch to an inch and one-half in diameter. The rawhide by which this sheathing was lashed in place can be clearly seen hanging from the rafters in Figure 106. One of the materials in wide use for this purpose was the bamboo-like giant reed, (*arundo donax*), a native of the warmer regions of the old world, and introduced into California by the missionaries. This reed grows rapidly and produces a stem about an inch or more in diameter. This material when lashed to the rafters served admirably as a surface on which to lay tile, or as a ceiling.[20] It was thought that this reed had been used at La Purísima.

For the roof of the *corredor*, one by four inch wooden strips had been nailed to the rafters about four inches apart. The board at the edge of the eave was made about two by eight inches in order to lay the eave tiles in proper position (see Figures 99 and 101).

Grilles: Remains of finished work such as doors, shutters, grilles, and stairways were fragmentary.

One partial window grille still remained in place in room number 22.[21] The measured details of this grille, seen in Figure 121, are shown on Plate XII. It was simply constructed of pine with a heavy frame, whose projecting top and bottom rails were firmly anchored into the adobe work. Vertical wooden spindles two inches square are set at a forty-five degree angle into this frame. A center rail is provided for additional strength. Joints are mortised, tenoned, wedged and glued. No shutter or other means of closing this opening was discovered.

Doors and frames: While no complete door remained in place details of ten partial door frames were recorded. All of these frames were made of yellow pine. Characteristics of these frames (as well as shutter frames) in common with those of other California missions leads to justifiable deductions of the procedure in their construction.

The jambs, head and sill pieces were sawn out and planed to the desired size. The side jambs were then tenoned into the head jamb and the sill, and wedged, so that the frame is rigid and strong. The rebate for the door was next cut out with a chisel all around. The depth of the rebate was found in most instances to be from one fourth to three quarters of an inch greater than the thickness of the door. This was partly overcome by insetting the hinge into the frame, and partly by offsetting the hinge strap. Cutting the rebate after assembling results in showing a portion of end grain in the rebate of the head and sill. The ends of the top and bottom members project into the adobe wall, anchoring the whole frame securely. Since it would have been impossible to install it after the brickwork is in place, this proves that the frame was set before the wall was built.

The only fragments recovered that could be associated with doors were three redwood pieces, each one and one quarter inches in thickness and moulded with a fillet and quarter round at the edge. Comparison with Historic American Building Survey measured details showed this section and profile to be identical with door panels found at Mission San Diego.[22] Since no similar detail was found except as door panels it has been assumed that these fragments were originally used for the same purpose. Thickness of stiles and rails could be definitely determined in those cases where the original nails were still in the straps of the iron hinges, of which numerous examples were recovered.[23] A hinge with nails complete is shown in Figure 144. The rail thickness is clearly evident from the distance from the strap to the point where the nails are clinched, which distance agreed with the San Diego Mission door. The reconstructed details of these doors are shown on Plate XII.

Shutters: A fragment of an original shutter was also recovered (see Figure 130) as well as examples of shutter hinges. This fragment showed the method of making a shutter to be similar to the doors already described. The mortising, tenoning, and rabbetting was carried out similarly, and into this rebate the panel had been fitted. The panel itself was missing, consequently any data for the design of these panels was dependent on other mission sources. Common methods found for treatment of panels were: (1) run panel moldings, flat in profile. These were crossed over at the corners of the panel, and not mitred, as at San Juan Bautista. (2) Incised vertical beading used to decorate the edge pieces forming the panel, same mission. (3) "River of Life" design — carved into the face of the panel, as at Santa Inés. (4) Moulded boards, with moulded vertical battens, as at San Fernando Mission. Examples from (1) and (3) were selected for reproduction.

Chapel details: The original chancel railing of the chapel could only be determined from photographs and one early date drawing. No remains existed. Figure 190 shows the simplicity and effectiveness of these flat spindles shaped to suggest a classical baluster, and painted to simulate the roundness of marble examples which decorated remembered Churches of the old country. Traces of the painted decoration can be faintly distinguished in Figure 102. A more detailed illustration of the railing from the sanctuary side can be seen in Figure 103, a pen and ink drawing made by Henry Sandham.[24] This picture is the only one known showing the choir loft, which utilizes the same spindle design in the railing.

Figure 103 also gives some detail of the pulpit and canopy, mainly silhouette. It indicates the painted design of the underside of the canopy, which Mrs. Jackson describes as "hanging awry." A fragment of the redwood panelling with moulded stile was recovered near this location which may very likely have been a portion of this interesting piece of woodwork (Figure 130). The panel was about three eighths inch in thickness, the stile about an inch. The panel mould was a simple cove mould.

Additional details of the design can be seen by careful study of the view from the choir loft shown in Figure 102. This picture forms the most valuable single view of the chapel as it appeared before going entirely to ruin. Although one copy of this print had been dated 1875, its date has not been conclusively ascertained.[25]

It is evident that the pulpit was one of the more elaborate pieces of wood craftsmanship — carved, panelled and decorated. The bottom pendant was carved in a rosette-like form, and from this the bottom is gracefully shaped to meet the floor of the pulpit in a reverse curve. The decorated treatment above this consisted of painted design, in the form of gilt, marbleized panels and running bands of simple pattern. The whole structure was supported on wooden cantilevers which can be seen projecting from the wall in Figure 104.

Another interesting example of woodwork is that of the two side niches above the altar which can be seen to better advantage with a good glass in Figure 102. As has been previously stated, it is believed that these features were removed from the older Church. These two niches were obviously made out of wood, and occupied a position above a continuous wooden shelf, supported partly on wooden corbels. While the central niche and the right-hand niche are difficult to see in the above view due to the damage caused by the leak in the roof above, the left-hand one can be made out in some detail. It appears that this piece took the form of a shell carving, decorated in color. Simple mouldings were used at the spring of the semi-circular head. The central niche was merely cut out of the adobe and decorated with color.

Figure 105, showing this wall in ruin, gives fairly accurate information as to the location of these niches.

Glazed windows: From the evidence of the original window openings, and from fragments of glass and of the sash themselves, there is no doubt that glazed windows were used in the lower and upper windows of the chapel.[26] Study of the historic photographs confirms the archeological evidence and gives information as to the design of these windows. It is very probable that some, or all of these were removed from the Church when it was dismantled.

From one well preserved fragment (see Figure 130) the details of the construction are known. The method of making window sash, like every other detail of the construction, was logical, simple and quite satisfactory. This fragment showed that the stiles, rails and muntins were made of yellow pine of about one and one-quarter by two inches, carefully mortised, tenoned and fastened with wood pins. These members were grooved to receive the glass. The tenons were made about three-eighths of an inch less than the mortise in one dimension, apparently for the purpose of allowing sufficient movement to permit glazing. The sash was fixed in place in the opening with no frame, by extending the top and bottom rails into the wall, and plastered in. Figures 73 and 75 indicate that the lower windows contained six panes, two panes wide and three panes high. The sanctuary sash had twenty panes — four wide and five high. One half of this sash can be seen leaning against the chancel rail in Figure 102. From the ruined openings glass fragments were recovered. The glass was very thin and of fair quality, originally clear, although now opalescent from long contact with the earth.

Plastering:

Types: Two types of plaster finish for walls were found in the Residence; (1) Lime plaster and (2) mud mortar. All walls were finished with one or the other type of plaster.

(1) *Lime plastering on adobe:*

Material: This was the preferred finish, due to its greater protection and smoother finish. Analysis and tests made of the samples of this material indicate its chemical and mechanical contents.[27]

The analysis of the composition of this mortar is calculated by weight, which shows eighty percent sand to twenty percent lime hydrate. This corresponds roughly to three parts sand to one part lime hydrate by volume.

Method: Since there is no bond between adobe brick (earth) and the lime plaster, mechanical means were resorted to in order to attach the plaster to the wall. The method was essentially the same throughout the mission buildings at La Purísima.

First the adobe brick wall was scored with grooves about one and one-half inches wide and about the same in depth, generally diagonally, about eight inches on center. These grooves were then filled with lime mortar and chips of roof tiles, so that the surface was about flush with the adobe.[28] This forms the bonding surface for the plaster coat which is then applied to about one-half inch in thickness over the adobe. Examination of the cross section of samples of plaster show that the finish surface (about one-eighth inch deep) is of a richer mixture of lime than the rest. This indicated that the plastering was done in two operations, first the three to one mortar mixture was applied, then followed up with a finishing coat, much as a modern "putty coat" is employed to secure a smoother finish.[29]

There seems to be a general agreement among the old residents and those Mexican workmen who learned the old methods that cactus juice was employed in plastering and in painting, both for whitewash and color. The cactus (opuntia) leaves were gathered, placed in a barrel, chopped up, and soaked in water. After about a week the resulting liquid was drawn off — a somewhat sticky fluid which appears to have produced qualities of adhesiveness and flexibility in the finish coating.

The finished surfaces, although reflecting the underlying "waviness" of the rough adobe wall, were smooth, and corners and edges are quite sharp. One almost might describe the plaster as "polished." Stones about three and one-half by five inches, oval in shape and smooth on one side from rubbing, with vestiges of white and pink plaster still clinging to them were recovered (see Figure 137). The smoothness and polish of the finish is explained by these stones, which were obviously used to rub the surface smooth.[30] Lime plaster was used on the exterior for the front wall and southwest end, and on the interior on all the rooms opening from the *corredor*, with the exception of the chapel. On all other walls, mud plaster and whitewash was used.

(2) *Mud plaster:*

Materials: Mud mortar was made from the same material as adobe bricks plus more sand, in order to reduce shrinkage and consequent cracking. It was applied directly to the adobe wall, without any necessity for the slow process of grooving and bonding required for lime. It averages about one quarter inch in thickness. After drying, it was treated with whitewash in the same manner as the lime plaster.

Care was taken to use mud plaster on outside locations least exposed to the rains.[31]

Character: When finished, the mud plaster has a slightly rougher appearance than lime. The coursing of the brick surface is more noticeable in this method, since it reflects more intimately the underlying construction. Edges were necessarily more rounded, and the whole appearance is cruder. While more subject to mechanical abrasion, it is a surprisingly effective finish and has the advantage of economy and rapid application.

Colored plasters: Integrally colored lime mortars were extensively used. Two colors were found in the Residence, pink and ochre. In the Church building, a dado of brilliant pink plaster was used on the exterior and interior, but in the Residence colored plaster was found only over stone masonry or brick work.

Use of this pink plaster was found in a great number of structures. It invariably occurs in water structures, such as reservoirs, aqueducts, fountains, lavatories, etc. It was also used to line the large vats of the tallow works, and the drainage flume leading from it. An interesting decoration was produced in the soffit of the arched opening into the "spring house" by making a pattern of crosses in two shades of pink.

Samples tested from the Church indicate a high content of sand and mineral coloring in proportion to lime, resulting in a mortar of brilliant color, but one of very low strength.[32] The lime content in colored plaster used on the Residence is greater, and while the color is less dense, the plaster is more satisfactory.

The pink plaster was produced with a red colored diatomite.[33] This material occurs along the banks of the Santa Ynez River, a range of colors from light pink (almost a coral shade) to a deep, purplish red. It was ground with pestles, screened and mixed as a plaster.[34]

The pink plaster was used in the base, cap, and flutes of the *corredor* columns. It was applied as a thin coat, approximately one-fourth inch thick, and rubbed to an extremely smooth, hard surface. The use of color in these columns adds greatly to their charm. At one period (about 1892) this was covered with white-wash, as can be seen in Figures 99 and 101, but this, fortunately, was not permanent, and the columns have now regained their former appearance.

The stone wall supporting the colonnade was originally finished in an ochre-colored plaster. Fragments still exist at the southwest end of the colonnade. This was produced simply by addition of earth ochres to the lime-sand mixture. Source of the coloring agent has not been ascertained.

Another interesting use of plaster is that of a finish for floors, and walks. No such use was found in the Residence, but walks in the cemetery, and the floors of the two sacristies of the Church were finished with a pink plaster coat, applied over a base of rubble and lime mortar. In addition, it was used for decorative purposes as described above. These colored plasters are to be distinguished from painted surfaces. A greater variety of colors and treatments are described below in the section entitled "Painting, Coloring and Decoration."

Painting, Coloring and Decoration:

Types of color treatments: In the archeological investigation of the Residence the following types of color treatments were identified:

1. Lime whitewash.
2. Lime whitewash plus color.
3. Color plus some vehicle, such as glue.
4. Gilt on gesso.

Oil paints, although used elsewhere, and probably here, were not found.

Colors: The following colors were observed, listed in the order of most frequent occurrence:

1. White — (whitewash)
2. Reds — (Light pink to deep burnt sienna)

3. Ochres — (From orange-yellow to straw color)
4. Grey — (Grey with a blue cast)
5. Blues — (Deep Prussian blue to light cobalt)
6. Bluegreen — (Pale)
7. Green — (Clear pure color)
8. Gilt.

Recovered color fragments have been identified as to chemical base, but it was not possible for the laboratory to state the exact material used as the coloring agent.[35]

Materials and Use:

Whitewash: This was used for all types of surfaces, and applied in many coats through the passing years. Considerable maintenance work was evidently necessary, for during the building's term of use it must have been whitewashed many times, building up to a coat of lime in many cases over one-eighth inch in thickness.

The exact composition of this material is not known except that it is essentially lime; to which tallow, or fat was added.[36] The laboratory reports indicate the admixture of fat in some form.

Tradition has it that the remarkable qualities of adhesiveness, elasticity and resistance to water of the old whitewash can be attributed to the use of cactus juice and tallow. There is no doubt that the early whitewash was of good quality. While modern formulas produce a good paint, the Padres produced a very satisfactory one from simple materials close at hand.[37]

Whitewash was used for walls, ceilings, ceiling beams and other woodwork. Frames and backs of doors and shutters were customarily treated in the same manner. No doors nor shutters existed, so no positive statement can be made regarding the treatment at La Purísima, but elsewhere it was customary to leave the front (obverse) sides of doors untreated by paint covering.

From photographic evidence, exterior rafters, stripes, beams, and other woodwork appear to have been left without finish, merely acquiring a natural weathered appearance during the course of time.

Reds and pinks were sometimes used as all-over colors as dados, as narrow stripes in deeper tones and as line decoration in the form of geometrical and conventionalized floral decorations on walls.[38] They are found in a variety of shades, from light rosy pink to deep burnt sienna.

Remains at the base of walls indicated clearly that the Residence originally was decorated with a pink dado, about 18 inches high. Traces of this dado are still visible at the southwest end of the *corredor.*

Burnt sienna stripes were found in the chapel and the baptistry, separating and accenting two other colors used in the dado. Traces of a stripe of color were found in the *sala,* but not sufficient remained to determine the nature of the decoration.[39] The width of the stripe was about one-half to five-eighths inch.

From the varieties of shades found, it was evident that reds were used both with lime, and pure in some clear vehicle such as glue or cactus juice. In general, where occurring in large areas, it is of paler shade, while stripes are of deeper shade.

Ochres were also widely used, since it was an earth color, lime-fast, and could easily be obtained. This color was used in connection with gray as illustrated in Plate XI. Traces of this color were also found in room number 4.

Blues, blue-greens and greens were also found in room number 4, but these were in such condition as to preclude definite statement as to any pattern. No colors were found in this room over six feet above the floor, but below this the above colors were found. Whether they were used as dados, or in all-over treatment cannot be stated. The colors themselves are clear and bright, and Plate XI gives closely matched samples. Laboratory tests showed all of the blues and greens to be copper compounds.[40] The blues were most probably derived from mineral azurites, and the greens from the copper carbonate group known as malachites. Grays were easily produced with either bone or wood charcoal, the latter being used in this building mixed into lime whitewash.[41]

Decoration on wood is known to have been used on the chancel and choir railings, the pulpit, and the niches above the altar. These having disappeared with the exception of the single fragment already described, the type of material used is unknown. It is very probable that this was carried out in oil paint over *gesso*, as was customary elsewhere.

There is little doubt that more decoration existed than what was found by this investigation. Time and weather obliterated nearly all of this work. Persons familiar with the building in early days describe the *sala* as being decorated with pictures painted directly on the walls.[42] However, La Purísima cannot be said to have been as highly decorated as was San Fernando, where recent investigations have revealed unsuspected wall paintings and decorations below layers of whitewash.

Hardware and metal work:

Materials: The metal articles recovered during the course of archeological work is perhaps the most valuable collection of artifacts secured through the excavation. Well over half of the total number of items catalogued are metal articles, such as tools, utensils, buttons, coins, and building hardware.[43] It is the hardware which is chiefly interesting in this discussion, although accompanying photographs of other representative items illustrate the character of the utensils and objects in use during the period. While the number of iron objects exceeds all others, the catalogue lists copper (cast and wrought), bronze (cast and turned), and silver (coins). Cast iron articles are also listed, but are apparently of later period.

Copper was extensively used, for the number of copper artifacts is nearly one half that of iron. Hardware, pots, kettles, buttons, eating utensils, and candleholders are typical objects made of copper. Nearly all were handwrought, possibly at the mission, from material brought from Lima, or Mexico. Bronze was also used for castings, such as door bosses, decorative nail heads, and candleholders. Whether these were cast and turned locally or imported is not known.

Articles of lead include bullets (musket balls), decorative buttons, a medallion (raised design), a decorative pin, and two cast spigots. Buttons and keys were found of brass, and coins were found of silver.

Door Hardware:

Hinges: Three types of door hinges were recovered from La Purísima. Numerous examples of each were found.

    1. The strap hinge — 2 types.
        a. with plain pin.
        b. with special pin.
    2. The butterfly, or surface butt.
    3. The H-hinge.

Photographs and measured drawings of these three types are shown on Plate XIII, and Figure 139. From the greater number of strap hinge fragments, it is evident that this type was most commonly used. It was no doubt preferred for its greater strength and simplicity of fabrication. An interesting variation of the above strap employing a special pin, designed for greater strength at the butt, is illustrated in Figure 140 and Plate XIII. This was found only twice on the entire site, indicating that it was only employed infrequently on larger or heavier doors requiring more support.

Several shapes of "butterfly" hinges were recorded. At Mission Santa Inés, this was frequently used in conjunction with strap hinges, as an intermediate hinge where a rail did not occur and the hinge was necessarily confined to the width of the stile.

A few examples of H-hinges were found infrequently. While it was a popular type in other mission work, it does not seem to have been a favorite here. The only method of fastening the hinge was long, hand-forged nails, projecting through the door, and double clinched.

Locks: Several good examples of locks were uncovered (see Figures 141, 147 and 151). The James Holloway Collection in the town of Lompoc contains additional originals from this mission.[44] One example in this collection is outstanding, having a case of heavy copper, and the working parts of iron.

Two types of locks were recorded:

    1. A simple half-mortised lock, using a common throw bolt, engaged by the key, with a metal strike.
    2. A sliding hand-bolt, which engages a hole in the jamb, or if a pair of doors, into a ring in the second leaf. The bolt locked into place as illustrated (Plate XIII).

The half-mortised lock was most common. It consisted simply of a plate, with the end bent around the edge of the door, and a slot cut into this for the bolt. The back was not enclosed — a smaller plate was held on legs rivetted to the front plate. The front and back plate were about an inch, to an inch and a half apart. The bolts are very simple — about one-fourth by one inch in section, sometimes heavier, with an S-shaped notch, into which a bit of the key fits to throw the bolt. Proper tension is kept on the bolt by a flat spring. The principal protection depends on the various shapes of keyholes, each one being different, and the keys fitted for that one alone. Decorative escutcheons were observed on the obverse face of doors at other missions, but no examples were found here.[45]

Thumb latches: Fragments of strikes and guards were identified as portions of thumb latches. No complete examples were found.

Bosses and decorative nail heads: These were great favorites for decorating doors, and their use dates back many centuries in Spain, where they were developed into many patterns, often of extravagant size.

Examples of forged iron, forged copper, and of cast and turned bronze bosses were found at the Residence, and are shown on Plate XIII, and Figure 146. The simplest forged types vary in size from an inch to two and one-half inches in diameter, securing interest by emphasizing the hammer marks. Cast and turned examples of bronze are of refined detail, suggesting that these were possibly imported from Mexico.[46] Since these were expensive, no doubt, and difficult to obtain, this supposition might explain the use of a crude copy of the last type made of a wrought copper disk probably used with a forged stud (see Figure 146).

Shutter hinges and fastenings: Simple butterfly hinges of smaller size were used for shutters. Marks remaining on existing shutter frames agreed in shape with several small hinges uncovered. One hook was found (Figure 143) suggesting that one leaf of the shutter was fastened to the other by means of a simple hook and eye.

Figure 117. The stone base of the colonnade. This stonework has but a few fragments of the buff colored plaster finish remaining. Its eroded condition does not reflect the original workmanship.

Figure 116. The characteristic stonework is well illustrated by the buttresses at the southwest end of the building. Originally, this work was finished with a lime plaster coating, which has largely disappeared. The pier in the center of the photograph is a restoration.

Figure 118, (upper). An original adobe brick, (lower) right and reverse sides of typical floor tiles (also used for masonry work).

Figure 119. The main walls of the building were four feet three inches thick, formed of adobes laid in the above manner. The alternate courses consisted of two headers. See also Plate V for detailed diagram of bond.

Figure 120. The exterior face of a typical window arch. The sill of this window had been raised by additional brick.

Figure 121. The interior face of the opening above after being excavated. Note the method of "keying" the arch by means of three bricks. This window contained the only remaining wood grille.

Figure 122. A typical window. This opening employed a wooden shutter (missing). The frame still remained. Note the remains of the tile sill, and sockets for the exterior wooden grille.

Figure 123. Portion of a window opening being excavated. This photograph illustrates the relationship of the inner and outer arches. Traces of whitewash are visible in the reveal, which was in process of being excavated when the picture was taken.

Figure 125. The short corridor west of the sala was paved with tiles. Some minor repairs had been made to this floor when this picture was taken.

Figure 124. Original tile flooring of *corredor* as excavated. This picture was taken north of the chapel entrance. At the outer wall of the *corredor*, the tiles are sloped sharply downward to form a gutter. This gutter extended only along the portion in front of the chapel.

Figure 128. Fragments of door panels.

Figure 130. Panel fragment, #4070; shutter fragment, #4064; sash fragments, #4074, #1071.

Figure 127. Plank fragment, (ceiling), and shutter frame.

MISCELLANEOUS WOOD DETAILS

Left (upper). The only remaining original wooden grille (Lower) A detail of the above grille, showing method of mortise and tenon joint, with wedge. (Center) A fragment of shutter frame, showing tenon and rebate for hinge. Right (upper), two fragments of redwood panelling, with moulded edge, assumed to be door planks. Lower (left to right), panel and panel mould, redwood with gilt on moulding over *gesso*, fragments of shutter, and two fragments of window sash.

Figure 126. Wood grille, partial.

Figure 129. Wood grille detail.

Figure 132. Method of scoring walls to receive lime plaster coating. The original plaster (upper right) though exposed for years still remained in place. The area in the lower left had just been excavated when the picture was taken.

Figure 131. A reconstructed window sash based on information furnished by fragments of the wooden portions and glass found in the ruin, supplemented by photographs. The arch is original. Sanctuary of the chapel.

Figure 133. A section of original wall and restored wall. Upper portion; new wall scored and filled with mortar and tile. Middle portion; original plaster as excavated. Lower; concrete underpinning (see Chapter 5, "Restoration").

Figure 134. The tile masonry of the *corredor* columns was finished with lime plaster. The shaft, with the exception of the flutes, was white; the caps, base, and flutes were a rosy pink plaster. The sharpness of detail is noticeable in the two original columns at the left. The column at the right is a replica.

Figure 136. Pink colored plaster was used as a finish surface for walks and floors. CCC enrollees are removing overburden from a walk in the cemetery in the photograph above, which was finished with pink plaster, and bordered with floor tile on edge. Both sacristies of the Church were finished with a similar material.

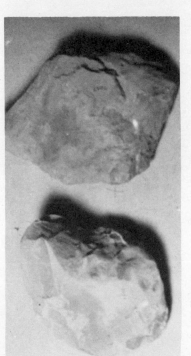

Figure 135. Fragments of calcined diatomite (native red mineral coloring) found in excavations, used for pigment in plaster and paint.

Figure 137. Three stones recovered in excavating, with remains of plaster, indicating original use as plaster finishing tools.

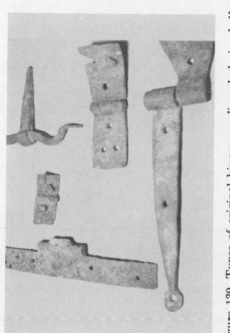

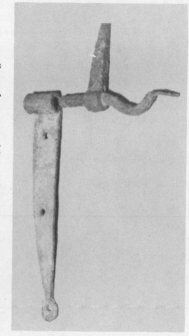

Figure 139. Types of original hinges; reading clockwise, half of H-hinge, a butterfly shutter hinge, a special pin for strap hinge, a butterfly door hinge, a typical strap hinge.

Figure 140. A strap hinge with a special pin, designed for greater strength. Catalogue No. 1199.

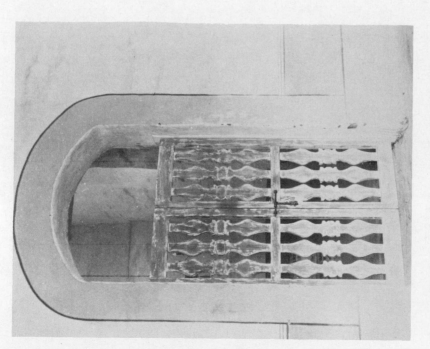

Figure 138. The wall decoration of the Residence at La Purisima relied chiefly on flat bands of color with accenting stripes carried around window and door openings. Above is the reconstructed opening from the chapel to the baptistry, with colors matched to recovered fragments.

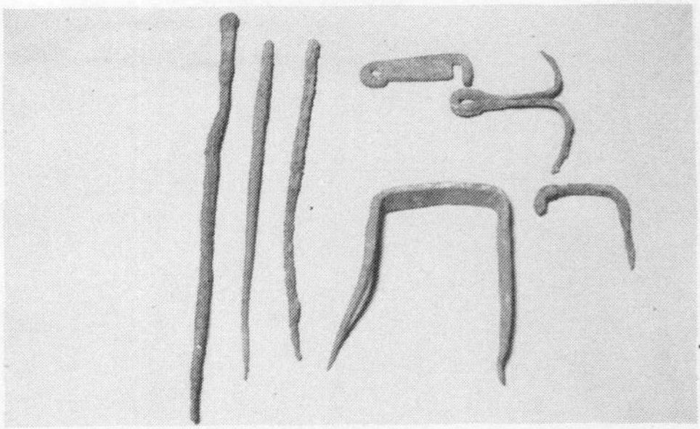

Figure 143. Leather awls #1117, #1126, and no number; latch #1247; ring, #1256; two U-spikes (latch guides), #1161, and no number.

Figure 146. Upper row, wrought copper, hand hammered bosses; end, forged iron boss. Lower (left) cast and turned bronze boss (right) hand wrought copper plate patterned from boss at left. Center (left) forged iron stud, (right) cast bronze stud with wrought iron nail.

Figure 142. Two bosses (1 large, 1 small); two candle cups, (left) cast bronze (not in Catalogue), center, #2022; crystal pendant.

Figure 145. Nine hand-forged nails.

Figure 141. Lock and key.

Figure 144. Strap hinge, #1195.

MISCELLANEOUS HARDWARE AND METAL OBJECTS

Upper left, an excellent lock case with key donated by Mr. Frank McCoy, which he secured from the Purisima or Santa Ynez region. (center) Candle cups of bronze and copper, and a crystal pendant were indicative of the type of lighting fixtures. (right) Leather awls, a hook and eye fastener, and typical U-shaped guides. Lower (left) thickness of door rails were indicated by the length of the nails in the hinge strap. (center) Typical hand-forged nails. (right) Types of door bosses.

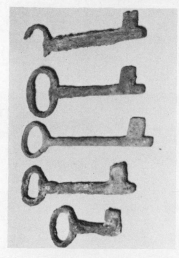

Figure 149. Five keys, #1232-1235, inc. One not in Catalogue.

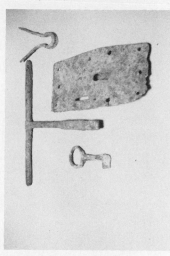

Figure 151. Lock, #1220; bar #1239; ring, #1257; key, #1232.

Figure 148. Lock, back, #1223.

LOCKS AND KEYS

Good examples of the hand forged locks, keys and strikes are shown on this page. The strikes (lower, left) are of wrought copper. At right is an assembly for a surface bolt lock. The bolt slides in two rings. The handle of the bolt has a U-shaped piece on the back, which fits into the upper left hand slot in the lock plate. The bolt of the lock engages this when moved by the key. (This assembly was not found together, but was assembled from scattered fragments for explanatory purposes.)

Figure 147. Lock, front, #1223.

Figure 150. Lock strikes, large, #2000, small fragment, #2001.

CHAPTER 5

RESTORATION

Objectives:

Although the value of historic ruins properly preserved as original documents is unquestioned, the members of the La Purísima Advisory Committee, after careful consideration of the various phases of this problem were of the opinion that the greatest value of the La Purísima monument could be obtained through the adoption of a policy of restoration. It was also recognized that, in addition to their value as a historical document, ruins have a certain romantic appeal to the thoughtful and imaginative mind. On the other hand, the picturesque quality of adobe ruins is lessened by excavation procedures. In order to obtain the essential information which they contain, it is necessary to detract from their appeal by stripping them to an unrelieved bareness. Not only does the enveloping earth mound which has accumulated from eroded wall material add an irregular and pleasing silhouette, but it serves to buttress and protect the weakened remnants of the former structure. Once this is removed, the heavy mass of adobe masonry, supported on a base softened by subsurface moisture and riddled by the burrowings of rodents, requires immediate additional support.

Other measures too, will be required, if adobe ruins are to have any degree of permanence. The principal problem is to adequately protect the adobe surfaces from the weather. Methods of treatment experimentally tried elsewhere have not been notably successful. If satisfactory treatment is available, it has not come to the attention of those seeking a solution to the problem of the La Purísima ruins.

In August, 1934, Dr. Owen C. Coy, Director of the California Historical Commission pointed out to a group meeting at the site the desirability of utilizing the La Purísima monument as an educational exhibit by restoring the economic features of a mission community, features which have largely disappeared in other California missions.[1] The Advisory Committee, impressed with the difficulties of successfully preserving the ruins, inclined toward the views expressed by Dr. Coy. It therefore recommended to the State Park Commission, in a letter dated March 27, 1935, that immediate steps be taken for supporting and preserving the existing walls, and that plans be prepared for the restoration of the building to be undertaken as funds permitted.[2] This recommendation was approved by the Commission March 28, 1935, and the National Park Service proceeded with plans designed to accomplish these results.

The objective of these plans, then, was to preserve the existing remains through incorporating them into a restored building which should reproduce as faithfully as possible the original.

[113]

Sources of data for restoration:

The foregoing chapters have presented detailed information secured from various sources. Summarizing and evaluating the information indicated that four sources were available for use in the proposed work.

Archeological remains and data provided the most accurate and valuable information of all. Furthermore, the original portions preserved, provided a "backbone" of authenticity and a model for much of the proposed restoration.

Pictorial evidence in the form of historical photographs, drawings, and sketches, listed in the order of their degree of accuracy, provided information on features no longer extant.

Documentary sources, including reports and letters of the padres, governmental and private individuals who described the mission and the writings of later observers who visited the mission varied in reliability, as is apparent from a comparison of the descriptions quoted in Chapter 3.

Finally word-of-mouth descriptions were secured by interviews with early residents who had knowledge of the building. These recollections although sometimes dimmed or distorted with the passage of years, were nevertheless studied for information they might yield.

Although the archeological information and data furnished by photographs and other sources provided considerable authentic information for the proposed restoration, exact knowledge of many details was still lacking. It was suggested, therefore, that details of hardware, lighting fixtures, doors, shutters, and the like, which had disappeared could be supplied by authentic and careful replicas of other mission examples. This policy would not restore the building to its exact original appearance as to these details. On the other hand, well executed replicas of other California mission details would be reasonably accurate in spirit, and furthermore would bring together a collection of educational value.

Thus a fifth source of information was added to those discussed above. Through published works, the extensive series of measured drawings available from the Historic American Building Survey, and through first hand study of existing mission features, a valuable supplementary source of information was available, which could be called upon after other sources had been exhausted.

The restoration of the Residence produced many problems, each of which was given full and frank discussion. Wherever possible, the duplication of the original, not only in spirit, but also in material and method became a basic objective. Where strict adherence to this objective would result in construction unsafe, or contrary to accepted procedure it was necessarily abandoned. It will be these deviations that the student will justly question. Faced with vexatious problems, those seeking the solution were at times forced to accept what seemed to be the prudent course rather than the historical ideal. It is hoped that a clear statement of some of the problems will serve to clarify the reasons for the solutions which were adopted and provide a permanent record of the work accomplished.

Problems and solutions:

The first problem to require attention was the structural security of the existing walls. Figures 12 and 13 illustrate the moistened and rotted condition of the base of the excavated walls. That additional structural support was imperative was forcibly demonstrated by the accompanying photographs (Figures 152 and 153) taken before and after excavating the north wall of the chapel. Removal of the earth accretion quickly resulted in the collapse of the wall.

Investigation showed that in most cases, the moisture had penetrated into the wall an average of twelve to fourteen inches, the height varying with the line of the unexcavated grade. This line would average about three and one-half to four feet above the floor lines. Since this moistened earth was of little value in supporting the weight of the wall, and penetrated approximately half the thickness, it followed that the pressure on the sounder central portion was doubled and as shown previously, the weight of the higher walls proved to be excessive, resulting in the crushing of the remaining adobe and the collapse of the wall. Furthermore, the instability of the wall was increased by the fact that the support was negligible in the outer portion and the mass of weight was actually balancing on a thin section of sound material in the middle.

Clearly, then, a means of supplying a solid "shoulder" on each side must be found. The method adopted is progressively shown in Figures 154 to 157 and diagrammed on Plate XIV. A reinforced concrete girder supported on concrete posts at close intervals, was employed on both faces of the wall. These girders were tied together at each post with steel and concrete ties. The "panels" of the new adobe brick occupying the space under the girder and between the posts carry no load, but act merely as space fillers and were used not only for economy, but because the surface texture is that of the original, and the surface of concrete is minimized. The method has so far appeared to be successful in its results. The feasibility of the method is demonstrated by the fact that not a single wall of the Residence building marked out for preservation was lost. It did nevertheless, call for extreme caution to prevent collapse while in the precarious stage shown in Figure 154.

Restored structural scheme: After the most careful work, the load-bearing value of such a wall is questionable. Therefore, any structural scheme which would require these walls to support heavy loads in addition to their own weight was ruled out. The extent of original wall which could be saved is indicated by the black areas on the diagrams of Plate VII.

Since the building had now become a public monument, requiring certain standards of permanence and safety, the adoption of a structural scheme which would eliminate the serious weaknesses of the original construction and which would offer all possible reinforcement to the original walls which were to be incorporated into the restored building was essential. At the same time, the structural design was controlled by the original dimensions, and modern structural members had to be entirely concealed from view in those portions of the building to be used for historic exhibit purposes, except where it might be desirable to illustrate original work and restoration methods.[3]

The solution adopted employs independent supports for all loads aside from the weight of the walls. Briefly, this makes use of a concealed concrete frame which receives the ceiling and roof loads on beams and transmits these loads to the footings through concrete columns. The top beams are flat and wide in section, intended to stiffen the walls and to resist lateral shocks, such as earthquakes. Tie beams are provided at each partition wall in order to secure the maximum bracing effect for the main longitudinal walls. It is of interest to report that, in the case of some of the original walls preserved, it was found that these walls were as much as eleven inches out of plumb in a height of about ten feet; hence the necessity of tying these walls securely can be appreciated.

As shown on Plate XIV, the ceiling beams are supported on a spandrel beam, which is connected to the center wall beam with tie beams at each partition. The top beam is designed to carry the roof trusses.

The original high center wall was eliminated for reasons of safety. This tremendous weight not only was an unsafe load to place on the lower walls, but formed a dangerous mass in the event of an earthquake. Its elimination, while regrettable from a historical point of view, permitted the adoption of trusses forming an additional tie through the entire building, which, by means of steel anchors, transmit lateral stresses to the concrete beam. None of this work is visible from the rooms on the first floor, since every room is ceiled.

The roof construction in the portion south of the passage differs slightly from the above, in that the higher ceiling did not permit the use of trusses. In their place are rafters bearing on a center girder. Ties are secured by means of the wooden ceiling beams of the chapel and cross beams in the loft. This condition is shown in the restored Section C-C, Plate IX.

Restored plan: Plate VIII represents the plan as restored. Through the decision to utilize three rooms at the north end of the building for custodial and convenience purposes, certain minor partitions were added. These internal modifications necessitated a variation from the original in the arrangement of openings on the west side and north end. It also required substitution of glazed windows in these rooms.

For the other areas where the archeological plan shows only the foundations, photographs were depended on for the location of former openings. Not all openings could be so located, due to lack of sufficient views. Instances where information was lacking were the doors between the two sacristies (Rooms 19 and 20), to the baptistry (Rooms 20 to 21), in the exterior opening arrangement in Room 18, the extreme northwest corner of the building, and the opening from Hall No. 2 to Room 15.

Aside from the unavoidable deviations in window arrangement resulting from the introduction of the modern living and convenience facilities, the openings in question were located in plan by what appeared to be the logical requirements for access and light to the rooms consistent with other known parts of the plan.

Determination of missing elements: Missing features such as walls, openings, roof slopes, as well as many details, were nearly all supplied by the historic photographic collection. The Figures 75 and 83 were invaluable to determine the roof slope and window locations of the southwest elevation. Plate XIV illustrates a perspective projection method whereby photographs were used to determine missing details of the southwest end. While reasonably accurate, this method was further checked by counting brick courses in other photographs to determine the height of the ridge and eave.

The slope of the building was evident from the fact that the height of the *corredor* columns remained constant. Columns existed at each end and the middle, and were found to be uniform in height. Since the relationship of the top of the column to the top of the adobe wall must remain fixed (unless the roof pitch varies) the elevation at any point along the top of the wall could be located. While the northeast end wall had been badly damaged as the result of a fire,[4] Figure 96 gives an excellent cut-away section of the original construction, and a check on the height at this end. In order to gain access to the public toilet room, the lower west window was changed to a door opening.

The remaining nine columns of the colonnade supplied models for the reproduction of the ten missing ones. The corbels and beam details are well illustrated in Figures 74 and 101. The rafter size was increased approximately two inches in depth over the original. The inadequacy of the originals is apparent from the photographs illustrating the final failure of these members.

Doors: Archeological data on doors has been reviewed in Chapter 4. Typical restored doors are based on those of Mission San Diego. The double doors into the *sala* and the chapel are copies of the entrance doors to the *sala* of the Santa Barbara Mission, which typify the "River of Life" design found very frequently in the California mission doors. The door to the short hallway leading from the west walk is a copy of the sacristy door of Mission San Juan Bautista. These variations were introduced since no mission studied utilized one single design throughout (Figure 128).

Shutters: One fragment of shutter was found, but the panelling was missing. A simple hand run panel moulding used at Mission San Juan Bautista was duplicated in these restored shutters. The general type employed in the restoration is illustrated on Plate XII, but variations employing a carved design from Mission Santa Inés were introduced in Room 5, and for a few additional openings on the west side (Figures 127, 130, 174, 175).

The grilles which originally occurred along the *corredor* had disappeared entirely except for the sockets. Restoration of these grilles was based on verbal descriptions,[5] characteristics of the surviving original and on a study of similar details at Mission Santa Barbara (Figures 126, 129, 174, 175).

The Chapel: The archeological remains afforded valuable information concerning the chapel. Almost the entire front wall, with the windows and door openings were preserved to a height of about ten feet. Location of the upper windows, types of window, chancel rail location, steps, pulpit location, choir loft beams, color decorations were wholly, or in part, determined from the remains. To supplement this information, photographs and drawings (Figures 102, 106), showing the chapel in progressive stages of ruin gave valuable assistance. Finally, the historical descriptions and reports added meagre, but at the same time significant details.

The details of niches, pulpit and decoration are not precise but represent the most careful replicas possible with the amount of information available. A hint of the type of decoration of the pulpit and chancel rail can be made out in Figure 102. The photograph indicates the characteristic marbleized treatment of the panels and spindles. The details of colors were obtained through the cooperation of the American Index of Design, a division of the Works Progress Administration. Information in the form of color plates from other missions and from color sketches of Santa Inés was used to supplement the information on file.

Lighting fixtures: Information regarding the light fixtures originally used in the residence was entirely lacking. A brief note occurs in the official reports concerning the acquisition of two chandeliers or candlesticks for the Church,[6] but beyond the fact that here, as elsewhere, chandeliers were used, very little is known. Two copper candlecups and a crystal pendant were uncovered; the pendant was similar to ones observed in old chandeliers at Santa Inés, which was considered suggestive.

Therefore, designs for lighting fixtures were dependent wholly upon originals from other missions. In order to secure this information, field trips were made to twelve of the missions to record the details of extant fixtures. It was found that few early fixtures exist, and the range of design was limited to about seven fixtures. From the measured drawings, photographs and color sketches, working drawings were made for the execution of the accompanying lighting fixtures.

An obstacle to carrying out the reproduction completely was the use of the buildings as a public monument, and since the restored rooms were to be used as public exhibits, it did not appear feasible to require the custodian to depend solely on candle illumination in the large number of rooms to be exhibited. Therefore a compromise was adopted which attempts to utilize old forms and designs with a minimum of alteration to adapt them for electric lighting. Certain fixtures, not required for illumination were copied *in toto*, as replicas for study.

The restored Residence makes use mainly of two exceptionally interesting chandeliers from Mission Santa Inés, supplemented by a lantern from Santa Barbara, which was adaptable to various situations. In the chapel, the chandeliers are adaptations of an old one from Mission Santa Barbara, brackets from an original at Mission San Juan Capistrano, and the sanctuary lamps from Santa Inés. A fixture from San Gabriel was copied for one or two minor rooms, but while appropriate in character, it is not believed to have been an original. Wall candlesticks were copied from an original at San Miguel.

Figures 193 to 200 illustrate these various fixtures and identify the original source.

The two fixtures from Santa Inés, Figures 193 and 194, were made of turned wood cores, probably made locally and decorated with oil paints in bands of colors employing white, orange black and green, with marbleizing carried out in ochre, black and white. On these cores were mounted cast and chased brass candle arms, of exceptionally delicate design and workmanship, which on more careful examination proved to be gold-plated. These were probably imported from Mexico. These arms were further decorated by crystal pendants. The whole fixture was suspended by a hand wrought brass chain. A measured drawing of the five armed chandelier is shown on Plate XIII.

Through the courtesy of the Capuchin Friars, who now act as custodians of Santa Inés Mission, original brasses were utilized as patterns from which new castings were made. The arms themselves are slightly heavier than the originals in order to carry the electric wiring. The cups were carefully hand-chased, after the manner of the originals. The chandeliers of the chapel were adapted from ones formerly in the living portion of Santa Barbara Mission. This fixture could not be seen in its original form, due to its recent covering of metal and was reproduced from a photograph. Hence the original colors could not be determined, but the same patterns were utilized. This fixture is a cruder variation of the Santa Inés fixtures, being simply a wooden core of graceful shape, with wrought iron arms terminating in a turned wooden drip-cup. The candles were merely stuck onto the sharpened ends of the metal arms. A tassel decorated the bottom.

A careful replica of the Santa Barbara lantern is shown in Figure 199. This lantern was adaptable for table use, being placed on a metal stand; for carrying in the hand, or could be used on the wall by slipping it into a ring. The ring was copied also from an old one in the museum case. The age of the model is not known. The lantern itself was made of tin and sheet iron with glass sides, and whether dating from museum days or not, it was felt to be so typical of Spanish work and so appropriate that it was used in many different ways in the restored Residence.

The candle-sconce illustrated in Figure 198 was found at San Fernando in the museum case. Its history is also unknown. Made of tin, with small pieces of mirror forming the reflector, it is an admirable design, and one found in other parts of the United States in early days.

Another wall candlestick is shown in Figure 200. The original is at Mission San Juan Capistrano. It is a simple, yet delicate design in wrought iron, with its modelled decorative leaves.

A replica of the sanctuary lamp of Santa Inés is shown in Figure 197. This is carried out in wood and brass, with the traditional oil reservoir of ruby glass in which floats the constantly burning wick. The wooden bowls and hanger are decorated in green, white, yellow and black, and a blue cotton tassel terminates the fixture.

A simple cross-armed wooden fixture of wood from Mission San Gabriel was utilized because of its appropriate simplicity and primitive character, but is no doubt of fairly recent manufacture.

It should be kept in mind by any person viewing these fixtures that they do not represent a collection of accurate replicas of original mission fixtures, because not only is the history of some of the models indefinite, but the concessions to modern needs alter the effect of the illumination, and to a certain degree, the proportions. They can be said to be essentially in the same spirit of the old work, and their delicacy of design and excellence of workmanship is surprising to the visitor who has held the belief that mission work was always crude and awkward.

Hardware: Although the fragments of original hardware which had been collected formed a good nucleus, it was evident that supplementary materials would be required to adequately hardware the building. Measured drawings secured during field trips to other missions were used as a basis. It was found that in most missions such examples were scarce. These notes and drawings so collected therefore represent a large proportion of the remaining original hardware in the missions. These field sketches were then developed into full size working drawings. A smith specially skilled in such work was assigned to execute these designs. The restoration utilized originals from La Purísima wherever possible. The supplementary designs were used for missing details.

Examples from six other missions have been used in addition to La Purísima examples. In the collection are three types of door bolts, four designs of thumblatches, two types of door stays, three of door pulls, and five different types of hinges. Three styles of bosses were copied from La Purísima fragments. Designs of locks differ only in minor details, in the missions visited. Each piece was made by hand, as nearly an exact replica of the original as possible.

The accompanying photographs of the executed hardware in place indicates the character of these replicas and identifies the location of the original from which it was reproduced.

Restoration Materials and Methods:

Historic methods: In carrying out a restoration of this type it was necessary to employ methods which are not ordinarily used in present day work. In order to understand the more ancient techniques, a knowledge of the conditions that the *padres* and their mechanics faced, the tools they used and an appreciation of the spirit in which they worked is essential.

When work got under way at La Purísima, experiments in duplicating originals soon revealed that modern materials given surface treatments to simulate the appearance of originals fell short of the true character. These experiments demonstrated that authentic materials, tools, and workmanship were requisite in order to achieve the desired results. This was forcibly illustrated in the case of wooden structural members, especially when attempts to resurface modern machined timbers failed to reproduce originals which had been worked out with whipsaw and adze. Adobes, tiles, plaster surfaces and metal work produced unsatisfactory results until the original conditions were approximated as closely as possible.

Dr. M. R. Harrington, curator of the Southwest Museum, after inspecting the work in progress, summed up the principle in an article entitled, "The Right Kind of Restoration": [7]

> It is said that the technicians of a certain Hollywood studio were greatly upset one time because they could find no way of simulating satisfactorily the sound of a barrel of water being poured upon some boards, which was called for in a picture then in the course of production. They worked on the problem several weeks and experimented with various devices: they rubbed pieces of sandpaper together; they poured peas on a drumhead; they tried everything they could think of, but still the sound was not quite right. Finally one of the technicians had a dazzling inspiration. Why not take a barrel of water and pour it on some boards? They did it, and the result was perfect!
>
> The same idea is worth thinking about in restoring historic buildings; if you use the old materials and methods, and follow the same plans, you are likely to get the old results; you may even recapture the quaintness and charm of the original.
>
> The restoration of the monastery at La Purísima Concepción Mission near Lompoc by the National Park Service is a shining example. It was handled according to this simple rule, and if there is a more authentic and appealing restoration in California I have yet to see it: and I have visited many. . . .

Many of the processes and techniques which have been developed have drawn wide interest. It is possible that the experience gained in developing these methods may be valuable in similar future work, and for that reason some of the more important phases of the restoration procedure are briefly reviewed.

Adobes: The manufacture of the 110,000 adobe bricks required for the Residence demanded production on a large scale. The first bricks were made by the CCC enrollees following very old methods under the direction of a Mexican *adobedero,* whose father taught him the method he learned at Old Mission San Diego. This man, after locating suitable soils on the site with the proper qualities, then puddled the material in pits about eight by twelve feet. During this process a quantity of straw was added, amounting to approximately twenty percent by volume. A plastic mass was secured by agitating the mixture with only the feet and shovels. It was placed in wooden forms; and the surplus struck off. After drying for several days in the sun, the forms were removed; the bricks were sufficiently firm to be turned up on edge to permit more rapid drying, and the bottom side cleaned of surplus soil. After drying, the bricks were stacked in piles awaiting use.

The laborious method of mixing in a pit was later supplanted by a pugmill powered with a gasoline engine. This machine doubled production and reduced the manual labor by one-third. In order to maintain required production of 2,000 bricks per day, this equipment easily handled eight cubic yards of material per hour.

Built on the principle of a clay pugmill, with the trough about ten feet long, a longitudinal shaft studded with vanes, or blades, at about four inch intervals chopped and stirred the mixture. The dry material was fed into one end, water and straw were added as the mixing proceeded. The mix issued from a gate at the lower end, from whence it was wheeled to the moulders in the field. The other steps of the manufacture remained unchanged.

Experiments with another method were carried on, but finally rejected. This method consisted of pouring the wet mixture into large frames. When partially dry, the large block could be cut into brick size. The bricks thus made were found to be objectionable when placed in a wall because the character of the surface reflected this mechanical quality.

Asphaltic emulsions for stabilizing the bricks against the effect of moisture were considered, but not adopted. Although excellent results are being achieved elsewhere through their use, it was believed that the original design of the building, and the plaster coating which was used made their use unnecessary in the present instance.

Tiles: While the manufacture of adobe bricks might be classed as a process not requiring a high degree of technical knowledge, the making of burned tile shapes, such as floor tiles, and roof tiles is decidedly less simple. In the earlier stages of the work, considerable doubt existed whether the work could be done by the forces at the camp. By experimenting with the various processes, and with the help of technical advice given freely by some of the commercial tile manufacturers, satisfactory methods and equipment were developed. Dr. Harrington has written a clear and interesting description of the process evolved at La Purísima, which is reproduced in Appendix C, illustrated with step-by-step photographs.

Timber: In the earlier stages of the work, commercial timbers were used for ceiling beams, planking and at other locations. Through the activities of the Civilian Conservation Corps in other park areas, it developed that timbers could be secured from the forests. Restoration work since the summer of 1936 has utilized timbers worked out partially in the forest and finished by hand at the site. These timbers are utilized for ceiling beams, planking, railings, etc.

Whipsaws, broadaxes and adzes were the tools of that earlier day, and these were all brought into use again in producing the lumber for the restoration. The enrollees after being taught the use of these tools have very often become unusually proficient and the results secured have been exceedingly satisfactory. Figures 226 and 230 furnish an interesting record of this work.

Not only were the rougher members done in this way, but hand methods were applied to the pieces requiring careful finish, such as the pulpit, canopy, railings, doors, etc. The finished articles have the indefinable character which can only be secured through hand work and simple tools.

Experience has shown the more skilled work such as the making of doors, frames and even window sash can be capably handled by the CCC enrollees, provided qualified supervision is available.

Restoration Plastering Procedure:

The original plasters found in this building, discussed in Chapter 4, were shown to be of two types: lime and mud.

Neither of these two materials is comparable for durability with modern cement plaster; reinforced with wire mesh and given positive attachment to the wall. Those favoring the more structural qualities of the cement plaster recommended adoption of this material to secure permanence and low maintenance, while others preferred adherence to authentic original methods.

Decision on the material and method adopted resulted from investigation and discussion by various technicians.[8] A compromise material was specified employing equal parts lime and portland cement containing a high percentage of silica; to which should be added three parts sand. The method of application followed that of the original, employing the ancient *rejuelos* (grooves) with no reinforcement.

Experiments were made to duplicate the texture of the original. It was found that the plastering trowels of today were not adapted to this work, since the unevenness of the adobe wall caused the sharp edges and corners to dig into the fresh plaster. Trials with the original stones shown in the previous discussion demonstrated that the tool must be made small, rounded, and cupped at the edges so that it would "ride" the surface, much as a toboggan rides the hillocks of snow. Consequently, special trowels were constructed from small cement finishing trowels, which produced satisfactory results. The various steps in the procedure involved are explained in the accompanying photographs (Figure 231 to 234 inclusive).

Mud plaster was replaced on the west side and north end of the building as well as the interior rooms where previously enumerated. Moisture from the drip of the eaves led to later adoption of a cement plaster base on these exterior walls to a height of eighteen inches, which is not noticeable after being painted.

Painting and Decorating:

The simplicity of the original color treatment in the greater portion of the building required only careful attention in existing samples. An exception was the decorative work in the chapel, where special talent was secured through the cooperation of the Federal Art Project to make color studies and execute the decoration of the pulpit, railings and other features.

This work could be based only on the most fragmentary evidence. Figure 102 shows unmistakable evidence that the pulpit and railing had formerly been decorated in a marbleized design similar to that at several other missions. The single fragment of paneling already referred to had been treated with gesso, and the moulding gilded. With these few clues, the Federal Art Project series of color plates of existing mission decorations were studied in order to supplement the restoration scheme. The executed pulpit is treated with panels of crudely marbleized green, white, and black, with mouldings in gilt. Stiles and rails are decorated with burnt sienna red with additional blues and greens in the carved ornamentation. The pendant is gilded. The canopy above employs gilt, ochres and blues, in a geometrical pattern, based on the indications in Figure 103. The spindles of the chancel and choir railings were marbleized in green, black, and sienna, with the central portion high-lighted to suggest a round baluster in the quaint manner then in vogue. The colored dados were matched as closely as possible to the preserved fragments. The borders around the doors and windows were assumed to be light blue from photographic evidence, and the color was matched to the sample marked 1-3 (Plate No. XI). No remains of two of the three narrow stripes at the top of the dado were found, and these also were necessarily assumed.

Except for necessary repairs, the remaining original columns were left exactly as found. The weathered appearance of these columns set a "key" for the treatment of the new work. Whitewashed surfaces were treated with a diluted acid wash in order to reduce the glaring whiteness. This treatment has an effect similar to that produced by several years of weathering, and approximates the warm color of the original plaster, which is illustrated on Plate No. XI. The pink of the dado was matched by securing and grinding the same native pigment for use as a paint.

Woodwork was treated with an acid stain mixture which reduced the new wood to a weathered gray. Exterior surfaces of doors were wire brushed and treated in a similar manner. Hardware was given acid treatment to hasten the weathering.

Mission Furniture:

Figures 244 through 258 present the collection to date of mission furniture replicas, made on the site by CCC workers supervised by National Park Service personnel. These replicas have been made from carefully measured drawings and photographs of the originals. The measured drawings were made during a series of field trips to twelve California missions.

In the photographs, location of the original is given.

Important Structures of the Water System:

Four original structures of the water system remained in various stages of ruin in the foreground of the Residence. In the year 1817 the Fathers reported the building of:

> . . . a fountain and its corresponding washing place; and to supply
> the Infirmary and other minor uses, there has been constructed in the

same *patio*, a fountain destined particularly for the Indians. The water that supplies both fountains has been brought from 800 to 1000 paces by pipes and aqueducts according to their distances.[9]

The "washing places" can be identified by the sloping stone rim. Both of these structures were found in a moderately good state of preservation, requiring minor repairs. The walls of the central octagonal fountain were almost entirely destroyed. A few courses of the tiles indicated the outline of the walls on the tile floor of the structure. The basins were gone. Features of similar fountains at Missions San Fernando and San Luis Rey were relied upon for the design of this restored fountain. (Figures 259-262.)

In addition to the fountains, remains of the masonry aqueduct leading from the reservoir about one-half mile northeast of the Residence to the foreground area have been restored to illustrate the method of irrigating. (Figure 263.)

Directly on the axis of the corridor is a very interesting vaulted masonry ruin which has been known locally for years as the "Springhouse" (Figure 264). It is actually the reservoir from which tile pipes lead to the central octagonal fountain. In 1933 moisture from the nearby spring caused the settlement of the foundation resulting in the collapse of the vault. A subsurface concrete wall has been constructed, shutting off the moisture, tie rods inserted to hold the building together, and the exterior line of the vault has been replaced with light framework and plaster.

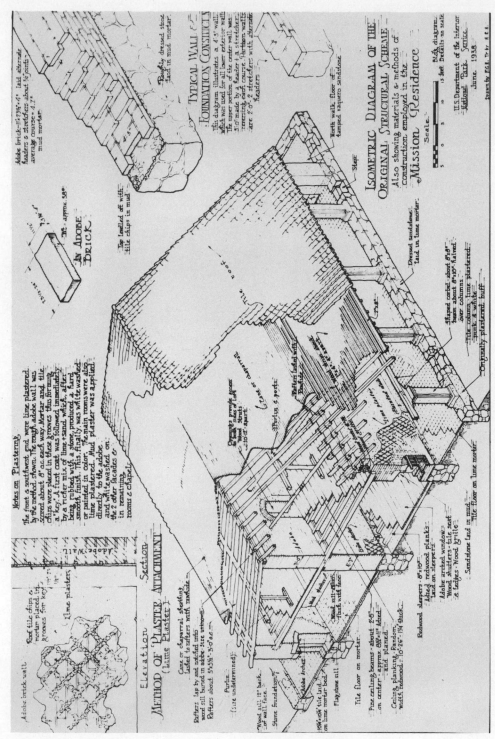

Plate No. V

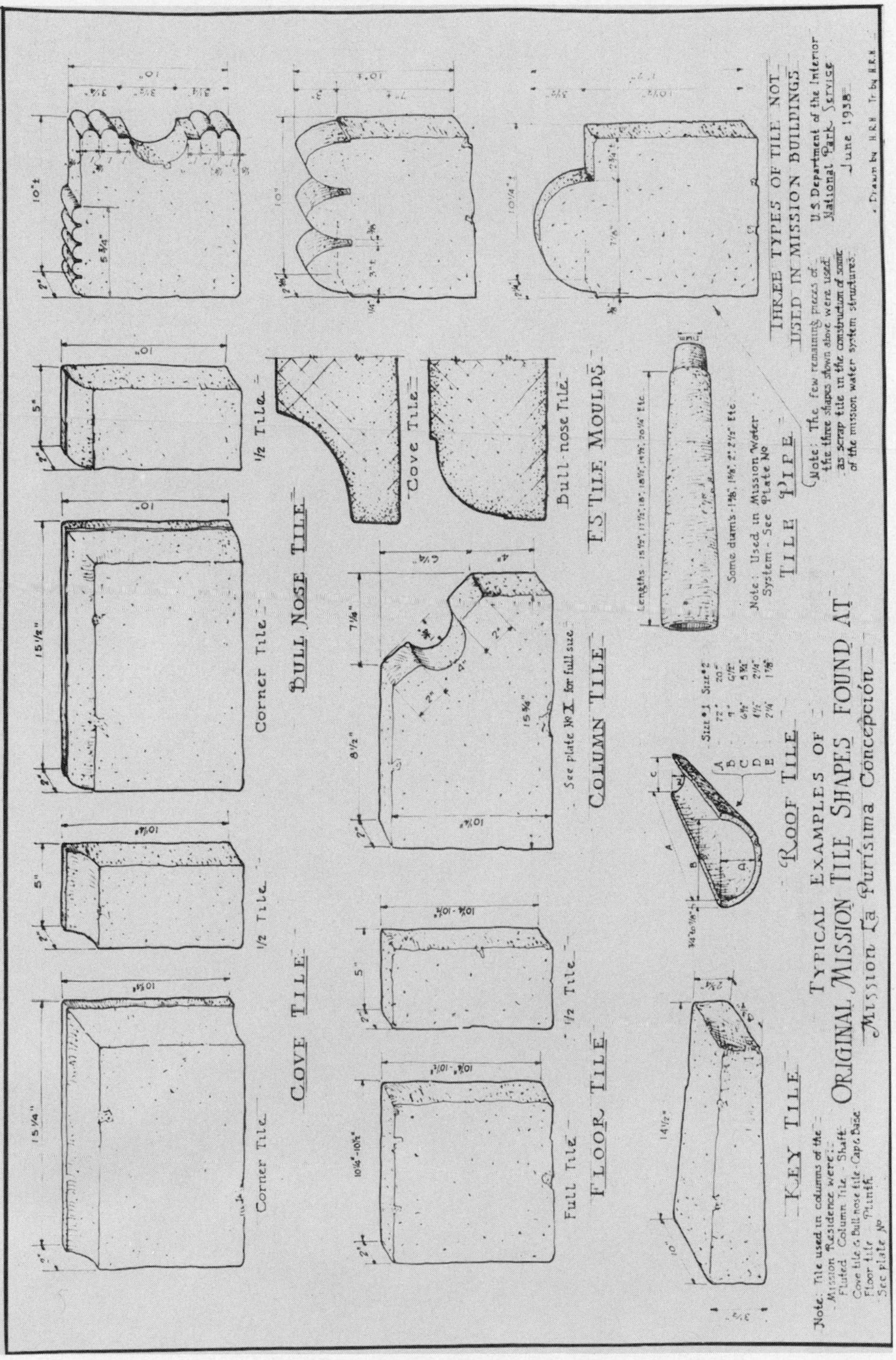

Typical Examples of
ORIGINAL MISSION TILE SHAPES FOUND AT
Mission La Purísima Concepción

Plate No. VI

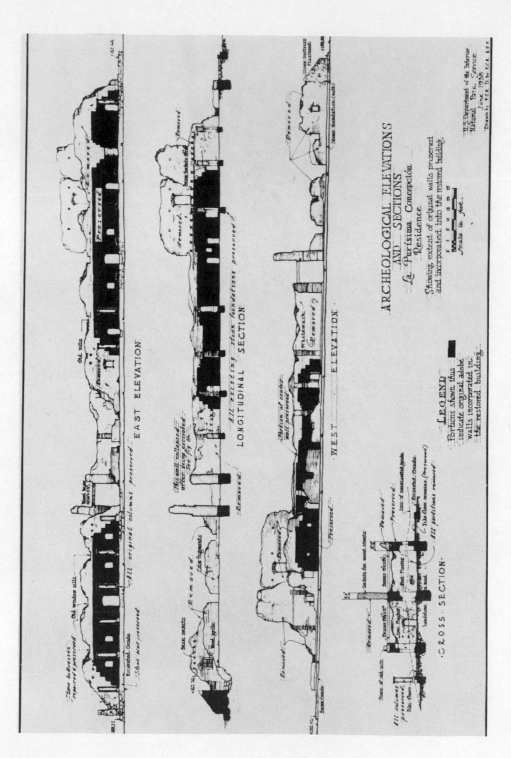

ARCHEOLOGICAL ELEVATIONS
AND SECTIONS
La Purísima Concepción
Residence

Showing extent of original walls preserved
and incorporated into the restored building.

Plate No. VII

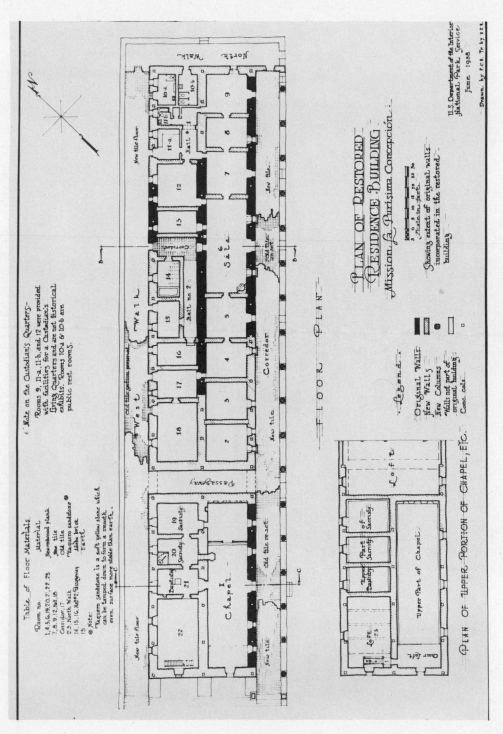

PLAN OF RESTORED RESIDENCE BUILDING
Mission La Purisima Concepcion.

FLOOR PLAN

Plan of Upper Portion of Chapel, etc.

Plate No. VIII

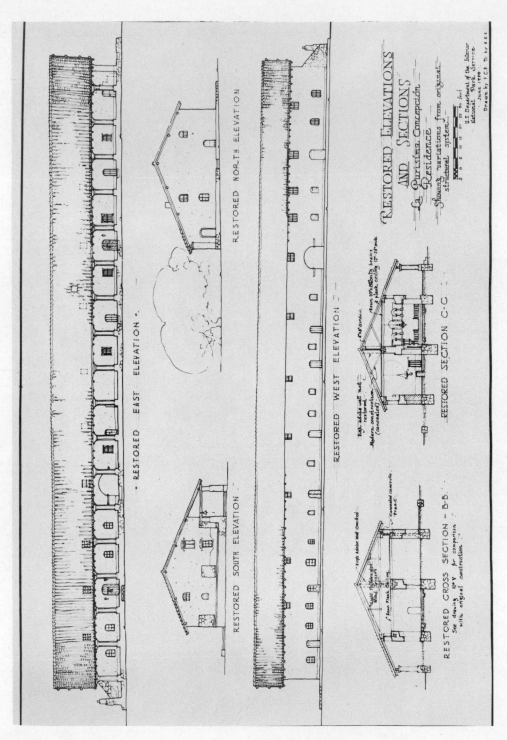

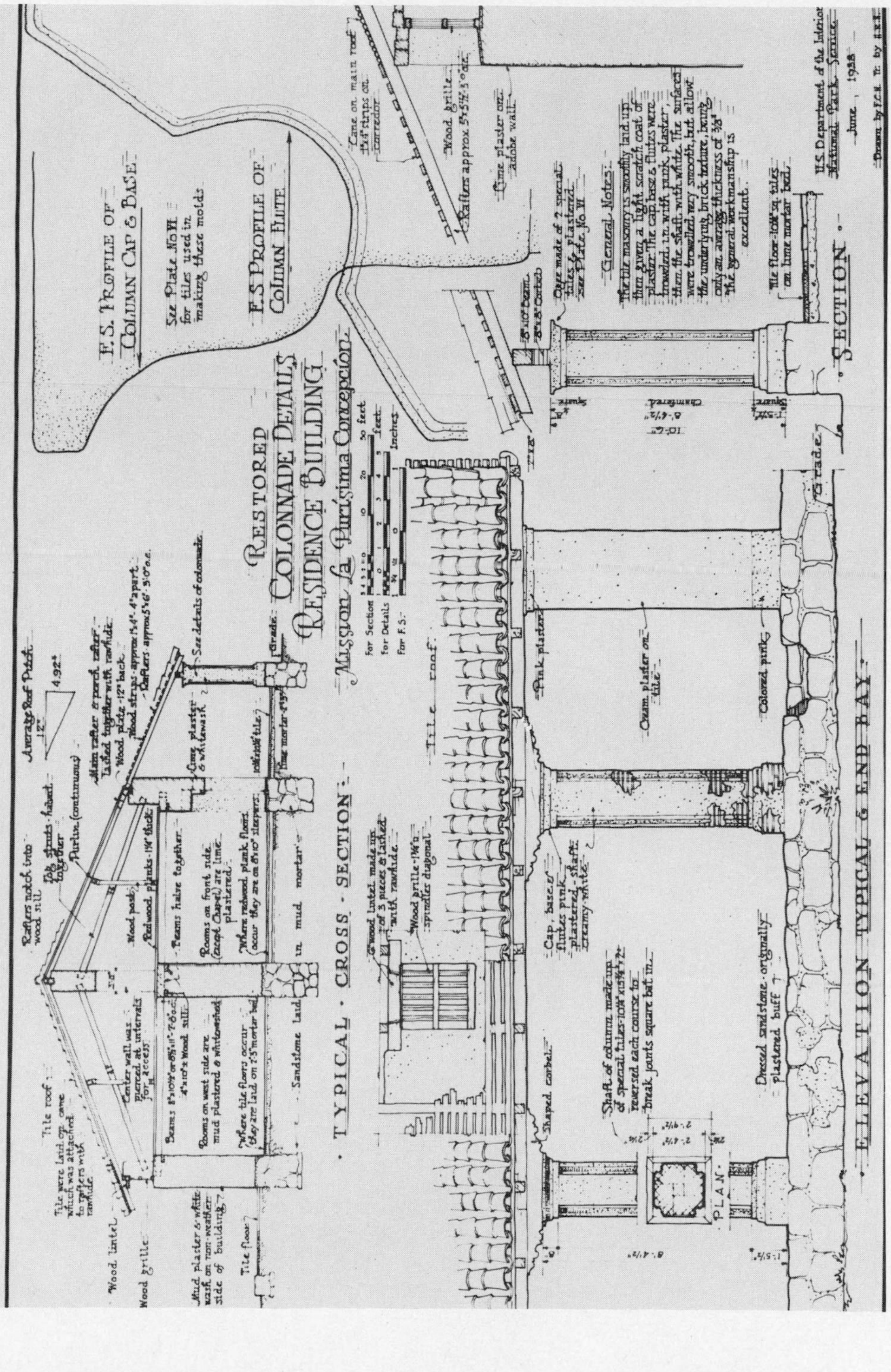
RESTORED
COLONNADE DETAILS
RESIDENCE BUILDING
Mission La Purísima Concepción
TYPICAL · CROSS · SECTION
ELEVATION TYPICAL & END BAY
SECTION
PLAN
F.S. PROFILE OF COLUMN CAP & BASE
F.S. PROFILE OF COLUMN FLUTE
General Notes:
U.S. Department of the Interior
National Park Service
June, 1938

Plate No. X

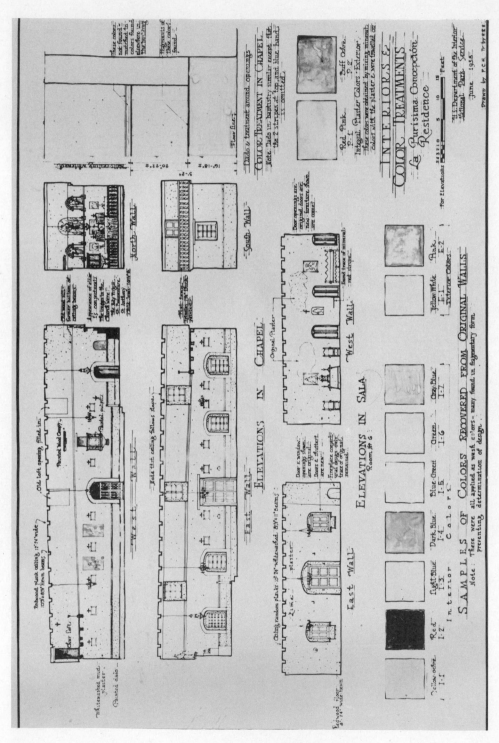

Plate No. XI

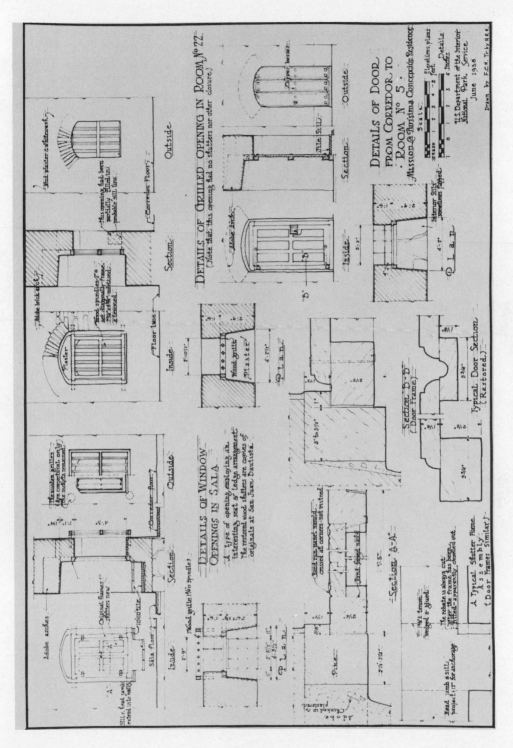

Plate No. XII

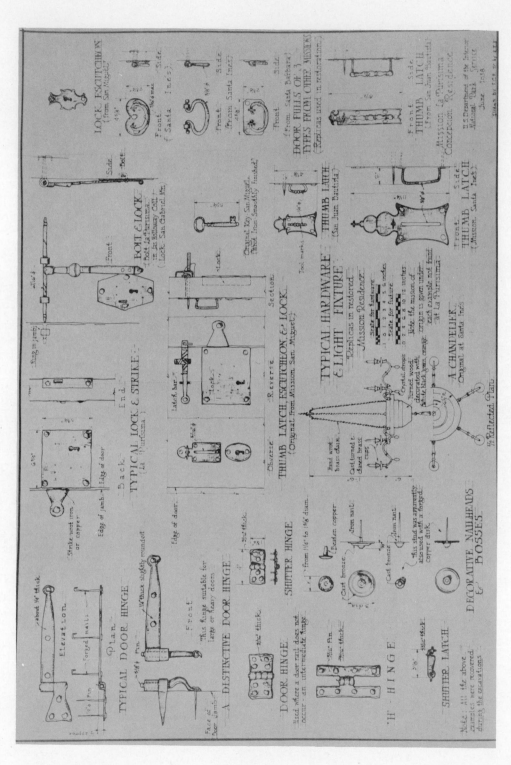

Plate No. XIII

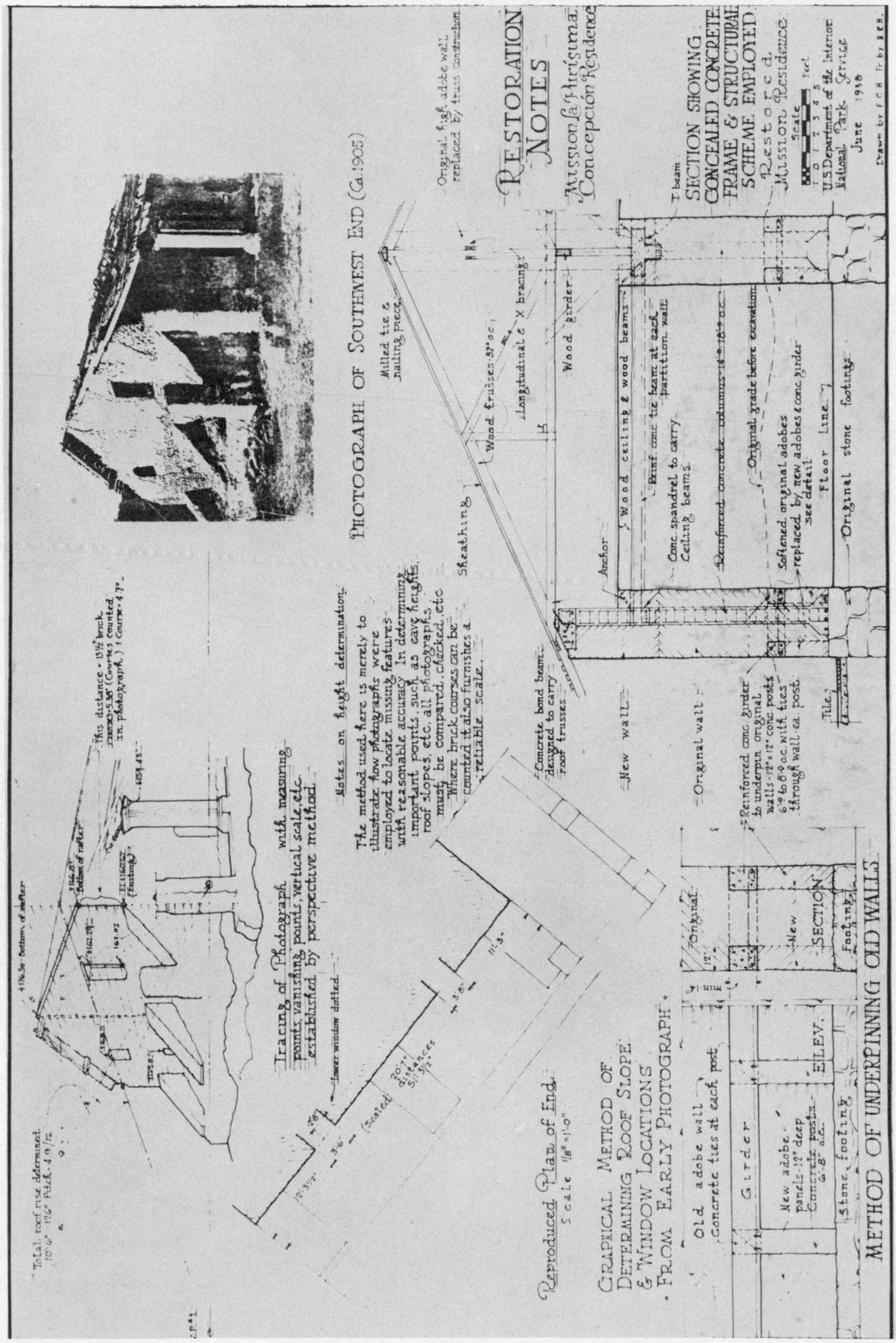
RESTORATION NOTES
Mission La Purisima Concepcion Residence
PHOTOGRAPH OF SOUTHWEST END (Ca. 1905)
Tracing of Photograph with measuring points, vanishing points, vertical scale, etc. established by perspective method
Notes on height determination.
The method used here is merely to illustrate how photographs were employed to locate missing features with reasonable accuracy. In determining important points, such as eave heights, roof slopes, etc., all photographs must be compared, checked, etc. Where brick courses can be counted it also furnishes a reliable scale.
Reproduced Plan of End Scale 1/8" = 1'-0"
GRAPHICAL METHOD OF DETERMINING ROOF SLOPE & WINDOW LOCATIONS FROM EARLY PHOTOGRAPH.
METHOD OF UNDERPINNING OLD WALLS
SECTION SHOWING CONCEALED CONCRETE FRAME & STRUCTURAL SCHEME EMPLOYED
Restored Mission Residence
U.S. Department of the Interior National Park Service
June 1938
Original high adobe wall replaced by truss construction
Milled tie & nailing piece
Wood trusses
Longitudinal & X bracing
Wood girder
Sheathing
Wood ceiling & wood beams
Reinf. conc. tie beam at each partition wall
Conc. spandrel to carry ceiling beams
Reinforced concrete columns
Original grade before excavation
Softened original adobes replaced by new adobes & conc. girder see detail
Floor line
Original stone footings
Anchor
Concrete bond beam designed to carry roof trusses
New wall
Original wall
Old adobe wall
Concrete ties at each post
Girder
New adobe panels
Stone footing
ELEV.
SECTION
Original
New
Footings
Tile

Plate No. XIV

A PROBLEM IN PRESERVATION: (1)

Figure 152. These were the walls at the north end of the chapel in the Residence prior to excavation. The earth mound acted as a buttress to the walls.

A PROBLEM IN PRESERVATION: (2)

Figure 153. A similar view shortly after excavation. The base of the walls, softened by the subsurface moisture, was incapable of supporting the heavy mass above, resulting in the collapse of the wall.

A PROBLEM IN PRESERVATION: (3)

Figure 154. The first step in stabilizing the wall was the removal of the softened section, usually extending about twelve to fourteen inches inward and varying in height. The wall at right is a new partition.

A PROBLEM IN PRESERVATION: (4)

Figure 155. Next these spaces were partially filled with panels of new adobe brickwork, leaving space for posts at about 8 foot intervals, and for the concrete girder which is to occupy the top space. Ties from the girder on one side to the other were provided at each post. (See Plate XIV)

[137]

A PROBLEM IN PRESERVATION: (6)

Figure 157. The concrete girder and supports after pouring was completed. Notice the varying line of the top of the girder, solidly poured up to the irregular bottom edge of the original wall.

A PROBLEM IN PRESERVATION: (5)

Figure 156. Reinforcing steel in place for the girder. The vertical steel is also placed for the concrete column forming a part of the structural frame.

Figure 158. The start of reconstruction, June, 1935. National Park Service Inspector P. T. Primm, re-laying one of the original adobes as the first brick of the reconstruction. County Supervisor R. M. Adam at the left of the man with the shovel. Note the condition of the original walls in the background.

Figure 159. Working up to the original wall seen in Figure 158.

Figure 160. Adobe laying in full swing, summer, 1935. Note the varying heights of the original walls, and keyways into which the restored partitions were fitted.

Figure 161. North section of Residence with adobe walls approaching the ceiling level. CCC Camp in the foreground.

Figure 162. Bonding new adobe work to the original. Note the underpinning in place in the section of original wall.

Figure 163. The big adobe arch of the passageway.

Figure 164. Steel reinforcing in place for the concrete columns. This wall is original, and was slotted to receive the column.

Figure 165. The spandrel beam at the ceiling level, on which rest the ceiling beams. Sockets have been left to receive these beams. The wall is now ready for the top beam.

Figure 166. The big Tee-beam, three feet across the flange, at ceiling level which caps the adobe wall and, together with the hidden concrete columns, forms the central support for the heavy tile roof.

Figure 167. The side wall, beam and columns completed. Note the steel anchors on both beams to secure wooden members. Steel in place for the tie beams across the tops of partitions.

Figure 168. A photograph of the study model.

A STUDY MODEL OF THE RESIDENCE

Before the working drawings for the restoration were completed, a study model was constructed at a scale of one eighth inch to the foot, painted to represent the condition as it appeared in the photographs taken about 1890. These photographs of the model can be compared with those of the building.

Figure 169. The model.

Figure 170. The southwest end, spring of 1936. Note the prefabricated trusses.

Figure 171. The last brick just laid on the gable of the southwest end. Original butresses. The heavy structural beam is visible at the left.

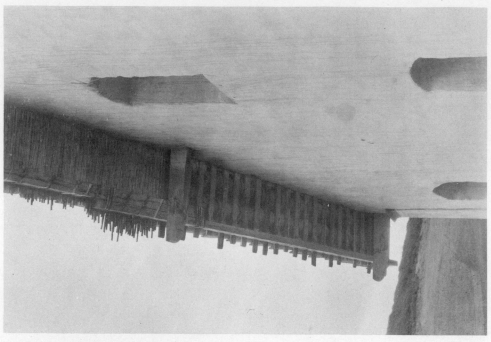

Figure 172, (above). The giant reed was gathered from river bottoms for sheathing under the tile at eaves and gables as pictured at right. Wood strips were employed over the porch. Rawhide was used to lash the timbers together.

Figure 173, (right). The underside of the north gable, showing the use of reed, wood strips and rawhide.

Figure 175. Typical restored exterior wooden grille of windows along the *corredor*.

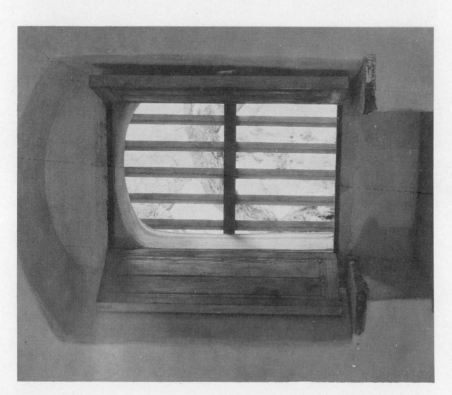

Figure 174. Interior view of a typical restored shuttered opening with exterior wooden grille. The arch is original, the frame partially original, the seat restored. Design of the shutter panels based on profiles at San Juan Bautista.

Figure 177. Restored door to the chapel, of the "River of Life" design. Copies of Santa Barbara Mission doors. Note the arch, which is original.

Figure 176. A typical restored exterior door, Room No. 9. Details of the panelling based on original fragments. Bosses are replicas of La Purisima originals, hand-wrought of copper. Door pull reproduced from Santa Ynez Mission. The arch is original.

Figure 180. Looking outward from the restored *sala*, past the ancient pepper trees. The doors are duplicates of the chapel pair. The door bolt and pull is from Santa Ynez Mission design, the lock plate from La Purisima.

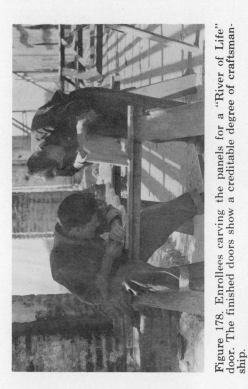

Figure 178. Enrollees carving the panels for a "River of Life" door. The finished doors show a creditable degree of craftsmanship.

Figure 179. The door to the corridor, west side. A copy of the sacristy door of Mission San Juan Bautista. The design of the door bolt is from the same mission.

Figure 181. A typical restored interior door. (From baptistry to sacristy.) A variation from others only in number of panel. The thumb-latch is from Santa Ynez.

Figure 182. Another exterior door. The cast bronze door bosses are replicas of La Purisima originals.

Figure 183. The restored stair to the choir loft from Room No. 22. No trace of the original stair remained. This one is based on construction details of the original at Mission San Miguel. No nails were used except for the railing stanchions. The treads are tenoned into the stringers.

Figure 184. Roof trusses were quickly lifted into place after being fabricated on the ground. These are actually double trusses; the center girder not having been placed when this photograph was taken.

Figure 185. Roof trusses in place and rafters of the restored *corredor* being placed. Tile is stacked on the north end of the building, the sub-roof of this portion having been completed.

Figure 186. Restored southwest end. Fall of 1936. Tile roof now in place, and the columns partially repaired.

Figure 187. Chapel after plastering, fall of 1936.

Figure 189. Restored steps from sacristy to the pulpit.

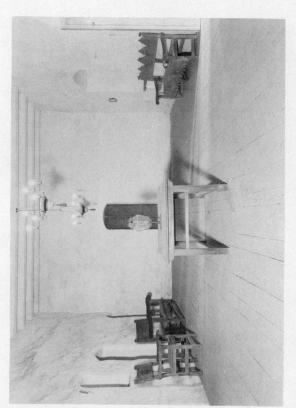

Figure 188. Restored *sala*, completed. The furniture in this picture was made by CCC workers to reproduce authentic originals.

Figure 191. Restored chapel showing the choir loft.

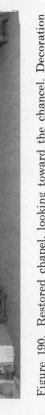

Figure 190. Restored chapel, looking toward the chancel. Decoration of the chancel rail executed by American Index of Design, division of the Works Progress Administration, based on fragmentary indications in ruins and early photographs, supplemented by color studies at other missions. The gate at the left leads to the baptistry.

Figure 192. A conjectural restoration of the fireplace in the *sala* of the Residence. Only the traces of the chimney breast across the corner, and a fragment of the flue was found. The date at which this fireplace was built is unknown. Archeological evidence indicated that it was not built at the same time the walls were erected.

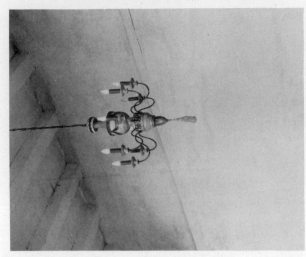

Figure 195. A fixture in the restored chapel, adapted from an original at mission Santa Barbara. This fixture has a turned and decorated wood core, with wrought iron arms.

Figure 194.

Figure 193.

Two fixtures copied from originals at mission Santa Ynez, employing gilded cast brass arms with chased cups. These castings were made from patterns furnished by the originals. The cores are turned and decorated wood.

Figure 196. A lantern on the *corredor* from a design at Santa Barbara. The holder was fitted with a ring for the lantern and a socket for a candle.

Figure 197. The sanctuary lamp (from Santa Ynez Mission).

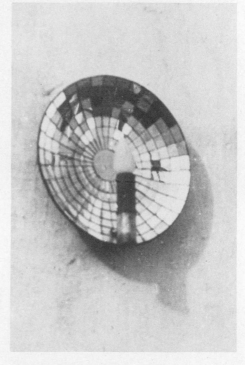

Figure 198. A mirror sconce from San Fernando.

Figure 200. Adaptation of the candelabrum shown below, photographed at mission San Juan Capistrano.

Figure 201. Original candelabrum at mission San Juan Capistrano.

Figure 199. Replica of the Santa Barbara lantern, of tin, glass and iron. The stand is removable, to permit carrying or placing in a wall ring.

Figure 203. Typical strap hinge. La Purisima Concepcion.

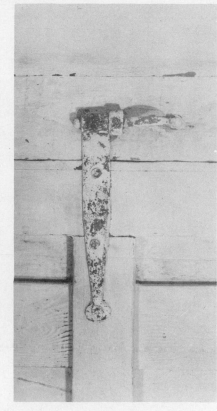

Figure 204. Strap hinge with special pin. La Purisima Concepcion.

Figure 202. Hook fastener on restored chapel door. It is based on example at mission San Gabriel Archangel.

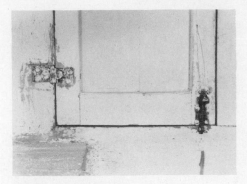

Figure 205. Typical shutter hinge. La Purisima Concepcion.

Miscellaneous hardware used in the restoration of the Residence building showing location of original from which replicas were copied.

Figure 206. H-hinge. San Fernando.

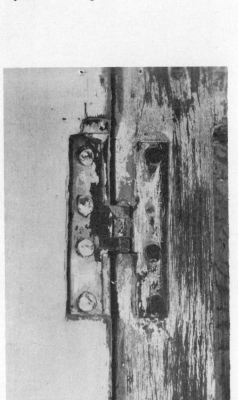

Figure 207. H-hinge of large size. La Purisima Concepcion.

Figure 208. Door stay. Santa Barbara.

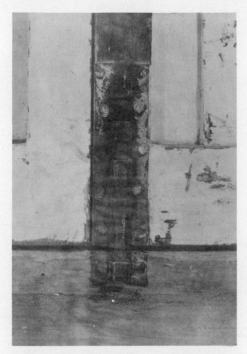

Figure 209. Door stay. San Miguel Arc-angel.

Figure 210. Thumblatch. San Miguel Arcangel.

Figure 211. Thumblatch. Santa Ynez.

Figure 212. Thumblatch. San Juan Bautista.

Figure 214. Key escutcheon. San Miguel Arcangel.

Figure 217. Door pull. Santa Barbara.

Figure 216. Door pull. Santa Ynez.

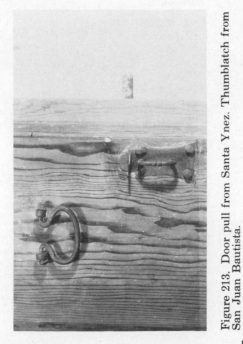

Figure 213. Door pull from Santa Ynez. Thumblatch from San Juan Bautista.

Figure 215. Shutter hook. La Purisima Concepcion.

Figure 220. Door bolt and lock bolt. La Purisima (Holloway Collection). Lock. San Gabriel.

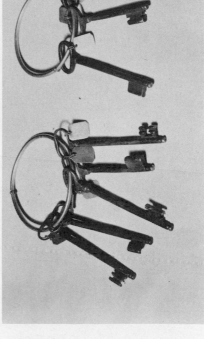

Figure 222. Keys.

Figure 219. Door bolt and lock. San Juan Bautista.

Figure 218. Door bolt, lock and pull. Santa Ynez.

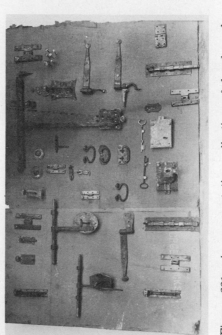

Figure 221. A representative collection of hand made replicas before installation.

Figure 223. The old time *adobedero* made his bricks by an ancient method. The mud and straw were mixed in pits.

Figure 224. Moulded in a wooden frame and allowed to dry in the hot sun.

Figure 225. Many an enrollee sighed with relief when this mechanical mixer supplanted the human ones. Dry earth shovelled in from the truck emerged properly mixed from the end where the man with the barrow is about to receive a load. Capacity is 2,500 bricks a day.

Figure 226. Timbers were brought 500 miles from Humboldt Redwood State Park, adzed and finished by CCC workers to the desired finish.

Figure 227. Split redwood puncheon from the forests, plank floors and ceilings after being hand finished by ancient methods produced highly satisfactory results.

Figure 228. Tools must be razor-sharp for this kind of work.

Figure 229. A whipsaw is a rare tool in these days. Here is a log being cut into boards in the manner of centuries ago.

Figure 230. Adzing requires a steady hand, an apraising eye, and skill.

Figure 231. Walls to be lime plastered were scored with hatchets, to form grooves about one and one-half inches deep and eight inches on center.

Figure 232. Into these grooves, lime mortar and chips of roof tile were inserted.

Figure 233. A lime-cement plaster was troweled on. Using small, rounded trowels, patterned after the original stones, enrollees rubbed the surface to a smooth finish, which follows the general texture of the wall.

Figure 234. The west side was plastered with mud. Here the wall is shown in process. The end wall was lime-plastered.

Figure 237. Restored pulpit, canopy, chancel rail, and niches.

Figure 235. Federal Art Project artist at work on decoration of the pulpit.

Figure 236. The restored canopy.

THE RESTORED RESIDENCE FROM MAIN ENTRANCE, APRIL, 1937

Figure 238. The parking area for visitors under construction in the foreground with one of the entrance piers at extreme right.

THE RESTORED RESIDENCE FROM THE HILLSIDE, SPRING, 1937

Figure 239. Development work in the foreground being started.

Figure 240.

Figure 241.

THE RESTORED RESIDENCE

The southwest end and front after some foreground treatment. Spring of 1938.

Figure 242.

Figure 243.

LA PURISIMA STATE HISTORICAL MONUMENT
SPRING OF 1938

Foreground planting and other development in progress. To the left of the restored Residence (Figure 243) is the Church and cemetery restoration in progress. Compare this view with Figure 63.

[171]

Figure 245. A table from Mission Santa Barbara.

Figure 246. Such craftsmanship requires application.

Figure 244. Replica of a pine chair from Santa Barbara.

MISSION FURNITURE REPLICAS

Figure 249. Chair from San Juan Bautista. (Original executed in a fruit wood, replica of magnolia.)

Figure 248. A replica of the San Gabriel chair.

Figure 247. Original chair at Mission San Gabriel.

Figure 250. Replica of a chair from San Miguel (pine). The leather back and seat covering not completed.

Figure 251. Replica of a chair from San Carlos Borromeo (redwood), the seat, back and arms are to be leather covered.

Figure 252. Replica of the San Gabriel chair (pine).

Figure 253. Replica of a bench from Santa Ynez Mission (pine).

Figure 254. Replica of a double bench from San Juan Bautista (redwood).

Figure 255. Copy of the La Purisima Bench (pine).

Figure 256. The original La Purisima bench. (Loaned by Mr. Frank McCoy, Santa Maria, California.)

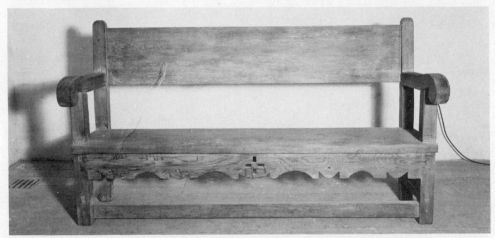

Figure 257. Replica of a bench from San Carlos Borromeo (redwood).

Figure 258. Replica of a bench from San Luis Rey. Original believed to have been made at Santa Clara, dated 1780. (Mahogany)

Figure 260. The central fountain restored. Little remained of this fountain except the floor and part of the base of the walls. The central basin is carved standstone, designed from characteristic California mission basins, and executed by the Federal Art Project.

Figure 259. The central fountain in the patio area being restored. This youthful worker is a descendant of an early California family.

Figure 261. The lavatory for washing purposes after being restored. This ruin was well preserved and required little repair. The carved water spouts are based on verbal descriptions and somewhat similar gargoyles at Mission San Luis Rey.

Figure 262. A lavatory similar in principal to the one in Figure 261 which operates from the overflow of the central fountain. The basin is a restoration. The olive trees are old trees moved into the area.

Figure 263. Restoring a section of masonry aqueduct, Compare the character of this work to the original pictured in Figure 5.

Figure 264. The ruined masonry reservoir known as the "Spring house" one-fourth mile east of the Residence. Preservative measures have since been taken to prevent further ruin. An interesting example of original vaulted masonry construction.

APPENDIX A

REPORTS ON ORIGINAL MATERIALS

Structural Stone from La Purisima Mission

The specimens of structural stone described in the following paragraphs were collected for identification and study from the ruins of La Purisima Mission, near Lompoc, California, by Senior Foreman Architect Frederick C. Hageman. The labels and descriptions are based on examination with hand lenses and tests for soluble carbonates with dilute hydrochloric acid. Notes on the positions and uses of the materials in the structures were supplied by Mr. Hageman.

1. A firm white, chalky limestone. A small proportion of clay-like material is insoluble in dilute acid.

A fairly strong durable rock, but its white color is objectionable for use with other materials in positions where it will be seen. It has been found chiefly in the sidewalls of some aqueducts.

2. A firm, thin-bedded, flaggy limestone; cream tinted to yellowish gray in color; some laminas and bedding planes stained a light ochre-yellow, due to the presence of hydrous ferric oxide (limonite); a notable amount of clay-like residue after solution in dilute acid.

Although not strong, the stone is firm and compact. It splits along bedding planes into thin slabs that are suitable for use as flagstone. It was used as door sills in adobe structures and as laundry slabs around the rims of fountains.

3. A firm, fine-grained, calcareous, pebbly sandstone; light gray in color. Contains numerous smooth flattish elongate pebbles of white to creamy white siliceous shale; also a few pebbles of white fine-grained calcareous sandstone and gray chert. The pebbles range in size from one-fourth inch to one inch in greatest diameters, and most of them are stained a light ocherous yellow on the surface, due to hydrous ferric oxide (limonite).

The stone is firm and suitable for use in foundations and walls, but the spotted appearance due to the pebbles would be objectionable in exposed positions. It has been found in foundations, where it did not show.

4. A firm, fine-grained, calcareous sandstone; pale grayish white in color.

A massive and fairly strong building stone of agreeable color and suitable for general building purposes.

5. A friable gray sandstone of medium texture; noncalcareous.

The stone is so fragile as to be easily broken by the hand and is too weak for use as a building material in important structures. The specimen was taken from an exposed position and has suffered from the effects of weathering.

6. A friable, medium-grained sandstone; noncalcareous; light yellowish brown in color, due to the presence of a little hydrous ferric oxide (limonite), which serves as a weak cement.

The stone is extremely weak and is not suitable for building purposes. The specimen was taken from an exposed position, and its fragility may be in part the result of weathering.

The insoluble residues from the limestones (Nos. 1 and 2) are clay-like in appearance, and the constituent particles are too small to be identified with the hand lens. Examination with the higher powers of a microscope would be necessary in order to determine whether or not diatoms and volcanic ash are present. Such constituents would not be surprising, in view of their abundance in many parts of the Monterey shale formation, which constitutes the bedrock in large areas of this region about Lompoc.

Respectfully submitted,
/s/ J. Volney Lewis
Regional Geologist

San Francisco, California
April 25, 1938

REPORT ON ADOBE BRICK

————

UNITED STATES DEPARTMENT OF COMMERCE
WASHINGTON

————

NATIONAL BUREAU OF STANDARDS
REPORT

National Park Service,   San Francisco, California,
Region Four,   April 2, 1938.
601 Sheldon Building,
San Francisco, California.

Subject: Tests of Adobe Brick.
Refer: Your letter of March 11, 1938.
Project: Restoration of La Purísima Concepción,
Lompoc, California

S. F. Lab. No.	07782	07783	07784	07786
Item	11	12	13	Box A
Description	old adobe from church	old adobe from church (fragment)	new adobe	adobe from estancia (fragment)

Dimensions, approximate

Length, inches	23⅜	24½
Width, inches	11⅜	12
Thickness, inches	4	4

Weight per cubic foot   88 lbs.   90 lbs.   108 lbs.   113 lbs.

Crushing strength (large size specimens)

Area in compression	86 sq. in.	138 sq. in.
Strength	190 psi.	305 psi.

Crushing strength (small size specimens for purpose of direct comparison)

Area in comparison	15 sq. in.	13 sq. in.	17 sq. in.	7 sq. in.
Strength	100 psi.	100 psi.	180 psi.	350 psi.

Organic binder material

(% by weight)	2.1%	2.3%	0.4%	0.2%

Sieve analysis (% pass)
Opening in mm.

9.4	100%	100%	98%	98%
2.0	98%	99%	98%	97%
0.5	97%	99%	94%	93%
0.074	54%	38%	45%	60%

Notes: Large size compression specimen on Item No. 13 shows inclusions of sandstone. Item No. 13 also slakes very rapidly in water in comparison with the other samples submitted. Weights per cubic foot and small size compression specimens were obtained by cutting fragments to approximately cubical shape.

Respectfully submitted,
San Francisco Laboratory,
/s/ Irving Furlong
Chemist.

Items as follows:
#11 and #12 — original adobe bricks from Church.
#13 — new adobe for restoration.
Box "A" — adobe from ruins, Salsipuedes.

REPORT ON TILE

———

UNITED STATES DEPARTMENT OF COMMERCE
WASHINGTON

———

NATIONAL BUREAU OF STANDARDS
REPORT

National Park Service,   San Francisco, California,
Region Four,   April 2, 1938.
601 Sheldon Building,
San Francisco, California.

Subject: Tests on Roof Tile.
Refer: Your letter of March 11, 1938.
Project: Restoration of Mission La Purísima Concepción,
Lompoc, California.

S. F. Lab. No.	07777	07778	07785
Item	7	8	Box A
Description	Fragment	Fragment	4 Fragments from Estancia.
Weight (oven dry)	5# 4 oz.	8# 6 oz.	1# 8½ oz.
Water absorption (five hours at room temperature)	12%	13%	11%
Thickness, range in inches	⅝-¾	¾-1	½-⅝

Respectfully submitted,
San Francisco Laboratory,
/s/ Irving Furlong
Chemist.

NOTE: Items as follows:

#7 — Fragment of roof tile — La Purisima

#8 — Fragment of roof tile — La Purisima

#9 — Fragment of roof tile — ruin at Salsipuedes.

REPORTS ON TILE

———

UNITED STATES DEPARTMENT OF COMMERCE
WASHINGTON

———

NATIONAL BUREAU OF STANDARDS
REPORT

National Park Service,   San Francisco, California,
Region Four,   April 2, 1938.
601 Sheldon Building,
San Francisco, California.

  Subject: Tests on Roof Tile.
  Refer: Your letter of March 11, 1938.
  Project: Restoration of La Purísima Concepción,
            Lompoc, California.

S. F. Lab. No.	07774	07775	07776
Item No.	4	5	6
Description	from monastery	from church	from church
Weight (oven dry)	14# 13½ oz.	10# 15½ oz.	13# 9 oz.
Water absorption (five hours at room temperature)	11%	14%	14%
Length, inches	22½	21½	22
Cross-section, large end:			
inside width, inches	*8¾	8	8⅞ **8⅝
inside depth, inches	*3¾	3½	4¾ **4¼
average thickness, in.	15/16	⅝	15/16
Cross-section, small end:			
inside width, inches	*7	5½	6¼
inside depth, inches	*3⅛	3	3
average thickness, in.	15/16	⅞	13/16

*Corners at ends of tile are broken. These measurements are made 6″ back from the respective ends.
**Additional cross-section 2″ from large end is as indicated. This tile is curved in longitudinal section on outside. Offset at center from straight edge placed across ends is 7/16″.

                              Respectfully submitted,
                              San Francisco Laboratory,
                              /s/ Irving Furlong
                                  Chemist.

NOTE: Items as follows:
  #4 — Roof tile from Residence.
  #5 — Roof tile from Church.
  #6 — Roof tile from Church.

UNITED STATES DEPARTMENT OF COMMERCE
WASHINGTON

———

NATIONAL BUREAU OF STANDARDS
REPORT

National Park Service, San Francisco, California,
Region Four, April 2, 1938.
601 Sheldon Building,
San Francisco, California.

Subject: Tests of Floor Tile.
Refer: Your letter of March 11, 1938.
Project: Restoration of Mission La Purísima Concepción,
Lompoc, California.

S. F. Lab. No.	07771	07772	07773
Item	1	2	3
Description	Tile from church	Tile from church Bldg. No. 2 end col.	Tile Fragment
Weight, oven dry	12# 2½ oz.	6# 11 oz.	3# 9 oz.
Water absorption (five hours at room temperature)	17%	15%	14%
Crushing strength, psi. (tested flat)	1900	2200	2800
Dimensions: (average)			
Length, inches	10½	10½	7⅞
Width, inches	10½	5¼	5
Height, inches	2¼	2¼	1¾

Strength tests were made on specimens which were oven dried after determining water absorption. Broken specimens indicate incomplete burning.

Respectfully submitted,
San Francisco Laboratory,
/s/ Irving Furlong
Chemist.

Items as follows:

#1 — Floor tile from Church.

#2 — Half tile from end column — building No. 2.

#3 — Tile fragment.

UNITED STATES DEPARTMENT OF COMMERCE
WASHINGTON

NATIONAL BUREAU OF STANDARDS
REPORT

National Park Service,
Region Four,
601 Sheldon Building,
San Francisco, California.

San Francisco, California.
April 2, 1938.

Subject: Tests on water pipe.
Refer: Your letter of March 11, 1938.
Project: Restoration of Mission La Purísima Concepción, Lompoc, California.

S. F. Lab. No.	07779	07780	07781
Item	9	10	10a
Description	Large pipe	Small pipe	Fragment
Weight (oven dry)	7# 10½ oz.	3# 15½ oz.	1# 0 oz.
Water absorption (five hours at room temperature)	13%	13%	14%

Dimensions:	Small end Transition Section	Small end pipe Section	Center pipe Section	Large end pipe Section	Large end Transition Section
S.F. No. 07779: Large Pipe					
Outside diam., in.	(2⅞-3¼)	3¼	3⅝	3⅞	3⅞
Inside diam., in.	1 15/16	2½		2	(2⅜-3⅛)
Av. wall thickness	¼″	⅜″		⅞″	(⅝″-⅜″)
Length, in.	1½				2 (inside)
Net length outside			20″		
Overall length			21¾″		
S.F. No. 07780: Small pipe					
Outside diam., in.	Broken	2½	(2 9/16-2 7/8)	3 7/16	3 9/16
Inside diam., in.	"	1¾		1¾	2⅜-2½
Av. wall thickness	"	⅜″		⅞″	⅝″
Length inches	"				1⅝ (inside)
Net length outside			15⅝″		
Overall length			not determined		

S.F. No. 07781: Fragment of pipe section:

	Small end		Large end
Outside diam., in.	2½		2 11/16
Inside diam., in.	1 7/16		1½
Av. wall thickness, in.	½		⅝
Length, outside, net., in.		4½	

Figures in ( ) indicate range of values along section.

Respectfully submitted,
San Francisco Laboratory,
/s/ Irving Furlong
Chemist.

Items as follows:
#9 – Large water pipe.
#10 – Small water pipe.
#10a – Fragment of water pipe.

REPORT ON TIMBER

Five samples of original timbers were submitted to Professor Emanuel Fritz, Division of Forestry, College of Agriculture, University of California, for identification as to species. The samples were as follows:

1. Portion of ceiling beam.
2. Spindle of wood grille.
3. Fragment (moulded edge) of door plank (assumed).
4. Fragment of door frame.
5. Fragment of (assumed) ceiling plank.

The report on species of these samples is quoted in full in the following letter.

UNIVERSITY OF CALIFORNIA
College of Agriculture
Agricultural Experiment Station
Division of Forestry
BERKELEY

June 4, 1938

Director
National Park Service
Sheldon Building
San Francisco, California
Dear Sir:—

The wood specimens from the Mission La Purísima supplied by F. C. Hageman were identified as follows, the numbers referring to corresponding numbers on samples:

1. Cottonwood (*Populus sp.*)
2. Ponderosa pine (*Pinus ponderosa*)
3. Redwood (*Sequoia Sempervirens*)
4. Ponderosa pine (*Pinus ponderosa*)
5. Douglas fir or Big Cone Spruce (*Pseudotsuga taxifolia or P. macrocarpa*)

These are being returned to Mr. Hageman.

There is a possibility that Specimen No. 3 may be Bigtree, although the anatomical evidence points to redwood. However, there is no clear-cut distinction between these two species, and it is not possible for me to say definitely that it is redwood, although I am inclined in that direction. Likewise, Specimen No. 5 may be Big Cone Spruce, since the Mission is located nearer the natural range of this species than it is to the range of the present commercially important Douglas fir. This particular specimen was quite badly decayed, and I doubt if it could be definitely ascertained as to which of these species it is. If information could be obtained regarding the locality where the timbers came from, then the identification could probably be made definite on that basis.

Very truly yours,
/s/ ROBERT A. COCKRELL
Assistant Professor of Forestry

UNITED STATES DEPARTMENT OF AGRICULTURE
FOREST SERVICE
LOS PADRES NATIONAL FOREST

Address reply to
FOREST SUPERVISOR
and refer to
S
Planting
Los Padres

SANTA BARBARA, CALIFORNIA
July 13, 1938

Mr. Fred C. Hageman
c/o National Park Service
La Purísima CCC Camp
Lompoc, California

Dear Mr. Hageman:

Reference is made to your telephone conversation of July 11 on timber and the possibility of use at nearby missions.

As you doubtless know, the closest zone of coniferous tree species extends from Figueroa Mountain (Elevation 4512 feet) easterly along the highest mountains to Big Pine, ending at Madulce Peak (Elevation 6546). The coniferous species are as follows:

Sugar pine	Pinus lambertiana
Ponderosa pine	P. ponderosa
Coulter pine	P. coulteri
Jeffrey pine	P. ponderosa, var. Jeffreyi
Digger pine	P. sabiniana
White fir	Abies concolor
Big Cone Spruce	Pseudotsuga taxifolia
Incense Cedar	Libocedrus decurrens

There are also a few California Juniper (Juniperus californica) and some recently discovered cypress known as Santa Barbara Cypress and identified by Dr. Jepson as Cupressus sargentii, var Raphaelensis.

From what we can gather locally, the most likely timbers used in nearby missions were Big Cone Spruce and possibly some Ponderosa Pine and California Juniper. On most of the above areas, one can find signs of old cuttings, but to what use these were put is a question.

I hope this information will be of use.

Very sincerely yours,
/s/ S. A. Nash-Boulden
Forest Supervisor

SANTA CRUZ PORTLAND CEMENT COMPANY WORKS

Davenport, California

December 24, 1935

Mr. R. A. Kinzie:

The enclosed memorandum by Mr. E. W. Rice, Chemist, gives you the analyses of the plaster and mortar from the La Purísima Mission, complying with your request of December 12. We are now making up several specimens designed to assist you along the lines suggested by Mr. Chas. B. Wing, of the Division of Parks, and expect to send these specimens to you for your inspection about December 26. (Signed) Joseph Riordan.

"Enclosed Memorandum".

Following are analyses of plaster and mortar from La Purísima Mission. These analyses have been recalculated to no ignition loss bases for comparison with our High Silica compound which is also included:

ANALYSES:	EXTERIOR PLASTER		BUILDING MORTAR		H. S. COMPOUND	
	Purisima Actual	Recalculated to no Ig'n. Loss	Purisima Actual	Recalculated to no Ig'n. Loss	Purisima Actual	Recalculated to no Ig'n. Loss
SiO_2	54.68	65.25	71.52	76.80	69.00	71.50
Fe_2O_3	1.19	1.42	1.19	1.28	3.87	4.00
Al_2O_3	6.41	7.65	8.09	8.70	8.53	8.82
CaO	20.27	24.20	10.64	11.45	13.92	14.40
MgO	1.23	1.47	1.31	1.41	1.30	1.35
SO_3	.11	.13	.32	.34	.07	.07
Loss	16.22	—	8.12	—	3.67	—
Insoluble	60.32	71.80	78.32	84.20	67.60	70.00

The building mortar most closely resembles our High Silica compound in analysis but the latter is too high in iron oxide. Mortar samples are gray in color, while our compound is iron oxide color. We have retained samples of these sand lime mortars for inspection.

(Signed) E. W. Rice, Chemist.

REPORT ON PLASTER AND MORTAR
SANTA CRUZ PORTLAND CEMENT COMPANY

Davenport, California

December 27, 1935

MEMORANDUM:—

We are sending under separate cover some experimental mortar pats that we have made in an effort to duplicate the mortar used on the Purísima Mission.

These pats are on glass and a description of each is on the back, but in case the pat should separate from the glass, the following description will serve as an identification:

MARK   DESCRIPTION

	1 part (1 part commercial cement) (2 parts lime hydrate) 4 parts fine sand.
1 hole	1 part (1 part High Silica cement) (2 parts lime hydrate) 4 parts Del Monte sand
2 holes	1 part (1 part High Silica cement) (2 parts lime hydrate) 4 parts fine sand
3 holes in a row	1 part (1 part High Silica cement) (4 parts lime hydrate) 4 parts Del Monte sand
3 holes triangular	1 part (1 part High Silica cement) (4 parts lime hydrate) (4 parts Del Monte sand (note by Colonel Wing — This very closely coincides chemically with the building mortar used by padres)
4 holes in a square	1 part (1 part High Silica cement) (1 part lime hydrate) 5 parts fine sand
4 holes in a row	1 part High Silica cement 4 parts Del Monte sand
5 holes in a row	1 part High Silica cement 4 parts fine sand

The pat with 4 parts lime hydrate mixed with 1 part High Silica cement with 4 parts Del Monte sand most closely approaches the color desired. It looks as if Santa Cruz High Silica cement can be used for this purpose if its color is toned down by admixture of the proper percentage of lime hydrate.

Of course, use of lime hydrate will cut down strength, but probably no great structural strength will be necessary over that needed for stucco.

Respectfully submitted,
Santa Cruz Portland Cement Co.
/s/ E. W. Rice, Chemist.

UNITED STATES DEPARTMENT OF COMMERCE
Washington

———

NATIONAL BUREAU OF STANDARDS
REPORT

National Park Service   San Francisco, Calif.
Region Four   April 2nd, 1938
Sheldon Building
San Francisco, California

      Subject: Tests of Outside Mortar
      Refer: Your letter of March 11th, 1938
      Project: Restoration of La Purísima Mission

S. F. Lab No. 36699 WHITE MORTAR (outside) Your item #14

The piece of mortar analyzed indicates an original mixture of approximately 80% by weight of white sand no coarser than #40 sieve, and 20% of hydrated lime.

S. F. Lab. No. 36701 PINK MORTAR (outside) Your item #16

Assuming your samples 17 and 18 marked "Diatomite (raw pink coloring)", are representative of the coloring material used in the pink mortar, then the pink mortar sample submitted was formulated by adding to the white mortar (see S. F. Lab. 36699 just above) an amount of diatomite of a weight about equal to the weight of the sand present in the white mortar mixture. That is, the composition of the pink mortar is approximately as follows:

      45% Sand
      45   Diatomite
      <u>10</u>   Hydrated Lime (now calcium carbonate)
      100% by weight

To some extent, such a formulation would have the effect of doubling the sand content in the pink mortar as compared with the white mortar. Such a dilution of the hydrated lime was evidently too much. The pink mortar is relatively weak, and otherwise has the characteristics associated with a lime deficiency.

               Respectfully submitted,
               San Francisco Laboratory,
               /s/ Irving Furlong
               Chemist

Items as follows:

#14 — Mortar sample from Residence.

#16 — Pink plaster from Church wall base.

Appendices

REPORT ON COLORED PLASTER
UNIVERSITY OF CALIFORNIA
College of Agriculture

Berkeley, Calif.

September 25, 1935

Mr. C. J. Durbrow
U. S. Department of the Interior
National Park Service
420 Underwood Building
San Francisco, California

Dear Sir:—

Your letter of September 18th to Professor John Burd has been re-ferred to me for answer.

I find no mercury in the sample of plaster you sent, but there is plenty of iron. My conclusion is that the coloring matter is iron oxide, frequently sold under the name of Venetian Red.

Very truly yours,
/s/ P. L. Hibbard

Note:

This sample was taken from the flute of the *corredor* columns, and was the pink colored plaster previously described. Deposits of this material were located and ground for use in the restoration.

F.C.H.

REPORT ON PLASTERING

Three questions were addressed to Mr. J. D. Long, in a letter dated Nov. 14, 1935, University of California, College of Agriculture, who has carried on research into adobe construction:

1. What material, or materials, and what method of attachment would you recommend for plastering the exterior walls of this mission? For the interior walls?

2. Do you feel that the original finish (sample enclosed) would be du-plicated employing cement plaster and a stucco coat?

3. Do you feel that if lime plaster were used, water proofing under the plaster should be employed? Over the plaster?

His reply is given below:

[193]

UNIVERSITY OF CALIFORNIA
COLLEGE OF AGRICULTURE
DIVISION OF AGRICULTURAL ENGINEERING

November 30, 1935

Mr. Frederick C. Hageman
Santa Rosa Park Camp, SP-29
Lompoc, California

Dear Mr. Hageman:

I am very glad to be of further service in the work you are doing on the restoration of the La Purísima Mission. I have enjoyed the booklet dealing with the work, and appreciate your desire to achieve the traditional results using modern materials. I shall answer your questions in order.

1. It has been my policy to consider a cement plaster properly applied on wire mesh reinforcing as standard exterior wall coating, both for waterproofing and protection against mechanical wear. Reinforcement should be 1″ 18 gauge galvanized netting stapled to the wall over ¼″ rods laid vertically on the walls at 30″ centers. If the wall surface is quite rough the furring rods may not be necessary. A two-course stucco coat is recommended proper attention being given to mix and curing.

Since the interior walls are not subject to either moisture or thermal volume changes, a lime plaster laid directly on the wall without reinforcement will suffice.

A traditional method followed on the headquarters building of the U. S. Forestry sub-Experimental Station east of Madera has given very attractive and very durable appearing results. The brick wall was carefully painted or "floated" with a wet burlap to minimize the brick texture. (It would be possible to apply a mud mortar of earth and sand properly proportioned to avoid shrinkage cracks, to secure any desired surface texture.) This was then given two coats of linseed oil sprayed on under pressure, and two coats of a white cold water paint (Dura Tone). This was used on both interior and exterior wall surfaces, and resulted in a soft mellow color closely approximating that of whitewashed adobe surfaces.

2. I doubt that the original texture could be secured by employing cement plaster. It would be necessary to use a 10% admixture of lime, based on cement quantity, in the final coat to secure the same "buttery" consistency of mix and smooth texture. Many of the commercial stucco preparations have some such admixture which enables the plasterer to secure this texture. A lime putty coat over cement stucco base should also prove satisfactory.

3. If lime plaster is used to approximately the thickness shown in the samples I doubt that it would be necessary in the climate at your locality to use waterproofing either on the adobe wall surface or on the face of the plaster. I can see no harm in so doing, however, and it might prove beneficial. Proprietary waterproofings are available but I would recommend

trial of ordinary fuel oil applied in a heavy coat to the adobe brick and allowed 3 days to penetrate, and sodium silicate on the plaster face.

I cannot appreciate all of the conditions governing your work, but I am inclined to recommend for your first consideration a lime plaster exterior coating and either a lime or mud plaster for the interior.

> Sincerely yours,
> /s/ J. D. Long
> Division of Agricultural Engineering

REPORT ON COLORS AND PIGMENT
UNITED STATES DEPARTMENT OF COMMERCE
Washington

———

NATIONAL BUREAU OF STANDARDS
REPORT

National Park Service   San Francisco, Calif.
Region Four   April 2nd, 1938
Sheldon Building
San Francisco, California

> Subject: Tests of Outside Plaster
> Refer: Your letter of March 11th, 1938
> Project: Restoration of La Purísima Mission

S. F. Lab. No. 36700 WHITE PLASTER (outside) Your item #15

This material, in thin section applied to the mortar, is essentially calcium carbonate.

A faint suggestion of oiliness to the feel, and an odor of animal or vegetable matter developed under heat treatment, suggest the presence of organic matter as an admixture. The sample was too small to attempt to carry the suggestion to any conclusion.

> Respectfully submitted,
> San Francisco Laboratory,
> /s/ Irving Furlong
> Chemist

NOTE: This report refers to the whitewash coating applied to the lime plaster.

F. C. H.

UNITED STATES DEPARTMENT OF COMMERCE
Washington

————

NATIONAL BUREAU OF STANDARDS
REPORT

National Park Service   San Francisco, Calif.
Region Four   April 2nd, 1938
Sheldon Building
San Francisco, California

Subject: Tests of Inside Plaster color materials

Refer: Your letter of March 11th, 1938

Project: Restoration of La Purísima Mission

S. F. Lab. No. 36698 Six samples of colored plaster chips

Your Envelope No.	Color	Coloring Material
1	green	A copper compound
2	orange-yellow	Yellow ochre
3	green	A copper compound
4	blue	A copper compound
5	blue-green	A copper compound
6	blue-grey	Wood charcoal

Respectfully submitted,
San Francisco Laboratory,

Chemist

APPENDIX B

RESTORATION POLICY

Meeting at Mission La Concepción Purísima

August 8, 1934

Present: Dr. Owen C. Coy, California State Historical Commission; A. A. Woodward, Curator Los Angeles Museum; Ronald A. Adam, Supervisor Santa Barbara County; Mr. Johnson, Camp Superintendent; Frank E. Dunne, County Forester; W. C. Penfield, Engineer County Planning Commission; Ed. Rowe, Landscape Architect; Arthur Darsie, Engineer; Fred Hageman, Architect; L. Deming Tilton, Director of Planning.

Dr. Coy stated his interest and pledged the support of the California Historical Society in the proposed plan for the restoration of the La Purísima Mission. He made statements on the following points:

(1) This and the Sonoma Mission are the only two now in public ownership. If this mission can be properly restored, it offers opportunity for the development of an exhibit of great historical and educational value, divorced in its management from secular interests.

(2) The mission restoration can be fully authentic, but no attempt at restoration should be made unless the work is organized with great care to assure the completion of the project along approved lines.

(3) Even if no restoration is attempted, the labor forces available at the camp should be used to do a considerable amount of excavating, measuring, mapping and general research at the ruins. This work will have great historic value. If any part of the mission is to be restored this is essential, and must be done first in preparation for the restoration.

(4) The desirable program of restoration would contemplate an eventual reconstruction of the entire mission establishment, as a means of showing the complete physical plant of the mission community, workshops, dwellings, chapel, granaries, reservoirs, tanneries, etc. If this cannot be done, one building might be restored and a model of the entire establishment shown therein.

After considerable general discussion the following conclusions were reached:

(a) The appointment of a competent research specialist is essential. Dr. Coy has recommended a young architect-historian named Miller who directed the restoration of the San Diego Mission.

(b) A survey and map of the property of the mission and environs is necessary. Engineer Darsie and Architect Hageman will undertake this at once.

(c) No excavations or interference with the ruins should be permitted until Miller is on the job.

(d) Under Miller's direction, or in his absence in case he is not appointed, under Hageman's direction, careful trenching should be started to determine the original outlines of each unit of the mission plant. This work should proceed with painstaking care to permit records, measurements and photographs to be taken of all findings. The results should be presented in well-drawn maps and diagrams.

(e) After the surveys and research have been completed, a decision should be reached as to the extent and character of the restoration work to be undertaken. Estimates should be made of the amount of material required, sources, costs, types of labor called for, time required for construction, special problems encountered, etc.

(f) If restoration is to be attempted, the property should be made a State Historic Landmark. The county, which now owns the land on which the ruins stand, has already indicated a willingness to transfer it to the State Park Commission, acquire additional property and enter into an agreement with the state for subsequent maintenance of the area.

(g) The restoration project, if approved, should call for the development of a well planned park and camping grounds in the vicinity of the mission. For this additional land is required, a minimum of 15 or 20 acres being needed to give the principal buildings and building sites adequate protection.

(h) The complete service of the camp in carrying on the restoration and research work outlined would include some activities at the site of the first La Purísima Mission in the City of Lompoc. This area, now private property, should become public. The ruins here should be excavated, measured and mapped and the principal walls and more interesting features of the site might be protected by a rough shelter.

It is apparent to any one, who studies the ruins at La Purísima, that the principal building can be restored if the work is not delayed too long. Much of the original adobe is available and can be used again. The main outlines of the structure are easily traced. The work will require skilled labor, which is available in the vicinity, including:

(1) Experienced adobe brick makers
(2) Plasterers
(3) Carpenters
(4) Tile and brick makers
(5) Masons

The most important need, however, is for competent, energetic, general direction of this particular work.

If a carefully-planned, systematic program of work is laid out for the men, much can be done during the period of the camp toward making this historic spot more attractive. Aqueducts, troughs, tanks and fountains which had such a large part in the life of the mission community are all in fair state of preservation. They can again be supplied with water from the original source. Trees, shrubs and lawns can be established in a pleasant park. The mission building restored can become a museum and educational center under the general management of the officials of Santa Barbara County. Their pride in the traditions and historic background of the county is assurance that this project will have sympathetic and responsible local support.

> L. Deming Tilton
> /s/ L. Deming Tilton
> Aug. 9, 1934

La Purísima Advisory Committee

The persons included in this group suggested by Mr. W. C. Penfield, Engineer for the Santa Barbara County Planning Commission, in his letter to Mr. W. E. Colby dated February 1, 1935 were:

Dr. Frederic Clements, Director of Santa Barbara Ecological Station of the Carnegie Institute.

Carleton Monroe Winslow, prominent architect of Santa Barbara and Los Angeles, vice chairman of the Historic Buildings Committee.

Kelley Hardenbrook, Lompoc Attorney, familiar with all legal transactions in the acquisition of the park.

Miss Marion Parks, Los Angeles and Santa Barbara research worker in California history and historian of the Santa Barbara Parlor of Native Daughters, an authority on early California history.

Miss Pearl Chase, general chairman of the Plans and Planting Committee of Community Arts Association of Santa Barbara, chairman of the County Roadside Committee.

As ex-officio members, the following were included for their technical advice and help:

Ronald Adam, County Supervisor of the Lompoc District.

L. Deming Tilton, Director of the State Planning Commission and Director of Santa Barbara County Planning Commission.

Frank Dunne, Santa Barbara County Forester.

Wallace C. Penfield, Engineer of the Santa Barbara County Planning Commission.

Figure 265. Standing (left to right): L. Deming Tilton, Director, Santa Barbara County Planning Commission; Ronald L. Adam, S.B. County Supervisor; E. D. Rowe, N.P.S. Landscape Foreman; Frank E. Dunne, S.B. County Forester; Harry Buckman, S.B. County Board of Forestry; Frederick C. Hageman, N.P.S. Architectural Foreman; Arthur L. Darsie, N.P.S. Engineering Foreman. Lower Row (left to right): Wallace C. Penfield, S.B. County Planning Commission Engineer; Lawrence Libeu, N.P.S. Fire Suppression Foreman; Arthur Woodward, Archeologist, L.A. County Museum; H. V. Johnston, N.P.S. Camp Superintendent; Dr. Owen C. Coy, Director of California State Historical Commission and Chairman of Department of History, University of Southern California.

In his reply of March 11, 1935, the Chairman of the State Park Commission concurred in the above list, and asked that a meeting be held in the near future, requesting that the Superintendent of the La Purísima Camp and such other members of his staff as he might designate be present.

Miss Marion Parks, although named, was unable to attend conferences and later resigned. Her name was replaced by *Professor William A. Ellison,* Professor of History, Santa Barbara State Teachers College.

The first suggestions for development policy were outlined in a letter dated March 27, 1935. (See Appendix B, post).

A more comprehensive report was submitted under date of September 24, 1935.

March 27, 1935

The State Park Commission.
San Francisco, California.
Gentlemen:

The first meeting of your newly appointed Purísima State Park Advisory group was held on Wednesday, March 27, at Lompoc.

At that time matters were discussed in relation to the development of the mission and certain conclusions reached which we feel should be submitted to your honorable body as recommendations. Under ordinary circumstances, it would be inadvisable to present a report of this type which considers only a few aspects of what must necessarily be a rather complicated problem. However, due to the necessity of immediate decision on certain fundamental matters concerning the mission project, your committee has carefully studied the situation from as broad a viewpoint as possible, and has further deemed it advisable to make known to you at this time the conclusions reached in order to facilitate your work in preparing estimates and plans.

1. The only excuse for a state park at La Purísima site is because of the mission ruins there. Any development of the park should be designed with the idea of preserving the mission ruins and surrounding them with a harmonious and appropriate landscape.

The walls of the ruins will not last another winter in their present state. Due to years of negligence, the bottoms of the walls have decomposed and will fall before long if no measures are taken to preserve them. For this reason it is recommended that plans be drawn immediately for a restoration of the better-preserved walls by means of concrete and steel. This may later be followed by similar work on remaining portions of the building and an ultimate restoration of the complete structure as money becomes available.

2. It is strongly urged that all restoration or reconstruction work be concentrated on the main building, and that all plans for caretakers quarters, service facilities, museums or other structures be included in this one

building, which is known to the public as La Purísima Mission. It is recommended that the first units of this plan be drawn immediately and approval secured so that material money now appropriated for this purpose and for caretaker's quarters be spent before the end of the fourth period to prevent a reversion of funds.

3. In view of the remarkable discoveries made through recent excavations of the old mission grounds, it is recommended that this work be continued until all of the old mission grounds have been explored, and that no new structures be built which could conceivably interfere with the archeological remains.

4. Due to unavoidable circumstances, the N.P.S. camp is located in what should be the mission garden area. It is recommended that such steps as are possible be taken toward placing the camp in a more favorable and permanent place.

5. Incidental immediate recommendations:

That the newly-excavated soap works be protected by a ramada or some other cover.

That a "rim road" be built for fire protection and access to the mesa section of the park.

That fire prevention work on the park be done according to the best standards available.

The committee does not hesitate to recommend restoration work on the mission building even though labor available is unskilled. It is the opinion of this group that the exceptionally fine camp staff at La Purísima is fully qualified to undertake this work.

Respectfully submitted,

WCP-MH

LA PURISIMA STATE PARK
ADVISORY GROUP

By: W. C. Penfield
    Secretary

Present:

Dr. Frederic Clements, Chairman
Miss Pearl Chase
Carleton Monroe Winslow
Ronald Adam

Frank E. Dunne
Wallace C. Penfield
H. V. Johnston
Fred Hageman

Copy
State of California
Department of Natural Resources
Division of Parks

420 Underwood Building
April 10th, 1935

Mr. H. V. Johnston, Superintendent
Santa Rosa, ECW Camp, DSP-3
Lompoc, California

Dear Mr. Johnston:—

The following preliminary policy has been outlined by the State Park Commission for restoration of the La Purísima Mission:

1. No buildings or other structures to be built on the Mission site other than those originally part of the Mission.

2. A portion of the eastern end of the Mission buildings sufficient to house a custodian to be restored during the Fifth period.
   Externally this restoration should conform to the original design of the buildings.
   Internally modifications necessary to provide as a minimum suitable living room, kitchen, bath, bed room, (two if practicable) and an office, if practicable.
   No part of the space originally used as a chapel to be used for Custodian's quarters or museum.
   If funds are sufficient, a small space for museum purposes can be included in the Fifth period restoration plan.

3. Decision as to further restoration of Mission buildings to be left until restoration under (2) is completed.

4. Work of exploration to proceed but as far as practicable plans should be prepared and executed for permanent landscaping along the excavated pipe lines and around structures connected therewith in order that the visiting public can have access to interesting portions of the work and at the same time be prevented from causing damage thereto.

The above is supplementary to letter of Procurement Office under date of April 9th.

Sincerely yours,

/s/ Chas B. Wing
Eng. in Chg.,
Fed. Co-op Projects
in State Parks

CBW-z

UNIVERSITY OF CALIFORNIA
DEPARTMENT OF HISTORY
BERKELEY

Mr. A. E. Demaray
Acting Director
National Park Service
Washington, D. C.

My dear Mr. Demaray:

In accordance with your request I went with Dr. Ewing to La Purísima Mission last week, spending two days on the trip. A large portion of one day was spent on the site of the mission and in conference with the superintendent, the architect and Dr. Ewing. As a result of what I saw, I am very much impressed with the opportunity there to provide for the public a rare educational feature — a complete mission establishment — such as it is not possible to prepare anywhere else in the United States. The popular notion of a mission is that it consisted primarily of a church, whereas it was a complete economic and social unit of vast importance in the history of two-thirds of the Western Hemisphere, all the way from Patagonia to California, to New Mexico, and to Georgia. Each mission was a self-sustaining community with fundamental economic, social and religious activities. The history of agriculture in two-thirds of the Western Hemisphere for three centuries centered largely around the missions, which controlled most of the agricultural land and of the agricultural labor. In the missions a large part of the native population of all this vast area — two-thirds of the Western Hemisphere — got its first contact with European civilization. The material remains of most of the old missions within the United States and the adjacent Mexican border, consist almost solely of the churches, thus accentuating the distorted notion of mission plants and mission life. Moreover, in most cases the mission remains are located in towns or cities with privately owned buildings hemming them in and making complete restoration impossible. At Purísima, on the other hand, a large area embracing most of the mission remains including not only the church and monastery, but the workshop, the fountains, the reservoirs, the Indian village, the orchard, and a considerable portion of the agricultural lands, is public property, making it possible to reestablish the whole plant much as it was when it was in active operation when the mission was it its height.

The work which has been done in the restoration of the monastery seems to me to be excellent. Mr. Hageman, the architect, has studied his problem with great care and devoted enthusiasm, and I feel that he has a very sensitive historical conscience, so that everything he does will be as nearly correct as it is possible to make it. To stop now with only the monastery restored would give as distorted a notion as that given in other places with only the church in evidence. The foundations of the work buildings are plain, and I think it will be possible to reproduce them faithfully. The same is true of the church, the cemetery walls, and the dwellings of the neophytes. The water system is surprisingly complete in its original form, and with very little reconstruction it will be possible to have it in actual operation.

Assuming that a preservation policy were more desirable than a reconstruction policy at Purísima, it is too late now, because the quite extensive remains of the church have already been destroyed to make way for reconstruction. Therefore it is only a question of stopping in the middle of the program or carrying it through, and I heartily recommend the latter, for the two principal reasons which I have stated above. Virginia has a reconstructed Williamsburg, Springfield has a replica of Lincoln's village. Here is an opportunity for much more authentic restoration of an equally significant and typical pioneer community in another section of the United States, with vast possibilities for a museum and other educational displays.

The State Park Service here has leaned more to the preservation policy than of restoration. But both Mr. Drury and Dr. Ewing agree with me now that it is too late to proceed on that basis. Mr. Drury hopes that it will be possible to carry out the reconstruction policy without reducing the sympathetic participation of the State Park Service in the promotion and utilization of the unique monument, because he believes that to do so would lessen its value for educational purposes. I share that hope.

Trusting that this report will be of service, I am

Yours very sincerely,

/s/ Herbert E. Bolton
Member, National Park
Advisory Board

UNIVERSITY OF ILLINOIS
College of Fine and Applied Arts
Urbana, Illinois

September 17, 1936

Mr. Wallace C. Penfield, Chairman
La Purísima Advisory Committee
Santa Barbara County Planning Commission
Court House
Santa Barbara, California

Dear Mr. Penfield:

I have returned from a 10,000 mile trip through the West and Southwest. During this trip of ten weeks I inspected many park and recreational ventures being carried out under various auspices. None was more interesting to me personally than the restoration work going on at Mission Purísima Concepción.

I examined carefully the building restoration work being carried out under the direction of Mr. Hageman. This, it seemed to me, was going forward in a highly commendable way, the concrete reinforcement of the walls, the secure support of the roofs and the generally accurate restoration of missing historic portions guaranteeing the perpetuation of a most important structure.

There are two schools of thought with regard to the preservation of historic monuments.

(1) One is simply to preserve (with or without some protecting shelter) what is left of a particular monument.

(2) The other is "to restore" in the best and most accurate spirit the total fabric of the structure, portions of which may in the course of time have disappeared.

In the past I have held mixed feelings about both procedures. I have seen the first method followed with the result that in time what was left has gone on to cureless ruin. Under the second procedure I have observed, upon occasion, historic relics so inaccurately "restored" as to destroy the whole original intent and spirit of them.

At Purísima I was considerably encouraged to see the second method being carried out in what I felt was workmanlike and archaeologically accurate manner. I discussed with Mr. Hageman and others their methods of research, the sources of certain details incorporated, etc., and was satisfied that they were proceeding in a commendable manner.

I came away with the matter pretty well settled in my own mind that Purísima could be made a splendid museum in which all the phases of mission administration could be made available to the public. This, due to various circumstances (church ownership among them) can scarcely be attempted elsewhere. I felt, however, that I should write your committee upon certain points:

I. I believe that, if the policy of making Purísima a true mission museum to show real mission administration is adhered to, further restoration of the buildings should be carried forward. This, of course, carries with it the implication that the work be put in the hands of competent architectural historians and archeologists.

II. An examination of the premises (principally the church, cemetery, and connecting structures) led me to believe that the plans for restoration could be quite accurately determined and in part the superstructure also. Old photographs, descriptions and a relatively complete knowledge of structural procedures elsewhere in my estimation make possible highly plausible restorations of the balance of the buildings. Excavated as it now is, the ruined church will go into further ruin unless it is accurately restored or adequately protected. Such protective structures, unless artistically carried out (as has been done in some of the early Lincoln structures in Kentucky) are likely to be either scenic eye-sores or as costly as restoration itself.

III.   I believe that with *good* research and historical study no real errors can result in the major portion of the project. I shall be glad to give the benefit of any knowledge I may have concerning disputed questions.

IV.   The proposed mission garden does certain violence to the whole idea of a "working" museum of mission culture. Of course in opening up such a structure to the public certain concessions must be made to that public. This usually takes the form of facilities for parking cars, toilets, food stations, etc. Would it not be possible in some way to keep these away from the main archeological features of the venture and thus keep the mission proper in as near its historic state as possible?

If you have visited any of the mission show places, you will have discovered that the crowds are never excessive. The location of Purísima, off the main truck highway, will further curtail crowds. Therefore the making of a garden with paths thirty to sixty feet wide is entirely unthinkable and unjustified. The old mission gardens were simple practical affairs, places where cherished plants, trees, etc., from Spain, Mexico, even Peru, could be protected and propagated. Sometimes the protection was a low adobe wall, sometimes a hedge of prickly pear. The location and width of the paths were determined by the line of travel of the padres and their neophytes in going from building to building. Usually these were paths in the real sense — just pathways. Around water basins, or in the padres garden proper, gravelled walks (tile bordered) or tiled pavements were in time put into place. Evidence of small cobbles (really large pebble mosaics) has been found. The Spanish habit of combining in the same garden vegetables and flowers, that is decorative and practical plants, like hollyhocks and squash, nasturtiums, and peppers, should not be lost sight of. I do want to appeal to your committee to keep the gardens in the same spirit of the old mission buildings, and above all do not let the thing become the type of place that lovely old Capistrano (picturesque as it may be in some respects) has become.

You have a magnificent opportunity to do a splendid piece of work. Do not let it escape you.

Yours very truly,

/s/ Rexford Newcomb
Dean of the College and
Director of the Bureau

RN:W

ST. BONAVENTURE COLLEGE AND SEMINARY
ST. BONAVENTURE, N.Y.

September 26, 1936

Mr. Frederick C. Hageman
Supt., La Purísima Camp, SP-29
Lompoc, California

Dear Sir:

Last summer the Franciscan Educational Conference met at Santa Barbara Mission and St. Anthony's College at Santa Barbara, California. The subject discussed at that meeting was Franciscan History in North America. We have all returned to our homes in the east and our minds still dwell with enthusiasm upon the wonderful things we heard and saw in your beautiful land on the Pacific Coast.

As President of the Franciscan Educational Conference, I feel it my duty to write a line to some of our hosts and friends along the Pacific Coast. I do this not merely to show our everlasting gratitude but also to say a word of encouragement to the leaders in that section of our country.

In reviewing my experiences in California, I can not but linger with a deep sense of gratefulness on the splendid work that is being accomplished at the Purísima Mission. And since you are the superintendent of that work, I feel that these lines should go to you.

I have visited excavation and restoration work in the far east and in other lands and I must say that I have hardly ever found such fine appreciation, such expert workmanship and such a wholesome sense of proportion as I discovered among the men under your charge at that Mission. Mr. Ed Rowe proved to be an excellent and most hospitable guide.

I cannot help but express my admiration at the aims for which your work of restoration is headed. You are not only unearthing the old ruins, and then take it for granted that all visitors are antiquarians. Your visitors are, for the most part, people who wish to see the living past in the living present. They want to see the grand old monuments of the Padres as they really were. There is a big difference between showing the remnants of history and showing revivified as it really was. For this reason your efforts will be crowned with a two fold success: the promotion of historical research and the re-awakening of an interest in the life of the past. Please let me congratulate you and your staff on your splendid achievement. All America owes you a great debt of gratitude for what you are accomplishing.

I sincerely trust that the sponsors of your efforts will continue to co-operate with you and stand by courageously until the entire mission, with all the buildings and appointments, will be fully restored. When that day comes, your sponsors will earn the gratitude of all high-minded citizens of this country and California will boast of a monument without a peer in this country and abroad.

Extending to you the congratulations and the admiration of all the members of the Franciscan Educational Conference, I am

Very respectfully yours,

/s/ THOMAS PLASSMAN
(Very Rev.)
Pres.
Thomas Plassman, O.F.M.

TP:J.G

APPENDIX C

MISCELLANEOUS

The Making of Tiles at the Missions
By M. R. Harrington
From *The Masterkey*, January 1938

On October 19th and 20th Mrs. Harrington and I visited La Purísima Mission near Lompoc, California where we were most hospitably entertained by Mr. F. C. Hageman, who is the architectural technician supervising the restoration of the Mission buildings by the National Park Service with C.C.C. labor. Among other things he illustrated for me the method of making roof-tiles or *tejas* and floor tiles or *ladrillos* probably used by the Indians under the instruction of the Franciscans in the Mission days.

The clay. In the case of La Purísima the clay is dug from a hillside near the Mission buildings. It seems to contain naturally the proper proportions of grit; but rich or "fat" clays would need an admixture of sand to prevent cracking and excessive shrinking in drying and firing the tile.

Modern tile-makers add what they call "grog" to such clay to reduce the shrinking. This is nothing but particles of burned tiles or bricks which have been ground up for the purpose. This material is inert and acts like the coarse aggregate in concrete. Pueblo Indian potters were familiar with this method, for they mixed ground-up potsherds with the fresh clay used in making vessels; in fact, they still do this.

At present the clay is ground between iron rollers and mixed by a special machine, but in Mission days it was doubtless broken up with mauls of some kind and mixed with hoes like adobe or mortar if there was need for haste; otherwise it was soaked in pits for a few days until it became thoroughly soft. Then it was mixed if necessary with sand, or other materials by the hoe method. Modern equipment for preparing clay is quite elaborate and expensive.

Equipment. Besides a table or bench to work upon, various pieces of plank or boards, and a rack, preferably roofed over, on which to dry the tiles, the equipment need for floor tiles is a square form of wood or iron (without top or bottom) a little larger than the desired size of the finished tile, a small piece of board and a bucket of water.

For roof tiles the form is larger at one end than at the other. For a type of roof tile used at San Fernando the length of the form would be about twenty-two inches, the width on the wide end about fifteen inches, on the narrow end eleven and one-half inches, the thickness a little over one inch.

At La Purísima, says Mr. Hageman, the roof tiles for the earlier Residence or Monastery building were thicker (a full inch) and slightly larger than those of the later buildings. This thickness was found to be excessive, or they may have improved their method, so that the later tiles are found to be three-fourths inch thick; a saving of twenty-five percent in material.

Another piece of equipment needed in making a roof tile is the tapering semi-cylindrical mold used to give it the necessary curvature. Anciently this was usually made out of solid wood with a handle on the larger end, or of narrow wooden laths nailed to two semi-circular pieces of board, with a hole cut in the larger one in lieu of a handle. For the San Fernando tile just mentioned the length would be twenty-two inches; the larger semi-circular end eight inches wide and four inches high and the smaller about six inches wide and three inches high, or a little less.

Tiles shrink somewhat in drying and firing so that they are slightly smaller when finished than the forms in which they are made.

Making the tile. For both kinds of tile the first shaping process is the same, although the forms are different in outline. The form is wet and laid on a sanded board or table, and a mass of clay mixed to a stiff uniform consistency is thrown into it and worked and patted down with the hands until the form is filled completely. Then the surplus clay is scraped off with the bit of board. The form is now lifted off and the shaping is complete so far as the floor tile is concerned. It is carried away on its plank and placed on the drying rack.

Modern tile makers, instead of sanding the table lay down a piece of paper first, to which the clay sticks, of course. This burns off in the firing process.

For the roof tile two other processes are necessary. The embryo tile is pulled with the side of the form to the front edge of the table and off upon the mold which has previously been wet, and which is gradually rotated to receive it evenly. Then the mold with the tile upon it is lifted upon the table and the workman, wetting his hands, presses it down to the mold and smooths it off if necessary. Then the mold, still with the tile on it, is placed on a shelf of the drying rack, and the workman, grasping the handle, pulls the mold out with a sudden jerk, leaving the tile to dry. If the clay was stiff enough it will not collapse.

There is not a particle of evidence to support the often quoted legend that the "Indians molded the roof-tiles on their naked thighs." One can picture long rows of Indians waiting with the wet tiles on their legs as the tedious hours dragged by the tiles slowly became dry enough to handle. Mission Indians were patient under various trials and tribulations, but not that patient!

Firing. After remaining on the racks until thoroughly dry — some say it took a month in average weather — the tiles were fired in a kiln. The tiles used in the La Purísima restoration, although shaped by hand in the old way are fired in a modern commercial kiln; but the old methods seem to have been something like this:

The kiln was made of adobe bricks laid up in a square form. At the bottom, on opposite sides were several low arched openings for firing connected by chambers built of burnt bricks laid some distance apart and corbelled so as to form a sort of arched passage. The floor of the kiln was

Figure 267. With the addition of a proper amount of moisture and a thorough mixing, the clay becomes a plastic mass which can be worked with the hands. This is the clay being taken from the machine to the moulders.

Figure 266. The dry clay, mined from the hillsides is fed into a crusher. The ground material passes through a screen, thence into the pugmill, seen in the background.

Figure 270.

A ROOF TILE IN THE MAKING

Figure 268, A quantity of the wet clay is cut out with a wire bow. Figure 269, The moulder places the metal form on a piece of paper, which prevents the clay from sticking to the board. Figure 270, The clay is placed in the form and firmly pressed into place. Figure 271, The surplus clay is scraped off with a hardwood stick. Figure 272, The form is removed from the sheet of clay. Figure 273, The clay sheet is pushed over a semi-circular wood core, which is rotated to receive it. Figure 274, The finisher forms the sheet around the core, and finishes the surface with his hands. Figure 275, After placing in the drying racks, the core is quickly removed. Figure 276, The fresh tiles remain in drying racks until they are sufficiently dry for moving to storage, where they remain until thoroughly dry. The final process requires firing in a kiln at a temperature of 1800 degrees. The burning process requires about five days.

Figure 269.

Figure 272.

Figure 268.

Figure 271.

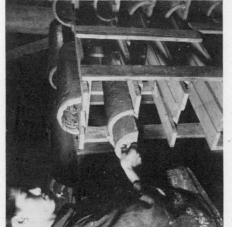

Figure 275.

Figure 277.

Figure 274.

Figure 277, (right). Moulding the floor tiles. The material is the same clay as that used for the roof tiles. The process for these tiles is substantially the same as for the adobe bricks. After thorough drying the tiles are burnt at a temperature of 1800 degrees F.

Figure 273.

Figure 276.

above these chambers and was formed of bricks also separated to let the heat through. In the kiln the roof tiles were stacked vertically, quite near together, several tiers high. Floor tiles were stacked like bricks in a kiln, with spaces between. Fire-bricks are used today for chambers and floors in the kiln.

The top was covered temporarily with a layer or two of floor tiles or adobes, laid loosely with openings between to let out the hot gases. The fuel, usually wood, was burned in the arched passages beneath the kiln and the heat passed up between the tiles. To make the best tiles it was said that a temperature of 1800 degrees F. should be maintained for 36 hours. Nearly all of the old tiles at Purísima are black inside although red outside. This is said to be the result of "flash" firing; of a higher temperature, say 2000 degrees F. for a shorter time.

The above information was obtained mainly from Mr. Hageman, although partly from other sources.

An Outline of Pigment Studies of the Wall Paintings in the Early Missions in Southern California

Warren W. Lemmon
Supervisor
Index of American Design
Federal Art Project

Pigments Used in Mission Wall Paintings
Spanish-California Period

REFERENCE: William R. Hayward, Geologist, painter and teacher of Santa Barbara, California

During the years 1908 and 1909, Mr. Hayward went to the Santa Inés Mission for a particular study of the pigments and methods of painting as used by the Indians. From this study the following information was obtained:

In the *red pigments*, hematite was not used, as we know it, but the softer parts of Monterey shale were burnt by the Indians or found in nature in a form of red oxide. They super-induced, to get different shades. Colors can be derived from this source from a very pale pink to an English Venetian red. These pigments are being used for distemper and commercial oil colors of today.

At Santa Inés Mission some evidence of cinnabar was found. This vermilion was not used in a pure state but gave almost permanent colors of purple and light brown. There is a red chalk deposit within a half mile of the Santa Inés Mission. However, the cinnabar used was from the quicksilver mines near the present site of the Gibraltar Dam.

[216]

The *yellows* were derived from the light Monterey shale which is found in many locations in this district. There are fine deposits on the Billings Estate and on the road to the present State College, Santa Barbara.

In Holland today a pigment is manufactured known as "Dutch Pink," which is really a primrose yellow (a term used by the housepainters fraternity). Yellow is derived from unexcreted fecal matter of the cattle which have been killed.

White pigment: Diatomacious earth, a pure white silica, which is almost indestructible, is used as a pigment today. The early inhabitants of this district took advantage of this material for their flat whites. Monterey shales were also used when found in light chalky deposits.

Black pigments: Ground charcoal was used almost exclusively. However, carbonized asbestos in a flaky form is found there near Santa Inés on the El Cielo Ranch and can still be found there. This carbonized asbestos will come off when touched. There is no evidence of animal blacks in the Santa Inés study.

Brown pigments: These were prepared from raw and burnt umbers quite prevalent and of a good quality in this district. An air bath was given to this pigment by the gravity process and the finer material, that which was suitable for painting, was obtained by this method. The heavier parts were used in mixing the by-colors.

Ochre pigments: These colors were made from the reds and yellows which are now exposed on the new and old San Marcos Pass roads and along the ocean escarpment. These are a peroxide of iron (a fine silt of earth mineral).

Green and blue pigments: The Indians ground a deposit known as "chert" to obtain a great range of colors from greens to blues.

Outcropping of copper oxide along the east range of mountains from the Santa Inés Mission have been the source of brighter greens and blues.

Wood obtained from a certain tree, name unknown at the present time, when dipped in water, turned the water blue.

Chrome yellow: Being a by-product of white lead, was too heavy to hold up in any solution used as a paint conveyor.

The Indians had primitive kilns in which they prepared their lime for their lime putty. Lime did not affect the natural colors used as such by the Indians.

The pigments were pounded to a powder rather than being ground in water as is customary, time and labor being no particular object in those days.

Oil colors were used on rare occasions. Poppy and olive oil were used sparingly. As these were non-drying oils, the early painters would use ground pigments on a pad, which they would pat onto the surface of the painting. These dry powders adhered to the non-drying oils without presenting the effects of being ground with the oil.

Distemper colors as used in this early period of Mission history were ground in water or in a process of distilled grain.

The vehicle for pigments was prepared by using the juice of cactus with tallow added. This tallow, mainly from sheep, gave a body to hold the colors in solution. It also aided in making the finished work impervious to water.

REFERENCE: John Gamble, prominent Santa Barbara artist. Corroborated by Bert Harmer (Santa Barbara artist), William R. Hayward (geologist, painter, and teacher of Santa Barbara), and Dr. Rogers of the Santa Barbara Museum.

"The gesso work was done by the Indians under the direction of the mission fathers. The binder for the gesso was the juice of the cactus known as the prickly pear (opuntia), which was pounded out and allowed to settle and then drained off and mixed with kilned lime. The best part of the lime was used in the finer work, and the other being used in the construction of the buildings."

REFERENCE: "In and Out of the Old Missions of California" by G. W. James.

"The colors used in the interior decorations of the missions are believed to be mostly of vegetable origin and were sized with glue. The yellows were extracted from poppies, blues from nightshade, the reds from pebbles found along the beaches (probably cinabar). The glue was manufactured on the spot from the bones of animals slaughtered for food."

— Page 333

REFERENCE: "San Juan Capistrano" by Z. Engelhardt.

An artisan named Mariano Mendoza was brought from Mexico to teach the Indians the art of dyeing products of the loom, but the experiment did not prove very encouraging so the neophytes were thrown back on their own resources. Dyestuffs used were campeachy wood, Brazilwood, Sacastal (a weed). The work of weaving and dyeing was inferior to that brought in from Mexico but was considered and accepted as good enough for the country.

— Page 36

Copy

Santa Barbara, California
June 20, 1936

Messrs. Whitsitt & Hageman

Gentlemen:

About forty years ago I visited the Purísima Mission then almost a ruin only one wing standing, and that was used as a barn or cowshed. It had been the refectory I believe, and the walls still showed traces of the painting that had adorned them. As from time to time I've read in the papers of the work being done to restore the mission and its buildings I have pondered over it, how the walls would be built again. The arches, windows and so on I thought of course that all had to be made over. About a month ago I again visited the ruins and my surprise was great indeed when I saw the old structure being as it were dug from its own grave. I was really thrilled, and I assure you I felt that great promise and credit should be given to all concerned in the work which to me at least is so wonderful.

I hope La Purísima will rise up again in all its glory a monument not only to the good Padres, under whose directions it was first built, to the honor of their Divine Master and to be a home for the poor Indians they had come to convert and bring to the knowledge of their Creator. Having lived amongst the pioneers for over forty years I have heard much about the early missions, and all connected with them since the days of Padre Serra. Mr. Bancroft at times his accounts are prejudiced probably by the persons from whom he got his information and in consequence not always accurate. Father Engelhardt on the other hand being a Franciscan and devoted to their work his "missions and missionaries of California" being the outstanding work of his life had only praise for the founders. I am acquainted with many who lived there after the secularization and sale. There is one little incident which I think worth being recorded if in the near future there would be a celebration of any kind, that is the baptism of J. C. Freeman there nearly 79 years ago, and the fact that the God father Don Juan Dana now nearly one hundred years old is still living as well as the Godson. The old man told of the doings of that day and how he had given so much money as he was called on "Bolo Padrino". It was a custom amongst the Spanish people of that time. It appears he was on his way to Santa Barbara and was followed by a bandit but he outwitted the robber by going over another trail. Old as he is the Don likes to tell of the stirring events he witnessed at that time. The baby baptized was the son of Dr. J. C. Freeman, an Englishman, then living on the Santa Lucia Rancho and his wife the oldest daughter of W. B. Foxen of Fremont fame, who was living on the Tinaquaic Rancho Foxen Canon. Members of the Foxen family often rode over the mission La Purísima to hear mass although as a rule they went to Santa Ynez Mission. The old Spanish families were all more or less connected with the missions. Juan Dana mentioned above was the son of Capt. W. G. Dana grantee of Nipomo Rancho and founder of the town of Nipomo. His mother was daughter of Don Carlos Antonio Carillo, one of the Governors of California. Nearly all of the old Californians were related by blood or marriage sometimes by both. I must apologize for this long letter but I give as an excuse, my great interest in the work.

Sincerely,

/s/ Mary E. Foxen

EARLIER EFFORTS TOWARD RESTORATION
THE LANDMARKS CLUB

In 1905, the Union Oil Co. of California owned the ruins of the Residence, as well as the surrounding lands. The Landmarks Club, founded in 1895 — "To conserve the Missions and other historic landmarks of Southern California," was carrying on an active program of conservation preservation of the missions, between Santa Barbara and San Diego, received the following communication:

Mr. Chas. F. Lummis,
   Prest. Landmarks Club,
      Los Angeles.

Sir: This corporation is the owner of the ruins of La Purísima in Santa Barbara County, together with contiguous lands.**** If your organization would care to take over the property with reference to restoring it, or any portion of it, or using it in connection with your organization, we will be very glad to convey the fee of the land upon which the ruin stands, and sufficient grounds about it to subserve any purpose for which it might be used.**** In the event you should care to take over this property, the titles would, of course, go with it. If you do not care to accept this proposition with the understanding that the society will at some time or other preserve the mission as a landmark, or use it for a commendable purpose, we shall be obliged to sell the tiles rather than allow them to be carried away promiscuously.

    An early reply will greatly oblige.

                Yours truly,
                /s/ Lyman Stewart,
                Prest. Union Oil Co. of California

To which the Club made reply:

Mr. Lyman Stewart,
   Prest. Union Oil Co. of California
      Los Angeles.

My Dear Sir: The directors of the Landmarks Club yesterday received with great interest, your communication of the 15th. By formal resolution we have accepted your offer and have pledged the Club to undertake the conservation and repairs of the mission La Purísima to the best of its ability.****
For obvious reasons sufficient surrounding land should be included so that the mission may be given proper elbow-room and not be belittled, when preserved, by the too close encroachment of other structures of any sort. We feel sure that this is a matter in which

you will heartily agree with us, and that you will make your generous gift in such shape that it will have the best efficiency and most permanent value.* * * *

We feel that your act merits the gratitude of all good citizens, and we undertake to do our best to make your gift effective for the public good and for the longest time possible.

Sincerely yours,

/s/ Chas. F. Lummis,
Prest. "Landmarks Club"

The story of this matter was published in the magazine "Out West," under date of September 1905, Vol. XXIII, No. 3, pp. 257-266 inc. Little was actually accomplished, apparently, for in "Out West" of August, 1909, Vol. XXXI, No. 2, appears an article entitled, "Saving a Landmark," pp. 721-728. It states that a deed was given by the Union Oil Company to the Landmarks Club which included six parcels of land, embracing the "noble monastery (290 feet long), the chapel and the scattered and extremely interesting out-work fountains, reservoirs, etc."

One condition of the deed was that "the Landmarks Club shall expend not less than $1500 in re-roofing and protecting the monastery."

"Mr. Hunt, chief architect of the club, and Mr. Lummis, the president, visited the ruin, measured it up, made architects' estimates for repairs, and marked out the reservations which would be necessary to make such a donation of the best public benefit. Fifteen hundred dollars will protect the enormous monastery for a long time to come. The rest of this handsome gift to the public will need no special expenditure at present. In a few years there will be no out-of-way corners in Southern California. With the growth of our Good Roads, with the increasing desire of our visitors to see something of interest besides sky-scrapers and orange groves, the value of this bequest will be better understood from year to year. The Landmarks Club will endeavor to make immediate repairs, trusting to the same public spirit which has already put in some $4000 each at San Fernando and San Juan Capistrano, besides the other missions repaired. The vital thing is to keep these splendid landmarks from going to decay at once. Later years and later generations may elaborate, but they will have no monuments to work upon unless we get busy now."

Apparently no further details were published, and the deed was allowed to void itself, through failure to comply with the performance condition.

It was this deed, however, eliminating these six parcels from the subsequent sale of the property which eventuated in the ruins becoming public property. The Union Oil Co., holding title for many years to the six parcels, finally made the gift of these to the County of Santa Barbara.

Figures 84 through 87 inclusive are reproduced from the 1909 article, which furnish interesting comparisons between the condition of the ruins as of 1906 and 1909.[1]

FIRES IN THE MISSION

During later days the Residence suffered severe damage by fire.

One such fire was reported in the *Sacramento Union,* under date of August 5, 1865:

"The old Mission, La Purísima, in Santa Barbara County, was destroyed by fire, together with $3,000 worth of goods and household furniture on July 25."

The building was not "destroyed" as stated, but may have suffered quite extensive damage. No other record of the fire of 1865 has been found but early residents are positive in their statements concerning a fire which broke out in the '70's.

Mrs. Virginia Tilley, daughter of Jesse Hill, living in the building, or on the "Rancho" at the time related the story of its occurrence, but gave the date as the early eighties.[2] Ford's etching, of the latter date shows the north end of the mission unroofed as do subsequent photographs. According to Mrs. Tilley, her father employed a negro cook. His cookstove was located in one of the northerly rooms, and the stove pipe led through the loft, which contained hay at the time. The hay caught fire, with the result that a considerable area of roof burned before it was stopped.

This portion was never repaired, and in the unroofed rooms it is said that sheep were kept. Numerous evidences of the fire existed in the ruins of this end of the building, and disintegration of the north wall was more advanced than in other portions.

Figure 280.

Figure 279.

Figure 278.

LA PURISIMA'S BELLS

La Purisima's bells were distributed to other Churches about 1875.[3] Of the five bells mentioned in the inventory of February 18, 1835, one was taken to the first Catholic Church in Lompoc and disappeared about 1923. One, and possibly two others were taken to Mission Santa Ynez. Figure 278 is a photograph of one of La Purisima's bells hung with its wooden stock in the *campanario* of that Church. The inscription on this bell reads, "Manuel Vargas Me Fecit, Ano de 1818, Mision de La Purisima De Le Nueba California." This bell was cast in Lima, Peru. The same bell was recently photographed, shown in Figure 279. A second bell at Santa Ynez is said to have come from La Purisima, but cannot be positively identified.[4] Figure 280 is the bell now hanging in the Church at Guadalupe, undoubtedly from La Purisima,[5] and also a Varga Bell from Lima, Peru, dated 1817. It is a companion to the second bell at Santa Ynez, marked M. V. 1817.

PART ONE

NOTES

Introduction

[1] Russell C. Ewing, *Mission La Purísima Concepción*, p. 238.

[2] *Ibid.*, p. 237.

[3] See Appendix C, pp. 220, 221.

[4] See Appendix B, p. 199.

[5] See Appendix B, p. 197, for recommendations on restoration policy by Owen C. Coy, Director of State Historical Commission.

Chapter 1. *Archeological Investigations.*

[1] The second or the Los Berros site will henceforth be referred to as La Purísima. The original site in Lompoc will be referred to as the *Mision Vieja*, or Old Mission, which is the term locally applied and appears on existing land maps.

[2] Before any organized plan of procedure was adopted, the mound covering Structure Number 9 was removed and the fountain partially excavated.

[3] These field books are on file at the La Purísima field office. They will hereafter be abbreviated as F.B.

[4] F. B. No. 1, p. 13.

[5] Harry Steinberger, *Catalogue of Historical and Ethnological Objects, La Purísima Mission.*

[6] [Frederick C.] Hageman, *Review of Data as Basis for Restoration of Church and Cemetery,* p. 2.

[7] Payeras, *Informe anual,* December 31, 1816, Santa Barbara Mission Archives (hereafter cited SBMA).

[8] F. B. No. 3, p. 23.

[9] *Archeological Report,* January, 1937, La Purisima Camp, p. 2.

[10] F. B. No. 5, p. 3.

[11] F. B. No. 3, p. 34.

[12] *Ibid.*, pp. 30-31.

[13] F. B. No. 4, p. 1.

[14] *Ibid.*, p. 2.

[15] F. B. No. 7, p. 3.

[16] *Ibid.*, p. 16.

[17] *Ibid.*

[18] *Ibid.*, pp. 1-2, 4-6.

[19] F. B. No. 4, pp. 7, 12.

[20] F. B. No. 7, p. 47.

[21] Ewing, *Mission La Purísima Concepción*, p. 252, note 7.

[22] Payeras, *Informe anual,* January 1, 1816, SBMA; Ewing, *Mission La Purísima Concepción,* p. 252, note 7, *Archeological Reconnaissance Report,* February to May 31, 1937.

[23] Zephyrin Engelhardt *Mission La Purísima de María Santísima* (Santa Barbara, 1932), p. 35.

[24] Payeras, *Informe anual,* December 31, 1836, SBMA.

[25] Engelhardt, *La Purísima,* pp. 57-58.

[26] Jesse D. Mason, *History of Santa Barbara County . . .* (Oakland, 1883), p. 30.

[27] Payeras, *Informe anual,* December 31, 1812, SBMA.

[28] See Appendix B, p. 202, Advisory Committee to State Park Commission, March 27, 1935.

Chapter 2. *An Historical Collection of Photographs, etc.*

There are no notes to this chapter.

Chapter 3. *The Mission Residence.*

[1] Payeras, *Informe anual*, January 1, 1816, SBMA.

[2] Maynard Geiger, *The Franciscan Conquest of Florida* (Washington, D.C., 1937), pp. 17-18.

[3] *Ibid.,* p. 16.

[4] *Ibid.,* p. 15.

[5] *Ibid.,* p. 18.

[6] The inventory of February 18, 1835, lists "Main Building with 21 rooms." Engelhardt, *La Purísima,* p. 57.

[7] *Corredor*: a covered walk, either on the front, or in the enclosed *patio* of Spanish houses, affording shelter from rain, sun and wind. We have no precise English term for this word, consequently the word *corredor* will be used throughout this discussion.

[8] Engelhardt, *La Purísima,* p. 31.

[9] Helen Hunt Jackson, *Glimpses of California and the Missions* (Boston, 1903), pp. 93-94.

[10] Mason, *History of Santa Barbara,* p. 31.

[11] George Wharton James, *In and Out of the Old Missions* (Boston, 1911), pp. 207-208.

[12] Rexford Newcomb, *The Old Mission Churches and Historic Houses of California . . .* (Philadelphia, 1925), pp. 237-238.

[13] Letter from Rev. Maynard Geiger, O.F.M., April 5, 1938, National Park Service File.

[14] Payeras, *Informe anual*, December 31, 1817, SBMA.

[15] Engelhardt, *La Purísima,* p. 44.

[16] Mason, *History of Santa Barbara,* p. 30.

[17] Engelhardt, *La Purísima,* p. 51.

[18] *Ibid.,* p. 52.

[19] *Ibid.,* p. 58.

[20] Engelhardt, *La Purísima,* pp. 84-86.

[21] Henry C. Ford, *Etchings of the Franciscan Missions . . .* (New York, 1883),

[22] Measurements of the altar wall of the Church proper showed a central, semi-circular niche, and portions of the smaller niche on one side, which meets the condition here stated.

[23] *Sacrarium*: "A receptacle in the sanctuary, or sometimes in the sacristy, into which is poured the water used in liturgical ablutions." [Information supplied by] Rev. Fr. Wand, pastor of Old Mission San Miguel.

[24] [Information supplied by] Emmet O'Neil.

[25] Mrs. Virginia Tilley (nee Hill), who lived in the building for several years after 1872, said in an interview, February 1, 1935, that she believed Ramon Malo built this partition and oven.

[26] The plaster extended into the corners, but "keys" for bonding the adobe brick of the fireplace occurred every four or five courses. The location of these "keys" was informative as the width of the former breast, and indicated that the breast extended the full height of the room.

[27] For example, the end room of the Residence of San Fernando, which was finely decorated and fitted with book cases, was, according to legend, reserved for visiting dignitaries.

[28] San Juan Capistrano, for example.

[29] The inventory of February 18, 1835, lists 139 volumes in the library valued at $655.75. Engelhardt, *La Purísima,* p. 57.

[30] According to Mrs. Teresa Malo de Janssens, daughter of Ramon Malo, born in the building in 1855 and residing there until 1864, at the time the main room was used as a general store, and the north rooms served the Mayordomo of the ranch and his family. The small room, number 13, was reserved for visiting padres, and one of the small rooms on the west side was occupied by the cook.

[31] Newcomb, *The Old Mission Churches and Historic Houses of California,* pp. 100, 103.

[32] The Church of San Juan Bautista was the only aisled Church in Spanish Alta California.

[33] Zephyrin Engelhardt, *Santa Barbara Mission* (San Francisco, 1923), pp. 63-64.

Notes

[34] Cloister: a private enclosure for monks or religious, a place for retirement, usually in architectural terminology, the arcaded porches in the quadrangle of a monastery or abbey.

[35] Study of Figures 112 and 115 shows that excessive deflection and eventual failure occurred in many of these rafters.

Chapter 4. *Original Materials and Methods of Construction.*

[1] J. V. Lewis, "Report on Structural Stone," La Purísima, April 28, 1938. See Appendix A, p. 181.

[2] "The new site was 5 quarter leagues from the old one. It was near enough to permit the use of old buildings for materials. Timber, stone, lime, etc., are even nearer than before." Bancroft Library copy of SBMA 6: 168-178, A.D. 1813.

[3] F.B. No. 2.

[4] J. D. Long, "Adobe Construction," University of California, Agricultural Experiment Station, *Bulletin* 472.

[5] *Ibid.*, p. 10.

[6] See Appendix A, National Bureau of Standards, "Tests of Adobe Brick," p. 182.

[7] Much valuable information concerning plant content of adobe bricks has been made available through researches of Professor George W. Hendry, University of California. His classification of refuses is divided into the following five general types: 1) crop residues; 2) manure from corrals; 3) pure weed mixtures; 4) grain field and other crop stubbles; 5) miscellaneous refuse accommodations, including kitchen garbage, yard and shop sweepings, etc. *An Approach to Southwestern Agricultural History Through Adobe Brick Analysis*, reprinted from the *University of New Mexico Bulletin*, October 15, 1936.

[8] The method of centering used is not known. According to Mr. Edward Borein, whose etchings of early California and Mexican life are well known, the Mexican workmen in Mexico today still cling to an old method which may have been used here. This method consists of filling the opening with loose adobe brick, then rounding off the top with a hatchet to the curvature desired. The arch is then built, and the centering can be quickly removed.

[9] Figures 102 and 103 furnish good pictures of the character of the old floor in the chapel (about 1880). Fragments of the planking and sleepers were recovered in the excavation.

[10] See Archeological Field Plans, Numbers 1 and 2, on file La Purisima camp.

[11] In the area north of the Church, adobe paving occurred in a double layer, with layers showing considerable wear. It was obvious that the area had been repaved over the worn surface of original bricks.

[12] Thin layers of this material were found in debris slightly above floor lines elsewhere during the excavation, suggesting that it may have been laid over the ceiling boards as a floor for the loft.

[13] See Archeological Field Plans, Numbers 1 and 2, La Purisima camp.

[14] Old cuttings of timber on Mission Pine (San Rafael Mt., U.S. Forest map) were reported as long ago as 1860 by Mr. Alfred Davis (Santa Barbara). Mr. Davis' grandfather was an early settler in this forest. Mr. Nash-Boulden, forest supervisor, U.S. Forest Service, states that nearly all stands of conifers in the above region were cut at various times, however.

[15] See Appendix A, p. 188, for report on "Identification of Wood Specimens From La Purisima Mission."

[16] Newcomb, *The Old Mission Churches and Historic Houses of California*, p. 76.

[17] Describing Mission Santa Barbara, one writer stated: "There is no native wood suitable for building close to Santa Barbara. Since it would be too costly and troublesome to bring down wood from the mountains seven or eight leagues away, timber is shipped via Monterey from the sawmills of Mission Santa Cruz." Eugene Duflot de Mofras, *Exploration de Territorie de l'Oregon, des Californias* . . . (2 vols., Paris, 1844), I, 196.

[18] An example of an early whipsaw was recovered in the excavation. See [Steinberger], *Catalogue of Historical and Ethnological Objects*, National Park Service file.

[19] An original timber was found in a shack built on the property west of the Church ruin by later owners. This timber was obviously taken from the mission, and measured five by six inches, a size which suggests that it was an original rafter.

[20] A. S. Hitchcock, *Manual of the Grasses of the United States* (Washington, D.C., 1935). An excellent example of an original ceiling of this material is still in place in the sacristy of the Mission San Luis Obispo.

[21] F.B. No. 2.

[22] The Historic American Building Survey, whose measured drawings form an invaluable collection, are obtainable through the Library of Congress.

[23] See items 1193-1210 in [Steinberger], *Catalogue of Historical and Ethnological Objects.*

[24] Published in Jackson, *Glimpses of California and the Missions*, [p. 74].

[25] A print furnished by Mr. Joseph R. Knowland from his files of the Landmarks Club.

[26] See measured details, F.B. No. 2, for window openings in chapel.

[27] See Appendix A, pp. 190-192, for reports on analysis and tests of plaster samples.

[28] Sometimes the use of pebbles inserted into the fresh mud mortar joints served a similar purpose. Example: San Antonio de Padua.

[29] The method employed by expert Mexican plasterers was described to the writer by Mr. Dave Couts, owner of the historic *Rancho Guajome,* San Diego County. Mr. Couts, desiring to re-plaster certain portions of the house, imported a crew of plasterers from Mexico. He watched the process, and described the method as follows:

The crew was composed of three men; one was the "boss," who directed operations. After the mortar mixture was made up (of about 3 or 4 to 1 mix) two men proceeded with its application to the wall. The master-plasterer had previously made up his special mixture of lime, some sand and the juice of cactus. As soon as sufficient area had been covered by the rough plasterers, the special finishing coat was rapidly applied by the "boss" while the preceeding coat was "green" and fresh. This was carefully trowelled down to a very smooth finish. Corners and edges were run with care.

[30] Later experiments in duplicating the original finish showed that modern plasterer's trowels would not serve the purpose, whereas these stones produced the appearance satisfactorily. The secret lay in the shape and rounded edges.

[31] Lime was a fairly valuable commodity, for, "Lime [was sold] at one real or 12½ cents a peck." Engelhardt, *La Purísima*, p. 30.

[32] See Appendix A, p. 192, for report on "Tests of Outside Mortar."

[33] Diatomite: a chalk-like accumulation of amorphous silica produced by microscopic marine plants known as diatoms.

[34] See Appendix A, p. 193, for report on pink colored plaster.

[35] See Appendix A, p. 196, for report on "Tests of Inside Plaster Color Materials."

[36] See Appendix A, p. 195, for "Tests of Outside Plaster."

[37] Mr. Irving Furlong, chemist, National Bureau of Standards Laboratories, pointed out that lime plus fat plus an acidulated juice such as fermented cactus juice would react to produce calcium stearate, which is the basis of numerous water proofing agents on the market today. However, no stearates could be identified in the samples tested, so while the combination, strangely, is chemically a good one for water proofing purposes, it is probable that the cactus juice was relied on to make the paint stickier and more resilient and the tallow to make it more water resistant.

[38] These designs, from fragments found in the excavation of the Church, were in such fragmentary form that a restoration of the complete design has not been possible. An attempt will be made to restore the complete design by the WPA unit known as the American Index of Design.

[39] See Field Plan No. 1.

[40] See Appendix A, p. 196, for report on inside plaster color materials.

[41] Research work on paint and pigment materials in this locality by the American Index of Design. A short paper on the subject is reproduced in Appendix C, pp. 216-218.

[42] See Appendix C, pp. 218, 219, for letter of Mrs. Mary E. Foxen.

[43] The [Steinberger], *Catalogue of Historical and Ethnological Objects, La Purísima Mission,* lists 792 items to date, of which 433 are classified as metallic.

[44] The collection of James Holloway, former owner of the La Purisima Rancho, contains 72 items; it is kept on loan to the Lompoc High School.

Notes

⁴⁵ Wooden bars were also evidently used across doors for additional protection. Sockets occurred in the interior reveals of the entrance to the *sala,* and one shutter opening which had no protective grille. These sockets were about 4 to 5 inches square.

⁴⁶ Identical examples of these bosses are to be found at Mission Santa Inés and San Gabriel.

Chapter 5. *Restoration.*

¹ See Appendix B, p. 197, for report of L. D. Tilton, "Meeting at La Purisima Concepcion Mission," August 8, 1934.

² See Appendix B, p. 201.

³ Room number 5 was chosen for educational purposes in this respect. In this room the visitor may see original work and the structural scheme of the restoration well explained.

⁴ See Appendix C, p. 222, for details of "Fires in the Mission."

⁵ In an interview, Mrs. Janssens, born in the Residence, 1855, described the wooden *rejas* on the windows, stating that they resembled the one found in the excavation.

⁶ Engelhardt, *La Purísima,* p. 44.

⁷ *The Masterkey* (January, 1938), p. 6.

⁸ See Appendix A, p. 194, for letter of J. D. Long; also p. 191, for report on plaster samples.

⁹ *Informe anual,* 1817, SBMA.

Appendices

¹ More detailed information: Letters, photographs, press clippings, records, etc., are to be found in the scrap books and official records of the Landmarks Club, which are preserved by the Southwest Museum, Highland Park, Los Angeles, Calif.

² Other residents state that this fire occurred in the seventies.

³ Mason, *History of Santa Barbara County . . . ,* p. 31.

⁴ M. T. Walsh, *The Mission Bells of California* (San Francisco, 1934), *passim.*

⁵ Mason, *History of Santa Barbara County . . . ,* p. 31.

BIBLIOGRAPHY

Printed Works

Benton, A. B., *The California Mission and Its Influence upon Pacific Coast Architecture.* (?)

Bolton, Herbert Eugene, "The Mission as a Frontier Institution in the Spanish-American Colonies," *American Historical Review,* XXIII (October 1917), 42-61.

Brewer, William Henry, *Up and Down California in 1860-1864. The Journal of William Henry Brewer* . . . edited by Francis P. Farquhar. New Haven, [1931].

Chase, J. S., *California Coast Trails from Mexico to Oregon.* New York, 1913.

Duflot de Mofras, Eugene, *Exploration du territoire de L'Oregon, des Californies et de la Mer Vermeille, exécutée pendant les années 1840, 1841 et 1842.* 2 vols. and Atlas. Paris, 1844.

Engelhardt, Zephryin, *Mission La Concepción Purísima de María Santísima.* Santa Barbara, 1932.

Engelhardt, Z., *Mission San Fernando Rey.* Chicago, 1927.

Engelhardt, Z., *Santa Barbara Mission.* San Francisco, 1923.

Ford, Henry Chapman, *Etchings of the Franciscan Missions. With the Outlines of the History, Descriptions, etc.* New York, 1883.

Geiger, Maynard, *The Franciscan Conquest of Florida (1573-1618).* Washington, D. C., 1937.

Hendry, George, "An Approach to Southwestern Agricultural History Through Adobe Brick Analysis." Reprint from University of New Mexico *Bulletin,* Oct. 15, 1936.

Hitchcock, A. S., *Manual of the Grasses of the United States.* Washington, 1935.

Jackson, Helen Hunt, *Glimpses of California and the Missions.* Boston, 1903.

James, George Wharton, *In and Out of the Old Missions of California.* Boston, 1911.

Long. J. D., *Adobe Construction.* University of California Agricultural Experiment Station, *Bulletin,* 472.

Mason, Jesse D., *A History of Santa Barbara [and Ventura Counties].* Oakland, 1883.

Newcomb, Rexford, *The Old Mission Churches and Historic Houses of California; Their History, Architecture, Art and Lore.* Philadelphia, 1925.

Robinson, Alfred G., *Life in California Before the Conquest.* San Francisco, 1891.

Simpson, Sir George, *Narrative of a Journey Around the World . . . 1841 and 1842.* 2 vols. London, 1847.

Smith, Frances Norris (Rand), *The Architectural History of Mission San Carlos Borromeo, California.* California Historical Survey Commission, Berkeley, 1921.

Storke, Yda (Addis), *A Memorial and Biographical History of the Counties of Santa Barbara, San Luis Obispo and Ventura, California.* Chicago, 1891.

Vischer, Edward, *Missions of Upper California. Notes on the California Missions.* San Francisco, 1872.

Walsh, Marie T., *The Mission Bells of California.* San Francisco, 1934.

Walsh, Marie T., *The Mission of the Passes, Santa Ines.* Los Angeles, 1930.

Periodical and Newspaper Articles

Harrington, Mark Raymond, "The Right Kind of Restoration." *The Masterkey.* Jan. 1938, Southwest Museum, Los Angeles.

"Saving a landmark: A report on the activities of the Landmarks Club." *Outwest*, XXXI (Aug. 1909).

"Report of the Landmarks Club, Recording Acceptance of a Deed by the Union Oil Co. to the La Purisima Ruins." *Outwest*, XXIII (Sept. 1905).

Sacramento Union, Aug. 5, 1865. California State Library, Sacramento, California.

San Francisco Daily Chronicle, Sept. 10, Sept. 11, 1903. California State Library, Sacramento, California.

Manuscript Material

Archeological reports, La Purisima Camp, Feb. 1936 to March 1938. National Park Service Regional Office, San Francisco, California.

Ewing, R. C., *Mission La Purisima Concepcion.* Manuscript report, Aug. 25, 1937, National Park Service Regional Office files, San Francisco, California.

Field Books numbered 1, 2, 3, 4, 5, 6, 7, 16, and 34. Paper covered field books on file at National Park Service Office, La Purisima Camp, SP-29, Lompoc, California.

Hageman, F. C., *Review of the Data Used as a Basis for the Restoration of the Church and Cemetery, La Purisima Mission.* Manuscript report to National Park Service Regional Office, San Francisco, California.

Informes anuales and Special Reports. Microfilm copies of yearly and biennial reports from the Fathers of Mission La Purísima Concepcion, for the years 1797 to 1832, inclusive were made from the originals in the Mission Santa Barbara Archives for the National Park Service Regional Office, San Francisco, California.

Miscellaneous

Landmarks Club Records, at the Southwest Museum in Los Angeles include correspondence, clippings, photographs, and photographic files.

Lemmon, W. C., *Pigments Used in Wall Paintings in the Early Missions of California.* Manuscript report, American Index of Design, Los Angeles, California.

Mission La Purísima records including:
1st and 2nd Books of Baptism, (*Libros de Bautismos*), April 9, 1788 to March, 1834

1st and 2nd Books of Death records, (*Libros de Entierros*), Feb. 14, 1789 to Sept. 15, 1851.

1st Book of Confirmation, (*Libro de Confirmaciones*).

1st Book of Marriage, (*Libro de Casamientos*), May 10, 1788 to 1851.

Account Book, Mission La Purísima.

Libro de Gobierno (accounts) 1824.

Padrones (or census books) 13, 14, and 15.

Padron, for year 1822.

Padron, for year 1836.

Padron, dated January, 1814.

Microfilm copies of the above records were made from the originals in the Archives of Santa Inés Mission.

Ruth, C., *Research Among the Ancient Chumash Village Sites of Northwestern Santa Barbara County.* Typewritten Manuscript. University of Southern California.

Ruth, C., *Research of Sudden Site No. 2.* Typewritten Manuscript. University of Southern California.

Steinberger, H., *Catalogue of Historical and Ethnological objects, La Purisima Mission,* manuscript report. National Park Service Regional Office, San Francisco, California.

Tilton, L. D., *Meeting at Mission La Concepcion Purisima,* Aug. 8, 1934 to Aug. 9, 1934. Santa Barbara County Planning Commission, Santa Barbara, California.

Historic American Survey. Measured drawings of the California Missions, Library of Congress, Washington, D.C.

Ford Sketches, from California State Historical Society, Los Angeles, California.

Figure 281. Panorama: Garden and monastery in foreground.

PART TWO

MISSION LA PURISIMA CONCEPCION, CALIFORNIA
By Russell C. Ewing

PREFACE

This monograph was prepared principally with a view toward assisting those charged with the development of a museum at La Purísima mission. The significant phases of the mission's history are narrated in six chapters, each of which should be given a prominent place in a museum of history at the mission site. The interpretation and organization differ from Engelhardt's *Concepción Purísima*. Much of the purely controversial matter has been omitted, and some information has been added. I have made generous use of the Franciscan's translations except where errors have been found or where I question his interpretation.

My researches have perforce been confined to local repositories of mission documents. No provision was made for an examination of pertinent materials in the invaluable Mexican archives. This must be done before any claim can be made to a definitive study of the mission. The present study is based on the materials in the Bancroft Library, the Santa Barbara Mission Archives, the California State Library, and the Mission Santa Inés Library. The sources therein were handled critically, and all facts have been checked in accordance with the accepted standards of scholarship. So-called legends of recent fabrication have found no place in this work. A reasonable amount of archaeological evidence has been used, and a select group of photographs has been appended to clarify the narrative. The absence of references to the Archbishop's and Bishop's Archives, located respectively at San Francisco and Fresno, was not an oversight on the part of the writer. Copies and abstracts of these materials dealing with the missionary history of La Purísima are to be found in the Bancroft Library. These I have made full use of. The Southwest Museum, Los Angeles, has many valuable historical Purísima photographs. There, too, is to be found correspondence on matters of a general nature relative to the mission. There are other collections of a similar nature to be found elsewhere. But since none of these has a direct bearing on the missionary history, I have not made use of them in this study. They more appropriately belong to the archaeological and architectural story, and they no doubt will be used by the architect in his final report.

A few editorial mistakes will be noted. Time has not permitted their correction, nor does their appearance detract from the accuracy of the textual information.

Russell C. Ewing,
Associate Historian, N.P.S.
August 25, 1937.

CHAPTER 1

FOUNDING

Some twenty-five miles north of famous Point Conception lies a small but beautiful valley. Hemmed in on three sides by rolling hills, a few of which reach mountainous stature, its fourth opens to the west and the Pacific. Close to the northern edge of the valley winds the Santa Ynez River, a small stream flowing lazily into the western sea. Refreshing, fog-laden winds blow up the valley during the summer months, and in winter torrential rains pour down upon fertile fields which are known the world over for their beautiful flowers and unsurpassed legumes.

This valley, the Lompoc — an Indian word of conjectural meaning — first became known to the white man shortly after the arrival in Upper California of Don Gaspar de Portolá and Father Junípero Serra. When Portolá and a handful of men made their historic journey from San Diego to Monterey in July-September, 1769, they camped on August 30th at the mouth of the Santa Ynez. To this stream they gave the names San Bernardo and Santa Rosa.[1] The Indians of the region, a small band of the relatively high-cultured Chumash, were much impressed with their visitors. They were decidedly hospitable, and made every effort to persuade one of the two priests who accompanied Portolá to remain with them.[2] The Spaniards, of course, declined.

For eight years thereafter the Spaniards gave little thought to the country of the Santa Rosa and its friendly natives. Then in the spring of 1777, when Father Serra proposed the building of three missions on the Santa Barbara Channel, "in order to make communications more safe between the southern and northern missions," attention was directed toward the Point Conception region. Serra made his wishes known to Governor Felipe de Neve, who approved of the plan, and recommendations to this end were sent to the viceroy by the frigate *Santiago*, which sailed for Mexico on June 9.[3]

The recommendations which Neve sent, dated June 3, 1777, were embodied in one of the important documents of early California history.[4] He pointed out that the Indians of the Santa Barbara Channel were in a peculiarly strong position to cut off communication between the northern and southern settlements. Besides the fact that the Channel Indians were somewhat more warlike than other California natives, they occupied a strategic position on the principal north-south highway. They should therefore be controlled. This meant that missions and a presidio must be established among them. Neve's plan called for a mission of San Buenaventura at Asunción at the southern extremity of the channel, a presidio and mission at Santa Barbara, and a third mission of La Purísima Concepción near Point Conception.

Two years passed, and no word came from Mexico authorizing the founding of the missions and the presidio. But Neve had not lost interest in the project. His famous *Reglamento* of June 1, 1779, again stressed the necessity of the establishment of the three missions.[5] As a part of his scheme for the military government of California, with which the *Reglamento* was concerned, there were to be a sergeant and fourteen men temporarily stationed at San Buenaventura and Purísima. At each of the missions already established, there were to be only one corporal and five men. Neve doubtless felt the need of extra forces among a people less amenable to European ways.

The Mexican authorities now began to take a serious interest in the proposal for the Channel missions. But, although both ecclesiastical and civil functionaries were eager to see the missions founded, further delay was occasioned by wranglings over supplies.[6] It was all very well for the viceroy to urge the founding of the missions, said Father Francisco Pangua, Guardian of the College of San Fernando, Mexico, but there could be no new missions unless the government provided the customary supplies. The government pleaded lack of funds. Very well, there could be no new missions, for implements and goods " 'are, as we have said, the bait and means for spiritual fishing.' " Why not release $1,000 from the Pious Fund? It had been created in 1697 for this very purpose, the founding of missions in California. This could not be denied, and the money was to be had early in 1781.[7]

But even the authorization of supplies did not move things along as rapidly as might have been expected. Father Engelhardt charges Neve with the delay.[8] The charge is doubtless true, in part, but the criticism is not quite fair in light of Neve's tremendous responsibilities. Civil and military matters justly received as much attention as religious affairs. Furthermore, Neve's disapproval of the missionaries' monopoly of Indian labor naturally displeased the Franciscans.

In 1785 definite steps were finally taken for founding Purísmia. On June 2, Pedro Fages, now governor, wrote Commandant General José Antonio Rengel suggesting that the mission be established on the Santa Rosa River (Santa Ynez), because "wood and pasturage were abundant, and the place . . . easy to irrigate from the same river."[9]

Rengel, residing at Chihuahua, was impressed with Fages's recommendation, and on March 24, 1786, advised the governor to select the site in accordance with the letter of June 2.[10] The commandant general was, however, somewhat confused as to the precise location referred to in Fages's communication, believing that Gaviota was the proposed site. This may have been the reason Rengel instructed Fages to make another survey in the same region. In conclusion, Rengel says that as soon as the site is agreed on, he will request that the $1,000 be sent for the mission.

Apparently the second survey was never made, and upon the receipt of Rengel's letter, Fages forwarded it to Father Fermín Lasuén, Serra's successor to the presidency of the California missions.[11] " 'I forward this to Your Reverence for your information,' " he writes, " 'and in order that I might be able to report the survey of the Río de Santa Rosa (Santa Ynez) which is the locality, not that of Gaviota, which by mistake is named in the foregoing order. The Mission may then be established in the coming spring and Your Reverence, if it pleases you, may accompany me so that the site, where the Mission should be located, may be chosen, entirely in accord with Your Reverence's pleasure'".[12] Lasuén was indeed pleased, saying "'I shall at the first notification comply punctually with Your Honor's wishes in this particular.'"[13]

Although it was Fages's intention to found Purísima in the spring of 1787, December 8 was appropriately chosen for the dedication, for this was the feast day of the Immaculate Conception.[14] On that day, at a site known to the Indians as Algsacupi, close to the base of the eastern hills of the Lompoc Valley, Lasuén performed the customary religious rites in the presence of Fages and presumably a small group of whites and Indians. Of that occasion Lasuén writes: "'On this day I, the undersigned *Presidente* of these missions, blessed water and with it the place and a large Cross, which we venerated and planted. I immediately celebrated the first holy Mass and preached, and we recited the Litany of All Saints. On the following day, Sunday, I said holy Mass, and in company with the governor I retired to Santa Barbara until the waters should subside.'"[15]

In April of the following year Lasuén returned to Algsacupi with goods necessary for the founding, and with Fathers Vicente Fuster and Francisco José de Arroíta, both of whom had been assigned to Purísima.[16]

Lasuén and his two religious companions found that Fages had not forgotten his part in making the new establishment a success. In March Fages had sent a squad of soldiers and several servants to the site under the command of Sergeant Pablo Antonio Cota. They were to bear in mind that the founding was for the purpose of christianizing the Indians. They were to exercise the greatest caution in their dealings with the natives, who were to be assured of good treatment. The new wards were not to be provided with arms, and the soldiers were always to be prepared to meet hostilities. Soldiers and servants were forbidden to visit the *rancherías,* unless under orders from their superiors. Severe punishment would be meted out for infractions of this order. The soldier or servant who struck an Indian was to be placed in prison, and the details of the case were to be made known to the governor. As a rule, and where possible, punishment of the Indians was to be avoided. Three to five men were to watch the horse herds. If any Indian complained that the horses were destroying his crops, the horses were to be removed. The sergeant was to make his troops understand that they were to assist in building the church, the fathers' residence, the guard house, warehouses and houses for their families. Two or three soldiers were to accompany the missionaries on their trips to the *rancherías,* and the sergeant was to maintain strict discipline and explore the best and shortest route to the Laguna Larga. Such were the instructions the sergeant was compelled to obey at Purísima.[17]

Mission Purísima had at last become a reality. Conceived during the administration of Neve and Serra, it took ten years of constant effort before it was actually established under the leadership of Fages and Lasuén. It was the eleventh of the final twenty-one California missions to be founded.

Figure 282. Panorama: church ruins in center foreground; restored monastery in background.

CHAPTER 2

PROMISING BEGINNINGS

The early years of a mission were the difficult years. Among a people of radically different culture, often obtuse and hostile, the missionary and soldier necessarily worked with great energy and much ingenuity. The native had to be converted from his wild, heathen state to civilized Christianity. He must learn a new standard of morals. He must pay allegiance to a government whose organization was too complicated and theoretical for him to understand. He was asked to accept the white man's agrarian and industrial economy. In fine, he must adopt new religious, economic, political and social philosophies.

Fathers Arroíta and Fuster, together with their military aids, faced their task with consummate ability and great zeal. Arroíta had been at his post only a short while, when he hurried off to a nearby *ranchería* to baptize a twenty-two year old convert *in articulo mortis.*[1] A month later six adults and two children were baptized in the Mission church, two of the adults being blessed in marriage by Father Fuster. This was an encouraging beginning, and other baptisms rapidly followed. Cota, writing on August 24, 1788, four months after the arrival of the friars, says that there were seventy-nine Christians at the mission.[2] Some of these no doubt were soldiers and their families, but the majority must have been Indians. At the close of the year there were ninety-five baptisms and twenty-five marriages registered in the mission books.

All that we know about building operations during the early years comes by way of conjecture. A church is mentioned, and we may reasonably infer that workshops, storehouses, and quarters for the missionaries, soldiers and Indians were erected. In accordance with customary procedure, the first buildings were probably crude, palisaded structures, which were later replaced with adobe, stone and brick buildings.

The mission soldiers had carried out their share in putting up the buildings and in abiding by Fages's orders. Cota made surveys for good highways, and apparently located the principal road which connected Purísima with the northern and southern missions.[3] He was also interested in encouraging families to settle at the new site. He states that in August, 1788, there were five families at the mission and that he had sent for two more. It is not clear, however, whether these were Indian or Spanish families. In September Cota was replaced by José M. Ortega, and by the close of the year there were fifteen soldiers at the mission, all of course detached from the Santa Barbara presidio.[4]

We know very little about the affairs of Purísima during the succeeding five years. Father Arroíta spent some time at San Luis Obispo, where he had been before his assignment to Purísima, and on several occasions he visited the mission at Santa Barbara.[5] Father Fuster was relieved of his post in the summer of 1789, to be replaced by Father Cristóbal Oramas, then serving at Santa Barbara.[6] Oramas had come to California in 1786 with Arroíta, and to him goes the distinction of having been one of the founders of the Santa Barbara mission. He was at Purísima for three years and he did his work well. In November, 1792, he retired to San Gabriel Mission, and about a year later he was forced to return to the College of San Fernando because of ill health.

It is from the pen of Oramas that we learn of an interesting and rare practice among the California missionaries. Oramas records that, upon learning of illness in the *rancherías* of Estayt and Sisolop, Casimiro, an Indian interpreter, was delegated to reach these people and administer baptism to them. Casimiro later reported that he fulfilled Oramas's instructions by baptizing three persons, all near death.[7]

Lasuén, always diligent in his position as president, made three visits to Purísima during this period; first in December of 1790, and then in June and October of the following year. It was early in the morning of December 8, the feast of the titular saint when he arrived in 1790, just three years after the founding. He inspected the mission books, and officiated at the baptism and confirmation of an Indian girl. On the following day he said mass, and instructed a group of neophytes and whites on the sacrament of confirmation. He told them that usually the bishop was the only one permitted to administer the sacrament, but that since there was no bishop in California the pope had empowered him to administer it. He concluded his remarks by saying that confirmation could only be received once. Lasuén then proceeded to administer the sacrament with the assistance of Fathers Arroíta and Oramas, the resident missionaries, and Father José Calzada of San Gabriel. By December 12, Lasuén had confirmed more than two hundred persons, some of whom were the soldiers and their families.[8] In June and October, 1791, he returned, administering confirmation to seventy-eight persons on the first occasion, and two hundred and fifteen received the sacrament on the second visit.

Spiritual successes, however, did not hold the missionary's attention to the exclusion of all other matters. Material gains were quite as important as saving souls. No mission could exist for long without decent living quarters, storehouses, an abundance of water, and an adequate supply of food. In these respects, Purísima did well. At the close of 1794 the fathers were able to report that during the year new and substantial quarters had been erected for the soldiers.[9] This building measured about thirty-eight feet long and seventeen feet wide. A warehouse was constructed of unknown dimensions, and two small rooms were built, one for the officials, and the other for pack animal outfits. Mention is also made of the addition of a brick corridor to the main building, which perhaps was the monastery. All these buildings were of adobe and tile. During the following year, 1795, a vaulted granary seven *varas* long was built, and joined to it was another structure of the same length. Each had tile roofs. The church was in bad condition and materials were gathered for a new one; but there is no record as to whether another was ever built. For the year 1796 we learn that "three capacious apartments were constructed for keeping implements and other things, and various structures were repaired or renovated."[10]

The crops grown at Purísima were much the same as those of the other missions of the period. Wheat, corn, and beans were the principal agricultural products. The productiveness of the fields was always of grave concern to the friars. Bumper crops meant plentiful food for the neophytes and soldiers. Lean years caused discontent among the mission's wards, and the Indian was not reluctant to complain to the authorities when his rations were curtailed. And Purísima had its good and bad years. In 1799 the missionaries reported the largest harvest recorded for the mission — 4,000 bushels of grain, most of which was wheat.[11] The smallest on record was for the year 1795, when only 1,200 bushels were harvested. The yield of a little over 2,000 bushels in 1800 was about the average for Purísima.[12]

A mission's material wealth also depended on its livestock. In this respect Purísima fared exceptionally well during the first few years. Nearly 6,000 head were reported for the year 1799. Cattle, horses, sheep and hogs were raised, and by 1800 there were 4,000 head of sheep alone.[13] Purísima was early famous for its fine stock, especially its cattle and sheep.

With an abundance of wool and a large supply of hides, Purísima was in an excellent position for the manufacture of cloths, blankets and leather goods. The Indians were instructed in these arts, usually by an experienced master weaver. In 1797, Antonio Enríquez was hired by the mission at the rate of twelve *reales* a day to teach the natives weaving.[14] Blankets were made from the wool, and if cotton were to be had, cloths of indifferent grades were made. Shoes also were among some of the principal leather articles turned out by the Purísima Indians,[15] and, although the documents are silent on this score, it may be inferred that saddles, beds and similar products were produced from the hides.

Skilled artisans were not only employed to teach the Indian handicrafts, but also to instruct him in building crafts. Engelhardt has few words of praise for the benefits the missions received from the skilled craftsmen.[16] No doubt these men often demanded exhorbitant wages, and at times exercised undue influence on the Indians, but they were nevertheless needed. In 1798, when plans were made for a new church at Purísima, the missionaries requested the assistance of able artisans. The fathers were afraid to attempt the job, fearing that the church might not be stable enough.[17]

Economic systems function only when there is a medium of exchange. Frontiers seldom have sufficient specie to serve the need, and consequently other media must be used. During the early California mission period, tobacco and soap were accepted for this purpose. "Let it be well understood that the money which circulates among the troops of Santa Barbara presidio is in the shape of soap and cigars. The same must be said of that of Monterey. Thus the soldier Agustín Marquéz in order to pay for some cavalry outfit, which he secured at this Mission (La Purísima), he had recourse to the comandante of Monterey, and what he gave him was $6.00 worth of cigars, with this he paid for the weapons' ".[18]

Thus, the missions were important economic institutions. They were not only self-supporting, but they were even asked to furnish the soldiers with supplies. The military was required to pay fair prices for goods received, but the missions often had just complaints to make against the inability or refusal of the army to meet their obligations. The presidio of Santa Barbara early became indebted to Purísima. In 1797 the garrison owed the mission more than four hundred dollars.[19] Surpluses were given to newly founded missions. In 1791 Soledad and Santa Cruz received goods from Purísima, and in 1797 goods were sent to San Miguel.[20]

By the opening of the nineteenth century Purísima could boast of several substantial buildings. In 1797 the temporary dwellings of the fathers were replaced by more suitable quarters.[21] In 1798 a guard house, doubtless replacing the earlier one, was built; and during the same year another storehouse and nine houses for the Indians were added. All were of adobe and roofed with tile.[22] In 1802 the garden, about two hundred yards square was enclosed with an adobe wall.[23] In 1798 the foundations were laid for a new church, and by February, 1803, it was completed.[24] Finally, in 1800 a large building one hundred and ninety feet long and nineteen feet wide containing eight rooms was built.

Although the missionaries were able to report that spiritual and material progress was encouraging, there were times when things looked dark. In September, 1794, some twenty neophytes of Purísima and San Luis Obispo, together with a band of gentiles, were arrested for inciting revolt at San Luis Obispo.[25] Five of the agitators were condemned to presidio work. Then the friars complained of a lack of sufficient church equipment to perform the necessary religious functions with the " 'decorum commanded by our holy Mother Church' ".[26] As if this were not enough to try the patience of the fathers, they were suddenly called upon to defend themselves against charges made by one of their own companions.

All California was shocked in 1800 when demented Father Horra of San Miguel accused the Franciscans of mistreating the Indians.[27] These charges reached the viceroy, who at once directed Governor Borica to investigate. The governor complied by requesting the commanders of the four presidios to answer fifteen questions bearing on the subject. Comandante Felipe de Goycoecha of Santa Barbara reported that the Purísima fathers were guilty of mistreating the Indians. The friars shortly thereafter were requested to explain their version of the controversy. After studying both the reports of the army and the missionaries, the viceroy felt that the charges were unfounded, and he thereupon exonerated the Franciscans.

Although Horra's charges were pronounced false, they did bring forth priceless documents bearing on the routine life of the mission Indian. And we are especially fortunate in having such a document for Purísima, which I here quote from Engelhardt's translation:[28]

"1. The Christian Doctrine is taught to the Indians in Spanish and Indian.

"2. Before baptizing them, the converts are instructed, as far as possible and according to their capacity, in the principal mysteries of our holy Religion, not exactly eight, ten, nor twelve days, but for as many days as are necessary.

"3. We Fathers speak Castilian, and we endeavor to have the neophytes learn and speak it. They also speak their own language. We Fathers, soldiers, and Indians converse together in another jargon, a mixture of Mexican, Otomite, Lipan, Apache, Comanche, etc., which is commonly in use among the troops.

"4. The Indians are not permitted to rove outside the Mission, or in the mountains, except for a limited time.

"5. . . .

"6. Every morning and evening the neophytes are given for their meals atole, and pozole for the mid-day meal, in sufficient quantity for their maintenance, without considering how little they labor generally, and without considering the frequent permissions that are granted them to collect wild seeds in season, which are calculated to take up almost half the year; nor do we consider the wheat which is given in addition on Sundays and some other feast days, when there is distributed to each one almost half a peck. Moreover, during this year one hundred and ninety-four head of cattle have been slaughtered for them and sixteen cattle have been sold to the troops, although according to the report of the past year, the herd of cattle consisted of only 400 head.

"7. For clothing, the neophytes are given a woolen blanket and suit of cotton cloth, which if treated with some care will last more than a year, even a year and a half. In addition the men are given two breech cloths of Puebla woolen cloth or of cloth at the Mission.[29] The women and girls receive gowns and skirts, and a blanket like the men.

"8. The habitations of the Indians are the same to which they were accustomed in the pagan state, because until now it has not been possible to provide more convenient lodgings. The construction of the necessary buildings for the storing of the crops and for keeping other goods left no time for it. The apartment for the single women is a room fourteen yards square. Almost all around the walls inside are the bunks constructed of good boards, a little more than five palms from the floor, and proportionately wide. There they spread their mats and sleep very comfortably. In the same apartment they have a convenient place for their necessities. During the day they are not obliged to stay within, nor in any other apartment, unless it be as punishment for some misdeed. The single men, after they have recited the prayers near the apartments of the Fathers, are free to retire to their homes, or to the *pozolera*, or they may remain to sleep in the corridors, which like the *pozolera* is outside the cloister.

"9. The number of hours allotted to the Indians for labor does not exceed five, and on most days they work scarcely four hours. There is no obligation to labor just so much and so long, except at such jobs that require piece-work: but that kind of work is proportioned with prudence and in no way is it increased, as has been done many a time at the presidios for the Indians hired from the Missions. — Pregnant, nursing, and aged women, and children are not engaged at more work than is necessary to keep the Fathers informed that they are at the Mission, for unless this be observed, they would not stay at the Mission, and the consequence would be that many of the aged would die in the mountains without the Sacraments of Penance and Extreme Unction, and the recently born would die without Baptism, as has happened many times.

"10. The neophytes are permitted all kinds of diversions which are popular among them. Likewise half the year, or almost one-half the year is granted them for gathering their wild seeds, in the various seasons.

"11. Not only are the neophytes permitted to deal with the white people, but they are taught how to deal with them. They are given permission to approach the guards, and the soldiers are allowed the services for their chores whenever they ask, although many times the Indians are over-burdened with work by the soldiers, or deprived of the fire and rest which those enjoy who labor at the Mission. The Indians then tell us that they do not want to go to work for the soldiers, but that they want to labor with the rest of the Indians. In such cases the Indians are allowed their choice and their freedom. They are punished if they leave the Mission furtively, especially at night, because then they forsake their wives, or because experience had taught us that such excursions have very bad results, for they solicit and lead away women, or steal, or do other things opposed to good order.

"12. The punishments which we apply to the Indians, of both sexes, are whipping, sometimes shackles, very seldom stocks, and also the lock-up. The misdeeds for which we Fathers chastize the Indians thus are concubinage, theft, and running away. When the transgressions are against the common good, like killing cattle, sheep, or firing pastures, which has occurred sometimes, the corporal of the guard is notified. . . ."

Such was Indian life at Purísima at the turn of the century. The resident friars could justly feel proud of their record. In 1799 the neophyte community had grown to 959, and there were only 397 deaths. "This was the largest proportioned gain and the smallest death rate in California."[30] In 1803 the baptisms reached a peak never again witnessed at the original site. Four hundred and fifty-one baptisms are reported for the year.[31]

The remarkable successes of the mission during these years were due in great measure to the energy and zeal of Father Arroíta. By his retirement to Mexico sometime after 1798 Purísima lost a great friend.[32]

CHAPTER 3

PAYERAS AT THE HELM

A long list of celebrated names are associated with Purísima, but few surpass that of Mariano Payeras in importance. Late in 1804 he was assigned to take Father José Antonio Calzada's place at the mission.[1] Calzada, long in ailing health and successor to Oramas in 1792, was now to be relieved by one of the most energetic and able Franciscans to grace the pages of California history.

In many respects Payeras's background and ability resembled Father Serra's. Both were sons of Mallorca, and both had received their early training in the Convent of Our Father Saint Francis in Palma.[2] Born in Villa de Inca in 1770, Payeras entered the convent while still a young man, and on September 5, 1784, he received the habit. In January, 1793, he left Mallorca for the New World. Here he entered the renowned College of San Fernando, where he remained until 1796. In that year he was called to Upper California, and in July he and two other friars,[3] Antonio Peyrí and José Viader, disembarked at Monterey.

Payeras was thus launched on his career of California missionary. He served for a short while at San Carlos before receiving an appointment to Mission Soledad, where he remained until the summer of 1803. He was then transferred to San Diego, and from here he was removed to Purísima.

Payeras, just thirty-four years old, entered upon his assignment with great vigor. In November he began officiating at baptisms, and was no doubt pleased with the large number of Indians he found attached to the mission. At the close of the year there were 1,520 neophytes under its jurisdiction. This was the largest Indian population on record for the Mission.[4]

Shortly after Payeras's arrival, Purísima was chosen as one of four missions to experiment in the growing of flax.[5] In 1781 the King of Spain had ordered the establishment of flax culture in the New World, but it was not until 1795 that special instructions were given for attempting its cultivation in Upper California. In 1804 Joaquín Sánchez, an expert in flax culture, was sent by the Mexican government to teach the Californians how to grow the plant, and he distributed flax seed to Purísima and the other three missions. Payeras and his companions may have carried out the King's orders, but there is no record of any such crop having been harvested at the Mission.

As an agricultural and industrial institution Purísima was now becoming one of the outstanding missions. The mission had been so successful in this respect that in June, 1805, it was able to send the newly founded Santa Inés an abundance of all sorts of products.[6]

The mission maintained a store for the white people. The names of several prominent Californians of the time appear in the account books. Lieutenant Raimundo Carrillo, Francisco Ortega, Juan Ortega, J. B. Alvarado, Antonio Reyes and others traded there.[7] As indicated, there was little coin in the country, and debts were paid in other media. Thus, in 1807, Reyes was permitted to satisfy his mission creditors with horses or colts at two dollars apiece. All the supplies, of course, were not produced solely at the mission. Each year the boats from San Blas, Mexico, the California base of supplies for many years, brought such things as china, sugar, fine cloths, and other commodities, which were exchanged for mission products. To this were added the supplies which the fathers received as their yearly stipend. Each friar was to receive four hundred dollars a year, all of which was paid in mission equipment.

Each mission also derived an income from the labor of the Indian. All that the native produced went to the mission. When he was hired out to the white people, usually for a wage of about twenty cents a day, his salary was turned over to the general mission fund.[8] Under existing conditions this was believed just, for the mission supplied all the neophyte's wants. The wages were paid in goods from the mission store.

Payeras and his religious companions made every effort to maintain the prosperity of Purísima.[9] In 1808 he was able to report that there would be a sufficient harvest for the year, and the rancho at Salsipuedes was being provided with irrigation and it was predicted that it would soon be productive. About the same time Payeras accepted the administration of the Reyes rancho, which proved to be a profitable venture. Of the latter Payeras says: " 'Since I accepted the management, mares for breeding, horses for work, cattle to be slaughtered . . . , hides to be tanned, were the advantages which I began to secure.' " In 1809 the rancho also supplied about 1,000 *fanégas* of corn; and a year later Payeras purchased 2,000 head of cattle and horses to stock the mission lands.[10]

Payeras was delighted with the material well being of his Mission. In a letter addressed to Father President Estevan Tapis on January 13, 1810, he says that there were 10,000 sheep at the Mission and as many cattle, and this meant that there would be " 'much wool for clothing, much meat to eat in the *pozole* and rations, much tallow for sale, etc.' "[11] He also expected $5,000 in goods from Mexico, and the mission would be able to purchase statues of saints for the church. Further, Payeras looked for a great improvement in the mission wines. He had recently transplanted the vineyard from Lalsacupi to a place called San Francisco, where the vines were bearing well, and he made a contract with the Ortegas for taking care of them. "Some day," writes Payeras to Tapis, "if God permits, Your Reverence shall drink some of the best of wines." The mission would have been even more prosperous had it not been for the strict trade regulations.

Payeras never lost his keen interest in his Indian charges. "The Indians are naturally docile and peaceable," he writes.[12] It was gratifying to hear them say their prayers and to see them happily at their work. He was pleased with their singing, and pitied them in their illnesses. They all died like good Catholics. There was one thing that worried him, however: the appalling number of stillborn infants. "At the beginning this was attributed to incontinence. They were instructed, warned and punished, but in vain; and we are not able to learn why such deplorable things happen." Payeras had also prepared a catechism, with the acts of faith, hope and charity. This was in the idiom of the Indians, and had been written with the assistance of interpreters. It was now hoped that the native pagan cult of Achup would be replaced with the worship of the true God. At the close of 1810 there were 1020 natives at the Mission. In this respect Purísima ranked tenth among the missions. San Diego had the greatest number, with 1611.[13]

Building operations continued. Some time late in 1809 or early 1810, Payeras renovated "the old building," which perhaps was the monastery, roofing it with tile and whitewashing it. Payeras also speaks of having completed an aqueduct. To assist in the work, Payeras hired José Antonio Ramirez. Besides helping to construct the vats, troughs, drinking fountains, and washtubs, he was to manage the carpenter shop. For his services, Payeras agreed to pay him two hundred dollars, and give him board for a year and two pounds of chocolate each month.[14] Francisco Xavier Aguilar seems also to have been employed by the mission, either as a mechanic or mayordomo. Aguilar was to receive twenty-five dollars a month and board. Thus, despite the contention that lay artisans corrupted the mission community, the missionaries apparently found that they had to have these men if the material progress of the mission were to be maintained.

In 1810 Payeras and his companions gave thought to the improvement of communications to Santa Inés and San Luis Obispo. Two roads were opened up through the mountains. They apparently followed the Santa Ynez River south, and were a league apart and each was forty paces wide. The northern route is not indicated.

Payeras's religious aid at this time was Father Gerónimo Boscana, who apparently remained at Purísima until May, 1811.[15] In August the mission was honored with the arrival of Father President Estevan Tapis, who officiated at the site until August of the succeeding year.[16] Tapis was then replaced by Father Antonio Ripoll.

The year 1812 gave promises of great success. Livestock was increasing at an encouraging rate, and the fields produced a fair amount of agricultural supplies.[17] At the close of the year there were 4000 cattle, 12,000 sheep, sixty pigs, 116 mules, and 1,150 horses; and there was a crop yield of 3,000 *fanégas* of wheat, fifty of corn, and twenty-seven of beans. The mission neophytes numbered 999, among whom was Chief Neuia, who was sixty years old and had just joined the mission community. Of these, thirty-six couples were married during the year, and thirty-three adults and thirty-one children were baptized.

But all this was suddenly offset by one of the most lamentable catastrophes ever to strike the missions. The year 1812 is remembered in California history for its terrible and ruinous earthquake. Practically every settlement in the province suffered from it, and many of the missions experienced irreparable damage. It was then that the beautiful stone church at San Juan Capistrano was all but totally ruined and Purísima completely destroyed. At the latter place slight shocks were first felt on the morning of December 8.[18] Little damage was done, however, and it was not until nearly two weeks later that the earth began to shake with disastrous results. On the morning of the twenty-first the shocks were so violent that it was difficult to stand. For ten days the ground trembled, and when the earth finally came to rest Purísima was a pitiful heap of ruins. Payeras has described the sad event in the following words:[19]

"'The extraordinary and horrible earthquake, which this Mission suffered on the memorable day of the glorious Apostle St. Thomas, entirely destroyed the church and vestry, buried under the walls the various images and paintings, and ruined the greater part of the furniture. The vestments have not suffered because they were inside the cases. Some of the workshops went down, but some more strongly built, may serve as habitations if not for minor uses which require no such security. One hundred houses of neophyte Indians and the *pozolera* or community kitchen, the walls of which were an adobe and a half thick, and roofed with tiles, have become inserviceable. The garden walls of adobe, covered with tiles, have either collapsed or threaten to fall. The damaged portion will scarcely afford material for rebuilding. The furniture and other contents of the Mission have likewise suffered; some of the contents are entirely crushed, some are broken and all are damaged.

"'The inclemency of the weather, and the very heavy rainfalls that followed, prevent digging out anything or covering what lies exposed. For the present, we have nevertheless dug out the most valuable things, and we have secured what is urgently needed. We have put up a church of palisades and in the most primitive way we have built two huts which are to serve as habitations for the two Fathers. We shall also go to work constructing from poles and grass what is indispensible until the earth becomes quiet. Experience may teach us the best method for constructing other buildings.'"

This was a hard blow to the missionaries, and had Payeras been made of weak stuff he could have painted a more dismal picture. He was not discouraged. On the contrary, he immediately set about the erection of a new plant. And he was no doubt thankful that there had been no fatalities. For eight years he had worked to make the Mission a success, and he was not now willing to permit his labors to go for naught. Payeras viewed it all quite philosophically:[20] "If God, like a father, chastizes and afflicts with one hand, with the other He helps and supports: in plain terms, that, if this Mission, as is known, was the one which suffered most, the said chastizement may be really called the most fortunate on account of sixty gentiles recently baptized, the remarkable and abundant amount of grain planted, and the copious waters which have filled the river and springs prodigiously."

CHAPTER 4

A NEW SITE

With characteristic energy Payeras undertook to repair the recent damages. Buildings were essential, and no time must be lost in their restoration. The Indians were willing to assist in the program, but they had become exceedingly superstitious about remaining at Algsacupi. In view of this attitude, the missionaries sought another site.

Payeras had further reasons for changing the Mission site, and it was his suggestion that the Mission be removed into the small draw about three miles north of Algsacupi. The proposed location was known as Los Berros — the watercresses — or, as the Indians called it, Amúu.[1] Payeras expected many advantages from this site. It was north of the Santa Ynez, which should improve communications with the mission. During the rainy season the river often reached such a height that a crossing of it was impossible; and since the *camino real* was north of the river and ran through the Los Berros ravine, it seemed only wise to establish the Mission at Los Berros.[2] The area also had an abundance of fire-wood, timber and building materials, and water was close at hand.

On March 11, 1813, the resident fathers petitioned for the removal of the site to Los Berros.[3] Father President José Señan forwarded the request to Governor Arrillaga, and on March 30 Arrillaga granted permission. On the twenty-third of the following month Purísima was officially established at Los Berros.

The fathers experienced some difficulty at first in getting things under way at the new site. Heretofore the missionaries could depend on financial assistance from the Pious Fund, but the wars for independence, which were now being waged in Spain's New World colonies, had shut off incomes from this source. Payeras and his companions, however, admitted no defeats, and they were soon laying the foundations of a new mission plant.

They apparently had little trouble in gathering the Indians at Los Berros. Indeed, by the end of the year they had more natives here than they had had at the old site. The aboriginal population was recorded as 1,010 souls.[4]

In nine months' time the Indians had erected temporary structures, and had made an encouraging start on the water system.[5] The buildings were all palisaded and roofed with tile (*techadas con texa*).[6] The tile was doubtless recovered from the old mission. "'A church was constructed of poles veneered with adobes. This holds all the people'." To maintain the Mission with water independent of the Santa Ynez, "'we are building a small fountain from which a ditch conducts the water to the foot of the Mission for a distance of 400 paces. To secure a greater volume of water, and to irrigate the field in summer, we have continued to this side of the river the same aqueduct that ran from the river to the old Mission. It crosses the river at the old pass of Santa Ynez. In due time it will bring to us its crystal and delicious waters to within 500 paces of our doors'." An orchard was planted with as many trees as were at hand, and for its irrigation the water from various springs were collected which, after emptying into tanks, promised abundant irrigation.[7]

As was the case at the original site, the Franciscans now employed skilled artisans to direct the erection of the new buildings. In October 1814, Ignacio Yguera was hired for twelve dollars a month and rations, and on July 20 of the next year he was employed especially to devote his skill and knowledge to the building of a church at the mission. The contract which he entered into with Payeras is interesting:[8] " 'The Mission will give, 1:— One dollar for every day on which he works. 2:— His board as heretofore, with the addition of one small bottle of aguardiente every week. It is to be noted that the liquor will be given him when it is made here; it will not be purchased. 3:— One or two men to help him when he needs them. In return for these wages he obliges himself to apply all his knowledge and energy in the service of the Mission, etc. This contract will continue until the church is finished.' "

In 1815, much was accomplished in the way of building operations.[9] The temporary church was strengthened and plastered and an unusually large building was erected.[10] This was 100 *varas* long, and recent excavations have shown the building to be nearly sixty feet wide. The walls were an adobe and a half thick, and a high wall ran through the whole length of the structure. This central wall divided the building into two rows of rooms, and it acted as the ridge-pole for the roof. This building, the present building known as the monastery, provided the residence of the fathers, contained rooms for the servants and guests, and there was some space for workshops and the chapel. A covered corridor with colonnades ran along the front, and a walk was built in the rear.[11]

The next year, 1816, was likewise notable for building activity. A special building for the workshops was constructed. It was 100 *varas* long and six wide, roofed with tile, and a corridor ran along both sides.[12] The walls were an adobe thick. This structure contained the guardrooms, quarters for the troops, rooms for the mayordomos, carpenter shop, and weaving rooms. In the same year the chapel was decorated, and two altar cloths and two altar covers were purchased. Two infirmaries were built, one for the exclusive use of the women. The general infirmary was fifty *varas* long, and both seem to have been made of materials salvaged from other buildings.[13] Two looms for new fabrics with necessary appliances were also made.

Meanwhile, Payeras had been named president of the California missions. On July 24, 1815, the guardian of the College of San Fernando appointed him to succeed Father Señan.[14] On November 22, Payeras notified Governor Pablo de Solá,[15] and for four years he held the office and continued to reside at his own mission. In ecclesiastical affairs he thus became the head of the friars in Upper California. The president also functioned as the direct representative of the bishop, who at this time lived in Sonora. He therefore exercised all the faculties and was charged with dispensations. There was only one higher religious dignitary in the territory, and this was the commissary prefect, a sort of visitor general who represented the commissary general of Mexico.

The extra duties which now fell to the lot of Payeras did not, as might be expected, cause him to neglect the interests of Purísima. He was too firmly attached to the welfare of the Mission to be detracted from his main purpose. In 1814 he had been able to report that the material progress of the Mission was decidedly encouraging; and the office of President was not now going to interfere with that progress. It was in that year that Purísima had 4,652 head of horses alone, the greatest number of horses ever reported in any one year for any of the missions.[16] Two years later, 1816, there were nearly 9,000 head of large stock at the Mission, and the sheep numbered 11,000.[17] And some of the fields were yielding over a hundredfold. In 1816 eight *fanégas* of maize were planted and 1,000 fanégas were harvested; 123 *fanégas* of wheat were sown and the yield was 2500; five *fanégas* of beans yielded 120 *fanégas*; and other crops were just as abundant. The mission vineyards, too, were receiving Payeras's attention. In December he wrote Solá a letter in which he thanked the governor for applying to the viceroy for twenty workers for the vineyard.[18] And it was at this time that Payeras mentions a garden somewhere north of the mission.[19]

The year 1817 proved a busy year for Payeras and the mission. Payeras says that the first few months were trying. There were a thousand jobs to do and he hardly knew how he could give them all his attention.[20] The activities of the Russians in the northern part of the province prompted Payeras to advise the Spanish king of probable dangers from that quarter.[21] Shortly thereafter the mission of San Rafael was founded as a buffer between Fort Ross and the Spanish settlements to the south. Besides serving in this more or less political capacity, Payeras was busily engaged with his duties as President and senior missionary at Purísima.

Payeras now had 958 natives to watch over at his mission, and, although most of them were good Catholics, there were always a few who clung to their pagan cults. The tale is told by an unknown father familiar with the Purísima neophytes that one of the Indians, who had been raised in the Catholic faith, called for the services of a native medicine man as he lay at the point of death.[22] After the medicine man had worked over the dying man for some time without favorable results, the native priest told his patient that he could do nothing for him because the Indian gods were punishing him with death for having worshipped the white man's God. The Indian would not submit to the Christian rites, and he died without the final ministrations of either heathen or Christian priest. Such, no doubt, were some of the problems with which Payeras had to contend.

The year 1817 saw continued building activities at the Mission. Foundations were laid for a new church, and the temporary church was repaired.[23] A cope with golden galloons was made; four damask curtains were received; two mantle cloths for the altar and three surplices were added to the church; five blue cassocks for the altar boys (*alcolitos*) were procured; and three gilded chandeliers were hung in the presbytery. Payeras mentions that all this was added to certain church equipment which had come from Mexico the year before, and from Lima. This same year, 1817, saw the erection of "a fountain with its corresponding lavatory between the house of the fathers and the *familias de razón* and the *ranchería.* For the use of the infirmary and for minor uses another fountain was constructed in the same patio, made particularly for the Indians. The water which reaches both fountains is brought from a distance of 8 hundred to 1 thousand paces in pipes and to basins at reasonable distances."[24] Building activities for the year seem to have concluded with the erection of a hostelry at a place known as the *Rancho de Larga,* nine leagues from Purísima. This structure was for the free use of any wayfarer who might need shelter. It was made of palisades and covered with tules.[25] The missionaries also made provisions for nursing the sick. On November 20th Guadalupe Briones was hired as an infirmarian at a salary of five dollars a month and keep.

The progress made at the Mission during the years 1817-1819 is all the more remarkable in view of the fact that Payeras seems to have been the lone resident friar during most of that time.[26] Occasionally he made trips to other missions, but he would always hurry back to his beloved Purísima. The neophytes needed his constant attention, and he never for long neglected the industrial and commercial affairs of the establishment. In 1819 he reported that the Mission had produced 500 *botas* of tallow. Each *bota,* or leather bag, contained about 200 pounds of tallow, making a total of some 100,000 pounds.[27] In addition Payeras sold saddles, weapons, blankets, and mules to soldiers, some of whom resided as far south as the Presidio of Loreto in Lower California. From this trade he received approximately $147.00.[28] The previous year the Presidio of Santa Barbara had purchased about $670.00 worth of goods from the Mission, the principal items of trade being blankets, shoes, serapes, hides, blankets and packing outfits.[29] The missions were also the source for much of the food supplies for the presidios. Thus, in 1817, of the $413 worth of commodities Purísima supplied the presidios, $232 were of corn and beans. The corn sold for $3.00 a *fanéga,* and the beans from $2.00 to $2.50 a *fanéga.*

The new site had met all the expectations of the missionaries. Purísima was once more a flourishing establishment.

CHAPTER 5

PORTENTOUS YEARS

Mission life was not always colorless. During the second decade of the nineteenth century Purísima received its share of excitement.

Since 1810 most of Spanish America had been experiencing the horrors of rebellion. Hidalgo, Bolivar, San Martín and many others were directing the efforts of Spanish creoles to free themselves from the mother country; and now, in 1818, California was made to feel that she, too, was playing a part in the great struggle.

In October, 1818, the Californians were informed that they were to be attacked by Hypolite Bouchard, who had been sailing the seas on a doubtful errand.[1] Ostensibly, he was in northern waters carrying the banner of the rebels; but there was good reason to believe that he was little more than a pirate. Pirate or rebel, the Californians objected to his designs. It was rumored that he was now fitting out in Hawaii, and that shortly he would descend upon the California coasts. Governor Sola at once took steps to defend the country. Provision was made to find safe inland refuge for the women and children and the livestock, and the governor called on the missions to provide as much military assistance as possible. Payeras complied by arming fifteen natives and ten *vaqueros* at Purísima, and then waited for further developments.

Late in November, Bouchard attacked Monterey, and, after sacking the town, headed down the coast. Payeras had stationed sentinels at Point Pedernales, and at three on the afternoon of December 1, they sighted the insurgents.[2] Bouchard's boats appeared to hesitate for a few minutes, as if undecided on which course they should follow. They apparently continued south, however, and as soon as Payeras received the reports of his sentinels, he advised the southern missions of the proximity of the insurgents. Next day Bouchard anchored at Refugio, where he sacked the houses in the vicinity and killed several head of cattle. He then made his way to Santa Barbara. Father Uría at Santa Inés became alarmed, and Payeras quickly sent forty armed neophytes to aid him. Fortunately, no more was heard of Bouchard at Purísima, and life once more returned to its normal channels.

The Franciscan authorities had long recognized Payeras's ability. His record at Purísima was second to none of the other missionaries, and all admitted that he fulfilled his duties as President with consummate zeal and tact. Therefore, upon the expiration of Father Vicente Sarría's six-year term of commissary prefect in October, 1819, Payeras was chosen his successor. This was the highest office among the California Franciscans.[3]

Meanwhile, Payeras had continued improving the physical aspects of the mission. Early in 1818 the temporary palisaded church collapsed, and Payeras immediately undertook the building of a new one. Of this he says:

"The (church) of palisades collapsed. A new temporary one was built of adobe on the same site, with a tile roof, a loft, a sacristy, and a *contra sacristy*. . . . "⁴ The neophytes applied themselves so assiduously that "begun in June of 18 they completed it in November of the same year."⁵ Among the principal items added to the church equipment were a cope, two red antependia, a portapaz of silver, an image of the Child Jesus a half-*vara* high, a fine alb, and an altar cover. The way of the cross, with framed pictures, was also placed along the interior walls. It appears that there were no other building activities for the year, but there were repairs made to the old mission tools and equipment and certain needed implements were added. In the following year nothing was done to the buildings save keeping them in repair.⁶ Payeras states that times were so miserable that nothing more could be done.

It would be interesting to know to what Payeras referred when he said "these miserable times." Perhaps a slight decrease in the material wealth of the Mission prompted the remark. But this seems hardly probable, since the statistics for the year show some 22,000 head of livestock at the Mission and 5,000 bushels of agricultural products harvested. This was only a little less than during some of the preceding years. Yet Payeras may have sensed the beginning of the decline of mission prosperity.

Payeras did, however, have reason to worry about his neophytes. For four years there had been a slow but definite decline in the native population at Purísima. In 1815 there had been 1019 Indians at the mission.⁷ Now, in 1819, there were only 888.⁸ A year later there would be just 840.⁹ This was food for thought. Furthermore, Payeras was ill; and, according to Engelhardt, "incessant demands of the military government of California that the Mission must contribute toward the maintenance of the territorial soldiers and their families, . . . had exhausted the resources of Mission Purísima. . . ."¹⁰ Miserable times indeed.

The years 1820-1822 proved to be busy years for Payeras. In the summer of 1820 he began his visitations of the northern missions.¹¹ By late October he had visited San Carlos, San Juan Bautista, Santa Cruz, San Francisco, San José and San Raphael. In April of the following year we find him at Soledad, where he wrote to the missionaries as far south as Santa Inés that Governor Solá had requested the missions to furnish workers to the presidio of Monterey.¹² Solá was asking for sixty-six laborers and artisans. La Purísima's quota was six, two masons and four laborers. The masons were to receive four reales a day, and the laborers one and one-half reales. In June Payeras was again at Purísima, where he was asking for supplies for the newly founded San Rafael. The *asistencia*, as it was then called, had 600 neophytes but only 1200 sheep (*boregos*).¹³ Consequently, the natives were without sufficient clothing. *"Esta desnuda."* Two thousand more sheep were needed, and Purísima was to provide 234 but sent 300. None of the other missions complied in full with the request, pleading exemption on the grounds that many of the animals had recently died.

Shortly thereafter Payeras resumed his visitations, proceeding this time southward. Toward the close of August he and his secretary, Father

José Bernardo Sánchez, arrived at San Diego.[14] After auditing the mission books, he resolved to make an excursion inland for the purpose of finding suitable sites for new missions. On September 10, he and his secretary began their journey east and north. At Santa Isabel he planted a cross, and soon arrived at Pala, an *asistencia* of San Luis Rey. The twenty-third found him again on his way. Within a few days he reached San Jacinto. Here he and Sánchez directed their steps toward San Gabriel, where they arrived on October 1. Payeras then hastened on north to Purísima.

At about this time Payeras began to consider the defenses of his mission. In 1822 there were six soldiers stationed there,[15] but Payeras doubtless felt that they would hardly afford adequate protection in case of a great emergency. Hence his rather elaborate plan for strengthening the military defenses of Purísima.[16] There were to be four *partidas,* or divisions, to this militia. The first *partida* was to be composed of thirty natives from the Santa Barbara Presidio. Eighteen of these were to be armed with bows and arrows, and twelve were to be mounted with lance and *reata.* The second *partida* was to consist of fifteen to thirty *vaqueros,* or others who were good horsemen. They were to be armed with lances and provided with strong *reatas,* and should go by the name of *partida de lanceros de la Purísima.* The third *partida* was to be a band of fifty natives under forty years of age, familiar with the Spanish language, armed with bows and arrows, and called *flecheros volantes de la Purísima.* The fourth and last division, the *partida de reserva de flecheros,* was to be made up of the remaining available persons, especially of those experienced with firearms. This last division would assist the *alcaldes* and *regidores* of the mission, escort persons leaving the mission, and to act as reserves in time of need. Such were the plans drawn up by this versatile man; but there is no reason to believe that they ever became more than written words.

Although Payeras was now a sick man, he continued to work with zeal and great vigor. In the spring of 1822 he was again at Monterey, where he took the oath of allegiance to the government of independent Mexico.[17] As commissary prefect of the missions, Payeras entered into a contract with William E. P. Hartnell by which the missionaries agreed to sell hides and other products to Hartnell's firm. Hittell says that this "started what may be called the first regular mercantile business in California."[18]

Payeras had other business to attend to while in the north. The government never relaxed its concern in the Russians' activities at Fort Ross. Consequently, when the imperial commissioner, Father Agustín Fernández, appeared at Monterey while Payeras was there, it was decided that a trip should be made to the fort. On October 11, Fernández and Payeras, accompanied by a small group of persons, began their trip north.[19] Crossing San Francisco Bay, they arrived at the Mission San Rafael on the nineteenth. Four days later they were at the Russian post. Payeras was impressed with what he saw, and he has left us one of the best descriptions of the post.[20] Although the nature of the visit was political, Payeras seems nevertheless to have had an eye for possible trade with these foreigners. How else are we to explain the good father's implication that there were Russians at Purísima two months later.[21]

Perpetual night was now fast approaching for the beloved father. Ailing for some time, and refusing to stop his arduous labors, Payeras soon lay in mortal exhaustion. On April 28, 1823, at the relatively young age of fifty-three, he died at Purísima. Next day he was laid to rest under the pulpit of the church.[22] Father Antonio Rodríguez made the following entry in the *libro de entierros*:

> "No. 2197. On the 29th day of April, 1823, in the church of this Mission of Purísima, I gave ecclesiastical burial to the body of the Very Rev. Fr. Mariano Payeras, Preacher Apostolic of the College of San Fernando de Mexico, missionary of the said Mission, and actual Prefect of these Missions. He received the holy habit in the Province of Mayorca. He died on the preceding day, disposing himself for this terrible ordeal with religious and exemplary edification to the Fathers as well as for the people *de razon* and the neophytes. He is buried under the pulpit of said church, and he received all the holy Sacraments. In witness whereof I sign this — Fr. Antonio Rodríguez."[23]

Bancroft, always hesitant in his praise of the missionaries, makes the following comment on Payeras:

> "There was no friar of better and more evenly balanced ability in the province. He was personally a popular man on account of his affable manners, kindness of heart and unselfish devotion to the welfare of all. It was impossible to quarrel with him, and even Governor Solá's peevish and annoying complaints never ruffled his temper. Yet he had extraordinary business ability, was a clear and forcible as well as a voluminous writer, and withal a man of great strength of mind and firmness of character. He was called to rule the friars during a trying period, when it would have required but a trifle to involve the padres and soldiers in a quarrel fatal to the missions. . . . His death just at this time, in the prime of life, must be considered as a great misfortune. . . ."[24]

The missions, and especially Purísima, were soon to miss the guiding influence of Payeras. His death marked the end of the halcyon days at Purísima. From that time on the Mission gradually fell into a long period of decadence. The year 1823 saw the last of the building operations. Two years before, in 1821, a belfry and cemetery had been joined to the church, and in the year of Payeras's death ten new houses, all roofed with tile, were built for the neophytes.[25] This closed the period of building activities. Most of the friars' efforts at this time were directed toward maintaining the structures already erected and toward acquiring needed supplies for the church. In 1822 three large mirrors and six glass lanterns were added to the church, and a small wheel with bells was acquired.[26] Three niches were made in the principal altar for mirrors. In 1823, a fine linen alb, a linen amice, a pair of glass cruets with plates, four large mirrors of more than a *vara* high, a pair of chandeliers, six oil paintings of various saints, and a new carpet for the presbytery were added to the church.

It might be well now to review the material status of the Mission during the closing years of Payeras's life. In 1820 there were some 22,000 head of livestock, 12,600 of which were sheep.[27] This number remained about constant down to 1824. The average crop yield was approximately 4,000 *fanégas*.[28] The lands belonging to the Mission were extensive. From north to south they covered a distance of fourteen leagues; and from east to west they varied from four to six leagues.[29] Most of this was, of course, pasture lands, but much of the surrounding flat bottom lands were devoted to grains, legumes, the vine and fruit trees.[30] But the missionaries must have sadly foreseen that the area was too vast to be properly worked. The Indian population, which supplied most of the labor, was fast dwindling away. By 1823 there were only 722 neophytes attached to the mission.[31] Perhaps no more than one-third of these were productive workers. Payeras's "mission of the first order" was doomed.

Purísima was now in [the] charge of Fathers Antonio Rodríguez and Blas Ordaz, the latter being stationed at the mission in the month of Payeras's death.[32] It was these two who were to witness one of the most unfortunate episodes in the mission's history.

Figure 283. Immediate foreground, foundations of original large structure (church); ruins of original permanent church, beyond; restored monastery in background.

CHAPTER 6

IN ARTICULO MORTIS

The missionary had always to contend with possible uprisings of his native wards. New World mission history is replete with many serious Indian outbreaks. Reasons for such disturbances are at times hard to discover. The willingness of both religious and civil authorities of the Spanish colonies to deny responsibility and cast aspersions upon each other has practically concealed the facts in a maze of contradictory statements.

Purísima early in 1824 experienced one such uprising. Engelhardt of course defends the missionaries and places responsibility on the laity.[1] Although we have no direct statements from the civil authorities, we may infer that they denied entire responsibility. Be this as it may, the revolt appears to have been plotted by the natives of Purísima and Santa Inés, and before it was put down it spread to San Luis Obispo, Santa Barbara, San Buenaventura and San Fernando.

The revolt was carefully planned.[2] Native couriers went from mission to mission plotting the uprising, which was set for February 21.[3] They kept their secret so well that the whites remained in ignorance of what was brewing until the instant of hostilities. Commandant José de la Guerra y Noriega of Santa Barbara is said to have been warned by one of his faithful servants; but he did not place much faith in what he heard.[4] The Indians were determined to free themselves for all time from what they felt to be an intolerable oppression.

On the afternoon of the appointed day the rebels attacked the whites at Santa Inés. These details need not interest us here. Suffice it to say that through the courageous actions of Father Francisco Uría and Sergeant Anastacio Carrillo the insurgents were soon discouraged in their efforts.

The same day the natives of Purísima fell on their white masters. Apparently the natives were well disposed toward the Corporal of the guard, Tibúrcio Tápia, and Father Ordaz, for they offered to allow them to escape if the Corporal would turn over to them all the arms. Tápia wisely refused, and he and the white families took refuge in their quarters. During the evening's conflict one neophyte was wounded, and four strangers were killed as they approached the Mission in ignorance of the uprising.

Next day Tápia and the other whites apparently managed to take refuge in the larger buildings, where they defended themselves with relative ease. The events of that day are not quite clear, but the fighting must have continued. The following day Ordaz was able to bury the four strangers who had been taken by surprise, and he and the soldiers and their families were permitted to withdraw to Santa Inés. Father Rodríguez found himself with the rebels, who undertook to defend themselves in the larger Mission buildings. No attempt was made to molest Rodríguez, and the natives now considered themselves in full possession of Purísima. They erected palisade fortifications, cut holes in the church and other buildings for their guns, and mounted two small cannon which the friars made use of on feast days. They now settled down to see what the authorities would do.

A month passed before Governor Argüello was able to relieve the Mission. After considerable effort he managed to raise a force of 109 men among the northern settlements. Lieutenant José María Estrada, who commanded the contingent, has left the following on this event:

" 'I have the satisfaction of placing before Your Honor for your further action the happy outcome secured against the factious neophytes of the said Missions of Santa Inés and Purísima by the valiant troops whom I have the honor to command and the account of which is as follows:

" 'Having left the Mission of San Luis Obispo, the point of our reunion, or let it be called quartel general, where we assembled to the number of 109, enlisted as artillery, infantry, and cavalry, with a field piece of four pounds. With this force I began my march to Purísima on the 14th of the present month of March. At the site of *Oso Flaco* the division passed the night after the precautions of war had been taken. In this place our advanced guard surprised two hostile couriers, who came from San Luis Obispo, which they had already reached on the 12th with three others. On the 15th, the march continued without anything of note, and then we camped at the foot of the Cuesta de la Graciosa. On the 16th, at two o'clock in the morning, after we had overcome indescribable obstacles on account of the declivity of the mountain, we succeeded in ascending and in dragging the cannon by hand. Observing that it was about time to operate it, after having placed it under cover for protection along with the munitions in charge of 28 horsemen under a corporal, I commanded that two advance guards, each composed of fifteen horsemen under the command of corporals Nicolas Alviso and Trinidad Espinosa, to separate to the right and the left, and in a circular movement proceed toward the Mission in order to prevent the flight of rebels, and make them meet our forces. In this manner, step by step, we approached the Mission until we were within shooting distance of our cannon. Protected by thirty-three infantrymen, this began firing at about 8 A.M., always advancing until we reached within shooting range of our muskets. From their loop holes, the Indians poured out a lively gun-fire at us with their one pound cannon, and also sent out a shower of arrows. Boldly despising that resistance, the artillery replied with brilliantly directed shots, and the musketry with a not less active firing.

" 'It seemed that the Indians wanted to take flight, but seeing that the cavalry had completely surrounded them, and that Don Francisco Pacheco with twenty horsemen and drawn sword hastened to intercept them, the Indians could not help seeing that they were completely cut off. They then availed themselves of the advocacy and favor of Fr. Antonio Rodriguez, the missionary of said Mission. He agreed to their clamors and sent a written supplication that the firing cease, and then he appeared openly in person. I commanded that firing stop. It was half past ten in the morning. The casualties of this glorious battle won by the small number of eighty men against 400 Indians equipped with all weapons were three wounded, one, the late militia-man Dionisio Rios, was mortally wounded, the other two only slightly so.[5] On the side of the rebels sixteen were killed and a considerable number wounded. Their two pedreros (swivel-guns) were taken, besides sixteen muskets, 150 lances, six machetes (cutlasses), and an incalculable number of bows and arrows. — Quartel General of Purísima, March 19, 1824. Jose María Estrada.'[6]"

These operations terminated the revolt at Purísima. Shortly thereafter Captain de la Guerra arrived with a few troops, and measures were taken to punish the Indians. Seven of the natives were adjudged guilty of murdering the five mission visitors on the first night of the uprising. These were condemned to die, and on March 26th, after receiving the sacraments of penance and holy eucarist, they were shot. Father Rodríguez buried them in the mission cemetery. The four ringleaders of the uprising, Pacomio, Mariano, Benito, and Bernabe, were sentenced to the presidio for ten years and perpetual exile from the province. Eight others received eight years' imprisonment at the presidio. Some of the missionaries, however, seem to have questioned the manner in which the military settled the affair. The charge was made that Lieutenant Estrada unwisely pardoned some of the rebels.[7] This Estrada denied.[8] In a letter addressed to de la Guerra on May 22nd, Estrada writes: "all that I said to Father Antonio Rodríguez was that this trouble would cease forever if the Indians would give up their arms. Neither have I promised anything else, nor do I believe that your honor would promise a pardon, as indicated in the letter of Father Ripoll to Father Sarria. . . ."[9] Whether or not the army was too lenient in its dealings with the rebels made little difference, for the neophytes soon returned to their Mission duties, and we do not again hear of armed resistance to the Purísima authorities.

The remaining months of 1824 seem to have been uneventful. Father Blas did not return, and in December Father Marcos Antonio de Vitoria became Rodríguez's companion.[10] At the close of the year the neophytes numbered 662, of which 366 were males, and the balance females.[11] There had been seventy deaths. The death rate in comparison to the baptisms was four to one. This could hardly have been encouraging. The year saw no further building activity; and the noted decrease in the harvests and the failure of the livestock to multiply were matters of concern. The total agricultural products of the year amounted to 2,035 bushels.[12] Two years earlier there had been 4,363 bushels. Livestock numbered 17,630 head. This was about 5,000 less than in the preceding year.[13]

Purísima as a mission was now looking into the dark abyss of oblivion. It missed the strong hands of Payeras, and, like the other missions, suffered from the rapid depletion of the ranks of the neophytes. The fathers faithfully and earnestly worked to maintain their establishment; but they were laboring against irresistible forces set on blotting out an institution practically synonymous with Spanish California history.

In 1825 two images, one of the seraphic doctor San Buenaventura and the other of San Antonio de Padua, were added to the church, and a "new throne of La Purísima Concepción" was made.[14] Two years later "two machines were made for grinding wheat and other seeds."[15] These seem to have been the last additions made to the mission property. At the close of the second decade of the century Purísima harvests amounted to 1,003 bushels, and there were a little more than 15,000 head of livestock.[16] The neophyte population had dwindled to 406.[17] The missionary in charge, no doubt Vitoria, complained that he was unable to perform the necessary religious exercises because he was alone and had to devote most of his time attending to the sick.[18] Alfred Robinson visited the mission at about this time, and he has left the following brief account of what he saw:[19] "In the morning we rode over to the Purissima, where we found two reverend friars, Fathers Victoria [sic] and Juan Moreno . . . though possessing abundant wealth, in cattle and planting grounds, yet it has been much neglected, and the Indians generally are ill clothed, and seem in the most abject condition."[20]

To all this was added a final destructive blow. In the early thirties decrees and acts of secularization were issued. By these measures the California missions were turned over to the secular authorities. The mission lands were distributed to the Indians and to the white citizenry, and in due time religious instruction was turned over to the secular clergy. This procedure, dating from the early colonial period, was usually opposed by the missionary. According to the laws of secularization, the mission and its Indians, after a period of ten years' tutelage, were to be relinquished to the seculars. It was assumed by these laws that the Indian would by that time have become sufficiently educated and christianized to support himself in a civilized manner. It was a theory, however, which seldom worked out in practice. At the end of the ten years the Indian was usually as much in need of instruction and guidance as at the beginning. This the missionary was not slow to point out, and the Spanish government in many instances suffered the missionary to remain long after the legal expiratory date.

In 1813 futile attempts were made to secularize the California missions. Nothing of importance again was proposed in this matter until after the arrival of José M. Echeandía, the first Mexican governor. On January 6, 1831, mission confiscatory decrees were issued by him.[21] In matters of government Purísima, together with the Santa Barbara and San Buenaventura missions, was to be under the jurisdiction of the Santa Barbara Presidio. Commissaries and mayordomos were to be assigned to the missions, although the fathers were for the present to administer the establishments.

There was great opposition to Echeandía's decree, and it was not until two years later that the question was again brought up. In that year, 1833, José Figueroa, the new governor, contemplated secularization. Father Narciso Durán suggested that before actual secularization be decreed, the plan be given a trial at the missions of San Juan Capistrano, San Buenaventura, Santa Barbara, Purísima, San Antonio, San Carlos, Santa Cruz, and San Francisco. Durán's plea, however, received little attention. Figueroa proceeded to the final acts of secularization. On August 9, 1834, he communicated authorization decrees to the friars, and on November 4, the final legislation on the subject was published.[22] Thereafter, curacies were established, and commissioners appointed to take over the missions. Purísima, San Juan Capistrano, San Buenaventura, San Fernando and Santa Inés were grouped into one curacy. On November 30 Domingo Carrillo was appointed commissioner of Purísima.[23] The true mission days of Purísima were thereby closed.

It would be well to pause for a moment to consider the general condition of Purísima at that time. When Father Marcos Vitoria officially delivered up the mission on March 1, 1835, its temporalities were valued at $61,976.37.[24] This, a secular appraisal, was about $1,000 less than the value placed on the properties by the church.[25] Mission credits amounted to $3,613.00, and debts to $1,218.50. The neophyte population, according to Engelhardt, who fails to give his authority, was 407.[26] In the year of secularization there were 2,047 bushels of grain harvested, and the livestock numbered 14,042 head.[27] At about this time the church seems to have become inserviceable, and the chapel in the monastery building was converted into a church. The inventory shows that there were fourteen structures belonging to the mission, five bells, a library of 139 volumes, three gardens and seven ranchos.[28]

The succeeding ten years saw the complete disappearance of Purísima as a mission establishment. The resident missionaries retired to Santa Inés shortly after secularization, and the last divine service was held in July, 1836.[29] In August, 1835, the commissioner Domingo Carrillo turned the mission over to his brother Joaquin.[30] The credits were now $1,174.00, and the debts $1,371.62. Two years later Carrillo reported the credits and debits being respectively $2,155.00 and $2,123.00.[31] On June 6, 1838, the mission was delivered by Carrillo to José María Valenzuela. Valenzuela seems to have been a fairly good administrator. By the close of the year he was able to show a profit in trade of $1,986.00; and for the first half of 1839 he recorded a profit of $4,103.00.[32] For this service the administrator and his assistants received a small salary. Valenzuela's yearly stipend was $600, while that of his mayordomo was $298.00, and the *llavero*, or keeper of the keys, received $84.00.[33] Many of the mission administrators, however, were not noted for their probity; and the charge has been made that through dishonesty and sharpness they made considerably more than their salaries. Eugenio Ortega and José Antonio de la Guerra followed Valenzuela as administrator, and when de la Guerra was asked to relinquish the position to Miguel Cordero in February, 1841, the latter found that most of the Mission property had been disposed of.[34] The best furniture was gone, and the inserviceable pieces that were left were sold at an exhorbitant price. Further, de la Guerra was accused of having killed and scattered the livestock. To this last charge de la Guerra replied that he had merely followed the government's orders. Eugene Duflot de Mofras, who visited Purísima at this time, also found the mission in utter decadence.

By proclamation, on March 29, 1843, Governor Manuel Micheltorena restored Purísima along with eleven other missions, to the church.[35] But Purísima was beyond any material benefit as a result. Cordero delivered the establishment to Father Juan Moreno, who nevertheless continued to live at Santa Inés. In February of the succeeding year Father President Narciso Durán was compelled to say: "After 9 years of secularization, nothing remains, neither property nor lands in which to sow. It still counts on a moderate vineyard. It is administered at present by the Reverend Father Juan Moreno, [who is] very ill, [and who is] assisted by Don Miguel Gómez, a recently ordained priest. Its population is about 200 souls."[36] No doubt many of these two hundred perished in the epidemic of smallpox which broke out at Los Alamos in July of that year.[37]

The government was not entirely satisfied with the secularization laws of the thirties. In many cases the Indians had abandoned the missions, and the lands were idle and abandoned. Such was the case at Purísima.[38] Furthermore, the income from such properties was in many instances insufficient to pay off mission indebtedness. It was for this reason, rather than for any personal animosity or cupidity, that Governor Pio Pico took steps in 1845 to sell mission buildings and lands. In the spring of that year laws were passed to that effect, and on October 28 Purísima, San Rafael, San Miguel, Dolores, and Soledad were offered for sale.[39] On December 4 Purísima was sold at public auction to John Temple for $1110. Meanwhile some of the Purísima lands, namely, the Santa Rita ranch, had passed into the hands of Ramon Malo. The mission thereby passed out of the hands of the church, to be partially returned by the United States government at a later date.

Shortly after the United States acquired California, the church began to press its claims on the missions. On February 19, 1853, Father Joseph Sadoc Alemany, Bishop of Monterey, petitioned the government for the return of Purísima.[40] Long and costly suits ensued. Finally, on January 24, 1874, President Grant signed the patent deeding the mission to the bishop. Little of original Purísima was recovered. During the interim the lands had been acquired by enterprising citizens, and they were able to retain their titles. Jesse Hill, a Virginian who had made his way across the plains in 1850, arrived in Santa Barbara in 1870 and purchased an interest in the ranchos of Santa Rita and La Purísima.[41] In 1880 he harvested 109 acres of wheat, 13 acres of barley, and 32 acres of flax on the Purísima ranch.[42] Others were also firmly established on the former Mission lands; and when the church acquired its interests in the site it received only 14.04 acres, consisting of an orchard, monastery, and the ruins of the workshops, church, cemetery and warehouse. On January 22, 1883, Bishop Francis Mora sold the church's holdings to Eduardo de la Cuesta for a nominal sum.[43] Sometime thereafter the Union Oil Company came into possession of the monastery, and the old mission church was returned to the bishop. And so Purísima at the turn of the century.

And he showed me a pure river of water, clear as crystal, proceeding out of the throne of God and of the Lamb.

In the midst of the street of it, and on either side of the river, was there the tree of life, which bare twelve manner of fruits, and yielded her fruit every month: and the leaves of the tree were for healing of the nations.

Figure 284. Two views of monastery as it appeared *circa* 1900.

Figure 285. Restored facade of the monastery.

Figure 286. Monastery as it appeared in 1927.

Figure 287. Rear view of restored monastery.

Figure 288. South end of restored monastery.

Figure 289. Part of monastery facade in process of restoration.

Figure 290. Part of monastery facade restored.

Figure 291. Restored door to monastery reception room.

Figure 292. Restored monastery door.

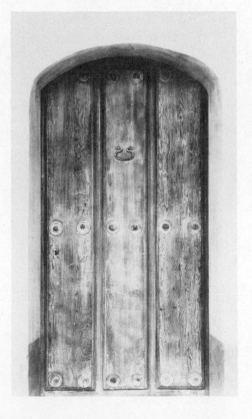

Figure 293. Restored monastery grill and shutter.

Figure 294. View of interior of monastery; original tile floor.

Figure 295. Part of monastery reception room restored; replicas of mission bench and chairs.

Figure 296. Part of restored chapel.

Figure 297. Replica of mission chair.

Figure 298. Replica of mission bench.

Figure 299. Ruins of church after excavation.

Figure 300. Church in process of restoration.

Figure 301. Ruins of altar and sacristy of church after excavation; Payeras's grave in right foreground.

Figure 302. Ruins of church sacristy after excavation.

Figure 303. Original door connecting church sacristies.

Figure 304. Workshop building foundations after excavation.

Figure 305. Ruins of bake-oven in patio of workshop building after excavation.

Figure 306. Ruins of mill building (?).

Figure 307. Ruins of mill (?).

Figure 308. (above) Ruins of small utility building (kitchen?).

Figure 309. (left) Ruins of fireplace in patio of workshop building after excavation.

Figure 310. Ruins of stoves.

Figure 311. Ruins of stove.

Figure 312. Ruins of tallow vats; modern *ramada*.

Figure 313. Front view of the ruins of one of the tallow vats.

Figure 314. Ruins of central fountain partly excavated.

Figure 315. Central fountain in process of restoration.

Figure 316. Left center. Central fountain partly restored.

Figure 317. Lavatory in process of restoration.

Figure 319. Replica of a mission fountain head to be used in the above lavatory.

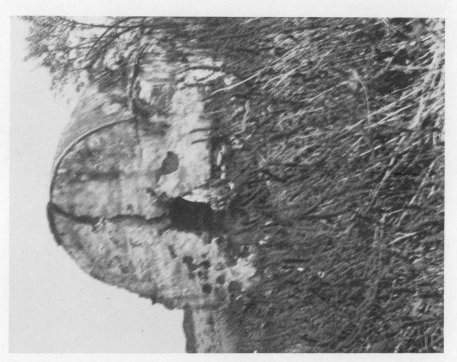

Figure 318. Ruins of spring-house.

Figure 320. Ruins of settling basin (above).

Figure 321. Ruins of reservoir (right).

Figure 322. Ruins of settling basin (above).

Figure 323. Only remaining pear tree of the original orchard (right).

NOTES

PART TWO

Chapter 1. *Founding*

[1] Herbert E. Bolton (ed. and trans.), *Historical Memoirs of New California by Francisco Palóu, O.F.M.* (4 vols., Berkeley, 1926), II, 165.

[2] *Ibid.*

[3] Zyphyrin Engelhardt, *The Missions and Missionaries of California* (4 vols., San Francisco, 1912), II, 218.

[4] Hubert H. Bancroft, *History of California* (7 vols., San Francisco, 1884-1890), I, 310.

[5] *Ibid.*, pp. 335-336.

[6] Engelhardt, *Missions and Missionaries*, II, 371-381; Z. Engelhardt, *Mission La Concepción Purísima de María Santísima* (Santa Barbara, 1932), p. 4.

[7] *Ibid.*

[8] *Ibid.*, p. 3.

[9] Fages to Rengel, Monterey, June 2, 1785, in Provincial Records, I, 192-193, Bancroft Library, University of California, Berkeley.

[10] Rengel to Fages, Chihuahua, March 24, 1786, in Provincial State Papers, VI, 112-113, Bancroft Library.

[11] Engelhardt, *La Purísima*, p. 5.

[12] Quoted in *Ibid.*

[13] Quoted in *Ibid.*

[14] La Purísima Book of Baptisms, located at Mission Santa Inés, quoted in Engelhardt, *La Purísima*, p. 6.

[15] Quoted in *Ibid.*

[16] Very little is known about the early lives of these first missionaries of Purísima. Father Fuster, originally from Aragón, Spain, had been Father Jayme's companion at the time the latter won a martyr's crown in the Indian uprising at Mission San Diego. Fuster was serving at San Juan Capistrano when he received his orders to go to La Purísima. Father Arroíta was a native of Cantabria. He left Spain and joined the Franciscans in their College of San Fernando, Mexico, in 1784 or 1785. He was appointed to California in April, 1786, "and came to his post with a reputation from the Guardian of being, like his companions, a good man, though somewhat lively and without much experience." He landed at Monterey in the fall of 1786 in company with five other Franciscans, one of whom was Cristóbal Oramas, who, too, was eventually assigned to Purísima. Arroíta was first stationed at Mission San Luis Obispo, where he was in the spring of 1787, when he received his appointment to Purísima. Engelhardt, *La Purísima*, 89; Bancroft, *California*, I, 675, note.

[17] Fages, "Ordenes generales que debe observar el sargento encargado . . . de la Purísima Concepción," Provincial State Papers, VIII, 21-26.

Chapter 2. *Promising Beginnings.*

[1] La Purísima Book of Baptisms.

[2] Cota to Fages, August 24, 1788, Provincial State Papers, VIII, 87.

[3] *Ibid.*

[4] "Estado de fuerza," Provincial State Papers, VIII, 89.

[5] Engelhardt, *La Purísima*, p. 89.

[6] *Ibid.*, p. 8; Bancroft, *California*, I, 664, *note.*

[7] Engelhardt, *La Purísima*, p. 82.

[8] *Ibid*, pp. 80-81.

[9] *Ibid.*, pp. 8-9; Bancroft, *California*, I, 676.

[10] Engelhardt, *La Purísima*, p. 9.

[11] Fernández to Borica, June 3, 1799, Archivos del arzobispado, I, 59, Bancroft Library; Bancroft, *California*, I, 675-676. See Engelhardt, *La Purísima*, p. 130, where the mission records show much less.

[12] Bancroft, *California*, I, 675-676; "Resumen gral . . . fin de Dizre. de 1800," in Juan Bandini, Documentos para la historia de California, 1776-1850, pp. 3-4, Bancroft Library. The sources which I have here used seem somewhat better than the La Purísima records. This raises an interesting problem which cannot be gone into here.

[13] *Ibid.*

[14] Engelhardt, *La Purísima*, pp. 9-10, is authority for the statement that Enriquez received twelve reales a day. There is some reason to believe, however, that the weaver received one-eighth of the value of the cloth woven under his direction, and that four-eighths were paid into the public treasury. See Fernández to Borica, May 27, 1797, Provincial State Papers, Benecia, Military, XV, 14, Bancroft Library.

[15] Engelhardt, *La Purísima*, p. 11.

[16] "The experience at other Missions told the friars that the neophytes received little benefit from the instructions of the artisans, not to speak of other drawbacks, *Ibid.*, p. 10.

[17] *Ibid.*, p. 11.

[18] *Ibid.*, pp. 16, 18.

[19] Goycoechea to the Governor, December 14, 1798, Provincial State Papers, XVII, 80.

[20] Engelhardt, *Missions and Missionaries*, II, 454; "Contribución . . . ," Archivos de las misiones, papeles originales, 1769-1825, II, 201, Bancroft Library.

[21] Engelhardt, *La Purísima*, p. 9.

[22] *Ibid.*, p. 10.

[23] *Ibid.*, p. 18.

[24] *Ibid.*, pp. 11, 18.

[25] Bancroft, *California*, I, 547.

[26] Engelhardt, *La Purísima*, pp. 10-11.

[27] *Ibid.*, pp. 12-13, and *Missions and Missionaries*, II, 549-585; Bancroft, *California*, I, 587-596; Theodore H. Hittell, *History of California* (4 vols., San Francisco, 1898), I, 482-483.

[28] Engelhardt, *La Purísima*, pp. 13-16.

[29] See Goycoechea to the Governor, October 14, 1798, Provincial State Papers, XVII, 72-73.

[30] Bancroft, *California*, I, 675.

[31] Engelhardt, *La Purísima*, p. 82.

[32] He died in Mexico on March 5, 1821. Lasuén to Borica, October 27, 1798. Provincial State Papers, XVII, 83; Engelhardt, *La Purísima*, pp. 89-90.

Chapter 3. Payeras at the Helm.

[1] Engelhardt, *La Purísima*, p. 21.

[2] *Ibid.*, pp. 91-92; G. W. James and C. S. Williams (eds. and trans.), *Francisco Palóu's Life and Apostolic Labors of the Venerable Father Junípero Serra, Founder of the Franciscan Missions of California* (Pasadena, 1913), p. 2.

[3] "Lista de misioneros . . . ," Archivos de las misiones, papeles originales, I, 330, Bancroft Library.

[4] Engelhardt, *La Purísima*, p. 36.

[5] San Luis Obispo, Santa Inés and San José were the other missions. Bancroft, *California*, II, 179.

[6] "Auxilios dada . . . a esta Misn. de Sta. Ynes . . . el día 11 de Junio de 1805," Archivos de las misiones, papeles originales, I, 308.

[7] Engelhardt, *La Purísima*, p. 30.

[8] *Ibid.*, p. 29; "Noticia de las misiones que ocupan las religiosos . . . en dicha prova.," Archivos de las misiones, papeles originales, I, 334.

[9] At this time, 1804-1810, Fathers Gregorio Fernández, Juan Cabot and Gerónimo Boscana alternated as Payeras's assistants.

[10] Engelhardt, *La Purísima*, p. 19.

[11] Payeras, "Comunicación . . . de la Purísima Concepción," January 13, 1810, Archivos de la mision de Santa Barbara, XII, 350, Bancroft Library.

[12] *Ibid.*

[13] "Noticia . . . en dicha prova.," Archivos de las misiones, papeles originales, I, 334.

[14] Engelhardt, *La Purísima*, p. 29.

[15] *Ibid.*, p. 21. Boscana seems, however, to have been considered officially stationed at the mission until the close of the year, for he is listed as being there as late as December. "Lista de las Misioneros . . .," Archivos de las misiones, papeles originales, I, 330.

[16] Engelhardt, *La Purísima*, p. 37.

[17] *Ibid.*, p. 36.

[18] Bancroft, *California*, II, 201.

[19] Payeras, *Informe anual*, December 31, 1812, in the Santa Barbara Mission Archives (hereafter cited SBMA). I have here used Engelhardt's translation, *La Purísima*, pp. 30-31.

[20] [*Ibid.*, p. 32.]

Chapter 4. A New Site.

[1] Payeras, *Informe anual*, January 1, 1814, SBMA.

[2] Engelhardt, *La Purísima*, pp. 31-34.

[3] *Ibid.*, p. 34; Señan to Arrillaga, March 16, 1813, Archivos del arzobispado, II, 89-90.

[4] Engelhardt, *La Purísima*, p. 38.

[5] Payeras, *Informe anual*, January 1, 1814, SBMA.

[6] Engelhardt, *La Purísima*, p. 35, translates this as "thatched roofs."

[7] Early in the spring of this year (1937) excavations at the site revealed the foundations of what must have once been a crude, but large building. "The stone foundations at the northern extremity of the ruin occur about fifty feet from the cemetery wall foundation. From this point the ruin extends to the south and measures about 177'-0" in length. The main part of the structure is formed by three rows of stone formations and the two outer rows are 18'-0" to 20'-0" apart. The wing at the south and east is similar in layout and is about 45'-0" in length." (See "Archaeological Reconnaissance Report, La Purísima Camp SP-29, Months of February to May 31, 1937," included with the papers attached to the present report.) A really remarkable discovery.

[8] Quoted in Engelhardt, *La Purísima*, p. 40.

[9] Payeras to De la Guerra, October 16, 1815, José de la Guerra y Noriega, Documentos para la historia de California, V, 12, Bancroft Library.

[10] Engelhardt, *La Purísima*, pp. 39-40; Payeras, *Informe anual*, January 1, 1816, SBMA.

[11] The beautiful colonnade, partially rebuilt, is said to have been of various materials. George W. James, *In and Out of the Old Missions* (Boston, 1905), says, after his visit to the site in May, 1904, "some [of the columns] are of stone, others of burned brick, and still others of adobe."

[12] Payeras, *Informe anual*, December 31, 1816, SBMA.

[13] *Ibid.*

[14] Engelhardt, *La Purísima*, p. 40.

[15] Payeras to Solá, November 22, 1815, Archivos del arzobispado, II, 103.

[16] Engelhardt, *Missions and Missionaries*, IV, 531.

[17] "Estado de las misiones . . . del año 1816," Archivos de las misiones, papeles originales, I, 378.

[18] Payeras to Solá, December 20, 1816, Archivos del arzobispado, III, 69.

[19] Engelhardt, *La Purísima*, p. 41.

[20] Payeras to Solá, March 20, 1817, Archivos del arzobispado, III, Pt. 2, 22.

[21] Hittell, *California*, I, 494-495.

[22] "Casos diferentes . . . de estos Indios," Archivos de las misiones, papeles originales, I, 319.

[23] Payeras, *Informe anual*, December 31, 1817, SBMA; Payeras to Solá, March 21, 1817, Archivos del arzobispado, III, Pt. 2, 22.

[24] Payeras, *Informe anual*, December 31, 1817, SBMA.

[25] Engelhardt, *La Purísima*, p. 42.

[26] "Noticia . . . en los años de 1817 y 1818," Archivos de las misiones, papeles originales, I, 380; "Lista de Abril 22, 1819," *Ibid.*, p. 422; "Lista de los misioneros . . .," *Ibid.*, p. 446.

[27] Payeras, "Memorial a los P.P.," June 2, 1820, Archivos de la mision de Santa Barbara. III, p. 163.

[28] Engelhardt, *La Purísima*, p. 48.

[29] *Ibid.*, p. 47.

Chapter 5. Portentous Years.

[1] Payeras to De la Guerra, October 12, 1818, De la Guerra Documentos, V, 36; Bancroft, *California*, II, 235-237.

[2] Payeras to Missionary Fathers, December 1, 1818, Archivos del arzobispado, III, Pt. 2, 36.

[3] Engelhardt, *La Purísima*, p. 93.

[4] Payeras, *Informe anual*, December 31, 1818, SBMA.

[5] "Noticias de las misiones . . . en los años de 1817 y 1818," Archivos de las misiones, papeles originales, I, 381.

[6] Payeras, *Informe anual*, December 31, 1819, SBMA.

[7] "Estado de las misiones . . .," Archivos de las misiones, papeles originales, I, 376.

[8] "Estado de las misiones . . .," *Ibid.*, p. 462.

[9] *Ibid.*, p. 468.

[10] Engelhardt, *La Purísima*, pp. 45-48.

[11] *Ibid.*, p. 93.

[12] Payeras to Missionaries, April 28, 1821, Archivos del arzobispado, IV, Pt. 1, 50-51.

[13] Payeras to Missionary Fathers, June 5, 1821. *Ibid.*, IV, Pt. 2, 63-64.

[14] Engelhardt, *La Purísima*, p. 93.

[15] "Quaderno de estados . . .," Archivos de la mision de Santa Barbara, III, 243.

[16] Payeras to Solá, 1821 (?), Archivos del arzobispado, IV, Pt. 1, [p. ?].

[17] Hittell, *California*, II, 44.

[18] *Ibid.*, p. 72.

[19] Engelhardt, *La Purísima*, p. 94.

[20] Payeras, "Diario," Archivos de la mision de Santa Barbara, XII, 411-430.

[21] Payeras to Missionary Fathers, December 15, 1822, Archivos del arzobispado, IV, Pt. 1, 101.

[22] Recent excavations at this spot have revealed the bones of what are believed to be the remains of Payeras.

[23] Engelhardt's translation, *La Purísima*, pp. 94-95.

[24] Bancroft, *California*, II, 489-490.

[25] Payeras, *Informe anual*, December 31, 1821; Rodriguez, *Informe anual*, December 31, 1823, SBMA.

[26] Payeras, *Informe anual*, December 31, 1822, SBMA.

[27] "Estado de las Misiones . . .," Archivos de las misiones, papeles originales, I, 468.

[28] *Ibid.*

[29] *Ibid.*

[30] J. D. Mason, *History of Santa Barbara County* . . . (Oakland, 1883), pp. 281-282, 291.

[31] "Estado de las misiones . . .," Archivos de las misiones, papeles originales, I, 668. The white population in 1822 was twenty. "Quarderno . . .," Archivos de la mision de Santa Barbara, III, 243.

[32] Engelhardt, *La Purísima*, p. 50.

Chapter 6. In Articulo Mortis.

[1] Engelhardt, *La Purísima*, p. 50.

[2] Engelhardt, *Missions and Missionaries*, III, 194-206, and *La Purísima*, pp. 50-54; Hittel, *California*, II, 59-64; Bancroft, *California*, II, 527-537.

Notes

[3] N. Van de G. Sanchez, *Spanish Arcadia* (Los Angeles, 1929), p. 111, says that the rebels were led by Chief Pacomio, "a youth of gallant presence, slender figure, great intelligence, unwearying perseverance, excellent judgment and proved courage. He had been given a superior education by the padres. . . ."

[4] Hittell, *California*, II, 59.

[5] It would be interesting to know what became of the balance of the one hundred and nine men who Estrada says enlisted for the campaign. Engelhardt questions Estrada's figures regarding the number of Indians besieged at the mission. Engelhardt estimates that there were no more than one hundred and fifty Indians who bore arms against the troops at the mission. *La Purísima*, p. 54.

[6] Engelhardt's translation, *Ibid.*, pp. 51-52.

[7] Estrada to De la Guerra, May 22, 1824, De la Guerra Document, V, 190.

[8] *Ibid.*

[9] *Ibid.*

[10] Engelhardt, *La Purísima*, pp. 45, 98.

[11] "Informe bienal . . .," Archivos de las misiones, papeles originales, I, 738.

[12] Engelhardt, *La Purísima*, p. 130.

[13] *Ibid.*, p. 131.

[14] Vitoria, *Informe anual*, December 31, 1825, SBMA.

[15] Vitoria, *Informe anual*, December 31, 1827, SBMA.

[16] "Estado . . .," Bandini, Documentos, p. 6; Engelhardt, *La Purísima*, p. 131.

[17] "Estado . . .," Archivos de las misiones, papeles originales, II, 343; Engelhardt, *La Purísima*, p. 129.

[18] Unsigned note, Archivos de las misiones, papeles originales, II, 497.

[19] A. Robinson, *Life in California Before the Conquest* (New York, 1846), p. 49.

[20] W. Colton, *Three Years in California* (New York, 1850), p. 448, says that there were some 80,000 head of livestock at La Purísima in 1830!

[21] Engelhardt, *Missions and Missionaries*, III, 379.

[22] *Ibid.*, p. 530; and *La Purísima*, p. 56.

[23] *Ibid.*

[24] Archives of California, State Papers, Missions, VI, 437-487.

[25] *Ibid.*, XI, 280-287.

[26] Engelhardt, *La Purísima*, p. 58. Duflot de Mofras, the famous French explorer, states that there were 900 neophytes at the mission at this time (*Exploration* . . ., I, 375-376). Both Engelhardt and de Mofras are perhaps in error. The official figures show a steady decrease in Purísima neophytes since 1816. In 1832, the year of the last trustworthy census figures, there were only 372 neophytes (Engelhardt, *La Purísima*, p. 129). De Mofras' figures were merely an estimate. If there was an increase, it must have been due to the influx of Indians not officially attached to the mission.

[27] *Ibid.*, pp. 130-131. De Mofras exaggerates also in this respect. *Exploration* . . ., I, 376.

[28] Archives of California, State Papers, Missions, VI, 437-487.

[29] Engelhardt, *La Purísima*, pp. 84, 86.

[30] Archives of California, State Papers, Missions, VI, 16.

[31] *Ibid.*, VIII, 3, 5, 11. An inventory of July 25, 1838, contained the following statistics: 3,824 cattle, 1,300 sheep, 1,532 horses, 90 mules, 3½ barrels of brandy, 1,500 pounds of tallow, 550 pounds of lard, 100 hides, 99 tanned skins, 210 *fanégas* of grain. Sixty *fanégas* of wheat barley had been planted; and there were 122 neophytes, some ill, and 47 natives had been freed and were living at Los Alamos. The debts were $3,696. Engelhardt, *La Purísima*, p. 59.

[32] Six hundred sheep had been lost in floods in February. Archives of California, State Papers, Missions. VIII, 4.

[33] *Ibid.*, p. 5.

[34] *Ibid.*, IX, pp. 5-6.

[35] Hittell, *California*, II, 323-325; Engelhardt, *La Purísima*, p. 62.

[36] Durán, "Informe . . .," Archivo de la familia Pico, I, 14, Bancroft Library.

[37] Engelhardt, *La Purísima*, pp. 87-88.

[38] Bandini, Documentos, p. 121; Hittell, *California*, II, 379-381.
[39] Engelhardt, *Missions and Missionaries*, IV, 445-450, and *La Purísima*, p. 64.
[40] United States patent quoted in *Ibid.*, pp. 66-73.
[41] Mason, *History of Santa Barbara*, pp. 289-290.
[42] Lompoc *Record*, September 11, 1880.
[43] Engelhardt, *La Purísima*, pp. 73-78.

BIBLIOGRAPHY

Alvárez, M. F., *Las fachadas de los edificios y la belleza de las ciudades.* Mexico, 1921.

Ames, J. W., *Opinion on Survey of Mission La Purísima,* in *Pamphlets on California,* XIII, No. 12.

Archivos del arzobispado, cartas de los misioneros. Bancroft Library MSS. Transcripts.

Archivo de la familia Pico. Bancroft Library MSS.

Archivos de las misiones, papeles originales. Bancroft Library MSS. Originals.

Archivos de la mision de Santa Barbara. Bancroft Library MSS. Transcripts.

Archives of California, State Papers, Missions. Bancroft Library MSS. Transcripts.

Archivo y Biblioteca de la Secretaria de Hacienda, *Coleccion de documentos Historicos: Las Misiones de la California. Tomo* II. Mexico, 1914.

Ayres, A. B., *Mexican Architecture, Domestic, Civil and Ecclesiastical.* New York, 1926.

Bancroft, H. H., *History of California.* 7 vols. San Francisco, 1884-1890.

Bandini, J., *Documentos para la historia de California, 1776-1850.* Bancroft Library MSS. Originals.

Beechey, F. W., *Narrative of a Voyage to the Pacific . . . in the Years '26, '27, '28.* 2 vols. London, 1831.

Benitez, J. R., *Las Catedrals de Oaxaca, Morelia y Zacatecas.* Mexico, 1934.

Benton, A. B., *The California Mission and its Influence upon Pacific Coast Architecture.* (?)

Blanchard, N. K., *The Santa Barbara Mission: An Architectural Study.* University of California MS. M. A. thesis, 1924.

——————, *A Memorial Chapel and Monastery Dedicated to the Franciscan Fathers.* University of California MS. Gr. in Arch. thesis, 1925.

Bolton, H. E., *Guide to Materials for the History of the United States in the Principal Archives of Mexico.* Washington, 1913.

——————, (ed. and trans.), *Historical Memoirs of New California by Francisco Palóu, O.F.M.* 4 vols. Berkeley, 1926.

Bossom, A. C., *An Architectural Pilgrimage in Old Mexico.* New York, 1924.

Browne, C., *Cloisters of California, with Illustrations of the Author.* Los Angeles, 1918.

"California Mission Buildings," in *The Brochure Series of Architectural Illustration,* IV, No. 7 (1898), 110-120.

Carter, C. F., *Missions of Nueva California; an historical sketch . . . with illustrations from drawings by the author, from photographs, and reproductions of old prints.* San Francisco, 1900.

——————, *Some By-ways of California.* New York, 1902.

Clinch, B. J., *California and its Missions: Their History to the Treaty of Guadalupe Hidalgo.* 2 vols. San Francisco, 1904.

Cole, G. W., "Missions and Mission Pictures: A Contribution Towards an Iconography of the Franciscan Missions of California," in *California Library Association Publication.* Sacramento, 1910.

Colton, W., *Three Years in California.* New York, 1850.

Crocker & Co. (pubs.), *Old California Missions.* San Francisco, 1889.

Dana, R. H., *Two Years Before the Mast.* New York, 1912.

Davis, N., *The Old Missions of California.* Oakland, 1926.

Deakin, E., *The Twenty-one Missions of California.* Berkeley, 1902.

Doyle, J. T., *et al, The California Missions.* San Francisco, 1893.

Duflot de Mofras, Eugéne, *Exploration du territoire de l'Oregon, des Californies et de la Mer Vermeille, exécutée pendant les années 1840, 1841 et 1842.* 2 vols. Paris, 1844.

Elder, D. P. (ed.), *The Old Spanish Missions of California.* San Francisco, 1913.

Engelhardt, Z., *Mission La Concepción Purísima de María Santísima.* Santa Barbara, 1932.

——————, *The Missions and Missionaries of California.* 4 vols. San Francisco, 1912.

Fages, P., *Ordenes generales que debe observar el sargento encargado de la escolta de la nueva mision de la Purísima Concepción, 1788.* Bancroft Library MSS. Transcript.

Forbes, A. S. C., *California Missions and Landmarks (and) El Camino Real.* Los Angeles, 1915.

——————, *California Missions and Landmarks, and How to Get There.* Los Angeles, 1903.

Guerra y Noreiga, J. de la, *Documentos para la historia de California.* Bancroft Library MSS. Transcripts.

Hall, T., *California Trails: Intimate Guide to the Old Missions.* New York, 1920.

Harding, G. L., *Don Agustin V. Zamorano, Statesman, Soldier, Craftsman, and California's First Printer.* Los Angeles, 1934.

Hayes, *Scraps, Missions.* Bancroft Library.

Hildrup, J. S., *The Missions of California and the Old Southwest.* Chicago, 1907.

Hittell, T. H., *History of California.* 4 vols. San Francisco, 1898.

Holway, M. G., *Art of the Old World in New Spain and the Mission Days in Alta California.* San Francisco, 1922.

Hudson, W. H., *The Famous Missions of California . . . with Sketches in color by W. H. Bull, and Many Other Illustrations.* New York, 1901.

Bibliography

Hughes, E., *The California of the Padres; or, Footprints of Ancient Communism.* San Francisco, 1875.

Hunt, R. D., and Sánchez, N. Van de G., *A Short History of California.* New York, 1929.

Jackson, H. H., *Glimpses of California and the Missions.* New York, 1882.

James, G. W., and Williams, C. S., (eds. and trans.), *Francisco Palóu's Life and Apostolic Labors of the Venerable Father Junípero Serra, Founder of the Franciscan Missions of California.* Pasadena, 1913.

——————, *In and Out of the Old Missions of California: An Historical and Pictorial Account of the Franciscan Missions.* Boston, 1905.

Kroeber, A. L., *Handbook of the Indians of California,* in Bureau of American Ethnology, *Bulletin 78.* Washington, D.C., 1925.

——————, "The Chumash and Costanoan Languages," in University of California, *Publications in American Archaeology and Ethnology,* IX, No. 2, 237-271.

Langston, K. L., *The Secularization of the California Missions, 1813-1846.* University of California MS., M. A. thesis, 1925.

La universidad nacional (pub.), *Iglesias y Conventos de la Ciudad de Mexico.* Mexico, 1920.

La secretaría de educación pública, departmento de monumentos (pub.), *Tres Siglos de Arquitectura Colonial.* Mexico, 1933.

(Lester, L.), "Old Spanish Missions," in *National repository* (June, 1877), 498-506.

Mariscal, F. E., *La patria y la arquitectura nacional.* Mexico, 1915.

Mission La Purísima Concepción books: (Santa Inés mission)

(1) *Padrón que contiene todos los neofitos de la Purísima Concepción.*

(2) *Libro de Casamientos.*

(3) *Padron 1835-1836.*

(4) *Libro Primero de Baptismos, Abril 9, 1788 - Marzo 24, 1834.*

(5) *Libro Segundo de Baptismos, Setiembre 26, 1834 - Mayo 30, 1850.*

(6) *Libro Primero de Difuntos dia 12 de Abril de 1788-1832.*

(7) *Difuntos Segundo Libro, 1832-1851.*

(8) *Padrón que Contiene Todos los Neofitos de Esta Mision de la Purísima Concepción, con exprecion de su edad y partida segun sur edad y partido segun se halla hoy dia 1 de enero de 1814.*

(9) *Libro Primero de Confirmaciones.*

[Mason, J. D.], *History of Santa Barbara and Ventura Counties, California with Illustration and Bibliographical Sketches of Its Prominent Men and Pioneers.* Oakland, 1883.

Mission Memoirs: The Franciscan Missions of California. (Photographs by Vroman; engravings by C. M. Davis Engraving Company.) Los Angeles, 1898.

Newcomb, R., *The Old Mission Churches and Historic Houses of California: Their History, Architecture, Art and Lore.* Philadelphia, 1925.

Provincial State Papers. Bancroft Library MSS. Transcripts.

Provincial State Papers, Benicia, Military. Bancroft Library MSS. Transcripts.

Provincial Records. Bancroft Library MSS. Transcripts.

Robinson, A., *Life in California during a residence of several years in that territory, comprising a description of the country and the missionary establishments, observations, etc.* New York, 1846.

Sánchez, N. Van de G., *Spanish Arcadia.* Los Angeles, 1929.

Santa Barbara Mission Archives:
    Annual and biennial reports, 1798-1832, for La Purísima.
    La Purísima account books.

Saunders, C. F., and Chase, J. S., *The California Padres and Their Missions.* New York, 1915.

Shurtleff, E. W., *The Old Missions of California.* Boston, 1897.

Smith, F. R., *The Architectural History of Mission San Carlos Borromeo California.* Berkeley, 1921.

Tip. de la oficina impresara de estampillas (pub.), *Las Misiones de la Alta California.* Mexico, 1914.

Truesdell, A. W., *California Pilgrimage, by one of the pilgrims.* San Francisco, 1884.

Truman, B. C., *Missions of California.* Los Angeles, (1903).

Tyler, W. B., *Old California Missions.* San Francisco, 1889.

Vischer, E., *Missions of Upper California, 1872. Notes on the California missions, a supplement to Vischer's pictorial of California dedicated to its patrons.* San Francisco, 1872.

Walsh, M. T., *The Mission Bells of California.* San Francisco, 1934.

———, *The Mission of the Passes: Santa Inés.* Los Angeles, 1930.

INDEX

Index

Indians, as military troops, 255, 257
Infirmary, 38, 42, 124, 252, 254
Iron, *see* Metalwork
Irrigation, *see* Water System

Jackson, Helen Hunt, 61, 92
Jalama site, 39
James, George Wharton, 62, 63
Janssens, Teresa Malo de; 226, *n. 30*; 229, *n. 5*
Johnston, H. V., 197, 200, 202, 203

Kitchen, *see* Food Preparation Area
Kittredge, Frank A., xx
Ladrillos, see Tile, Floor
Laguna Larga, 239; *see also* Rancho de Larga
Lalsacupi, *see* Algsacupi
Land Acquisition, *see* Property Ownership
Land Ownership, *see* Property Ownership
Landmarks Club, xxvi, 51, 220, 221.
La Purisima Concepcion, Mission, xxv, 233-235, 237-242, 247-249, 256, 261, 262, 265
La Purisima State Historical Monument, xxvi
Lasuén, Fr. Fermín, xxv, 238, 239, 242
Latches, *see* Metalwork
Lavatory, *see* Water System
Lead, *see* Metalwork
Leather articles, 243, 254
Lemmon, Warren W., 216
Lewis, J. Volney, 83, 182; 227, *n. 1*
Libeu, Lawrence, 200
Lighting fixtures, 114, 118-120, 156-158
Lime, 72, 83, 94-96; 228, *nn. 29, 31*
Livestock, 39, 243, 249, 253, 254, 256, 259, 263-265
Locks, *see* Metalwork
Loft, storage or *Tapanco,* 60, 69, 116
Lompoc Produce Company, 39
Lompoc Valley, xxv, 237, 239
Long, J. D., 85, 194, 195
Loreto, 254
Los Alamos, 266
Los Berros, xxv, xxvi, 37, 42, 43, 251
Lummis, Charles F., 220, 221

McCoy, Frank, 110, 176
Malo House, 2, 43, 82
Malo, Ramon, 226, *nn. 25, 30*; 266
Marquéz, Agustín, 243
Matanza, 39
Materials of construction, 72, 83-99, 181; 227, *nn. 2, 17, 19*; 251
Mayordomo quarters, 6; 226, *n. 30*
Measurements, 1-8, 35-37, 40, 59, 61, 63, 64, 73, 252; 295, *n. 7*
Metalwork, 5, 72, 91, 97-99, 109, 111, 114, 120, 134, 148-150, 159-163; 228, *nn. 43, 44*; 229, *n. 46*
Mexican Archives, 235
Mexico, allegiance to, 257
Micheltorena, Manuel, 266
Miguelito Canyon, 37, 83

Mill, 7, 39, 283
Missions, *see* individual mission
Mission Vieja, xxvi, 32-34, 37, 40, 227, *n. 2*; 238-250
Mofras, Eugene Duflot de, 31, 69, 70; 227, *n. 17*; 265
Monastery, 59, 60, 64, 68; 227, *n. 34*; 260, 269-273
Monterey, 247, 255-257; 293, *n. 16*
Mora, Fr. Francis, 266
Moreno, Fr. Juan, 264, 266
Mortar, mud, 83-85, 93, 94, 123, 167; 228, *n. 28*

Nash-Boulden, S. A., 189; 227, *n. 14*
National Park Service, xxvi, xxvii, 113, 121, 124, 139
Neasham, Aubrey, xxiii
Neve, Felipe de, xxv, 237-239
Newcomb, Rexford, 63, 64, 71, 72, 205-207
Niches, 36, 67, 69, 76, 77, 92, 97, 118, 168; 226, *n. 22*
Numbering system for buildings, 9

Old Mission, *see* Mission Vieja
O'Neil, Emmet, xxii, 67, 226, *n. 24*
Oramas, Fr. Cristóbal, 241, 242, 247; 293, *n. 16*
Orchard, *see* Plantings
Ordaz, Fr. Blas, 259, 261, 263
Ortega, Eugenio, 265
Ortega, José María, 241, 247
Ortega, Juan, 247
Oso Flaco, 39, 262
Oven, 69

Pacheco, Francisco, 262
Padre's Quarters, 60, 69, 70
Painting, *see* Color Decoration
Pala, 257
Palisade Construction, *see* Post Construction
Pangua, Fr. Francisco, 238
Parks, Marion, 199, 201
Partitions, *see* Walls
Passageway, 4, 60, 68-70, 81, 82, 141
Patio, 6, 38, 74, 88, 125, 254, 284
Payeras, Fr. Mariano, 37, 38, 40, 59-61, 70, 247-259, 280
Pear Orchard, 43
Penfield, Wallace C., xxiii, 197, 199, 200, 202, 205
Peyri, Fr. Antonio, 247
Pico, Pío, 266
Pigments, *see* Color Decoration
Pillars, *see* Columns
Pioneer Society of Lompoc, xxii
Pious Fund, 238, 251
Pipelines, *see* Water Systems
Plans, Building, 2, 3, 7, 37, 38, 60, 63, 64, 69, 71, 113, 114, 116, 117, 129, 130
Plantings, 39, 171, 178, 199, 203, 207, 236, 252, 291

[305]

Index